The Gentle Giant
of the 26th Division

By
Carolyn McKinney

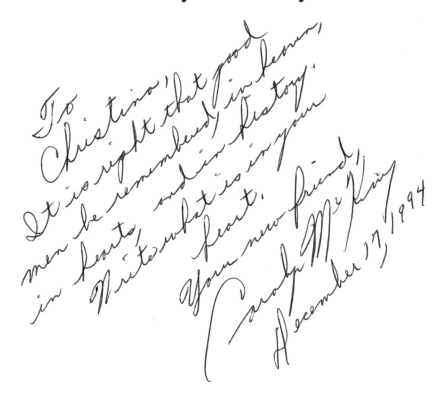

To Christina! that good
It is right that in heaven,
men be remembered in history.
in hearts, and is in your
Writes what is in your
heart.
Your new friend,
Carolyn McKing
December 27, 1994

Headline Books, Inc.
Terra Alta, West Virginia

The Gentle Giant of the 26th Division

A Headline Books, Inc. Publication
May, 1994

Library of Congress Catalog Card Number:
94-77268

For Information Address:
Headline Books, Inc.
P.O. Box 52
Terra Alta, WV 26764

ISBN 0929915119

First Printing, 1994

PRINTED IN THE UNITED STATES OF AMERICA

Table of Contents

ACKNOWLEDGMENTS

For the sake of Alfred's biography, there have been many crossing my way who deserve gratitude and thanks:

First of all to my husband David, who has stood behind me all the way and believed in me. My boys who have never complained, and all of them for keeping the home fires burning while I hopped a plane.

To my Dad, and especially Mom, whose saving instinct led her to the day when she laid a box of letters in my lap, and for dredging up the memories of her dear brother when it was painful to do so.

A thank you to Alfred's family for sharing their brother in whatever way they could. Uncle Melvin, for letting me rummage through his attic and pester him from time to time. To my Uncle Harold and Aunt Winifred who regaled me with the details of life from the early days.

My cousin, Esther Winters in Colorado, for obtaining old photographs and acting as a sounding board for me every summer.

A big thanks to my brother Alvin, and to Beverly for lending me her ear, Dick and Shirley who helped me out financially, and to big brother Bill, for being there when I needed him the most.

To Captain Dee Jepson and family, I can only say that God couldn't have put in my way a finer family in Germany than these Mormon folks.

It was a great pleasure to meet Marie Shaw and I shall not forget her very soon.

Bill and Ann Walls who helped light the fire with inspiration, encouragement, information, and remaining my constant support through the last four years.

To my best friend Bonnie Knieriem, who always listened (sometimes on the telephone), read my journal without a comment, and stood beside me during the tough times.

To her sister-in-law Jennie Knieriem who generously gave me a camera to take to Germany.

A special thanks to all the men of the 328th Regiment for allowing me to attend their reunions. A big thank you to each man who allowed me to interview him and who contributed information about my uncle.

To Robert Clapp, their secretary, I will always be indebted to as he was a constant source of help.

To Mike Sajna, writer and author, I couldn't have done it without your help. Because of your encouragement, I became a published writer. Words seem inadequate.

To my niece, Kathy Leer, for digging in at the last moment and putting this manuscript into disc form, well, what can you say about someone who reaches in and pulls you out of the fire, all my love and thanks.

To my friends at Salem's Children's Home and everyone else who gave me the courage to turn my dreams into a reality, I extend my heartfelt thanks and gratitude.

Carolyn McKinney

DEDICATION

This book is dedicated to God, that through Alfred's life, many will be guided and inspired; to the men of the 328th Infantry, 26thDivision; and to my mother, for saving Alfred's letters and giving permission to publish them.

These pages are a tribute to all the heroes, who were, who are, and who may tomorrow, find that they too must pay the price.

PRELUDE

On a gently sloping hill overlooking Fairchance, PA., Union Cemetery reposes in the quiet morning. Red, blue and white flags, silent sentinels over the dead, flutter in the cool breeze.

Small artillery weapons can be seen standing some piece off. Their appearance does not seem unnatural in this place of solitude and peace, but they had little in common with the nature of the one who lies at my feet. Ironically, they had everything to do with his death.

Alfred Wilson's grave is a simple square stone. In one corner the congressional Medal of Honor stands out in relief. It reads:

CONGRESSIONAL MEDAL OF HONOR
AWARDED TO
ALFRED L. WILSON
CPL MED. DET. 328TH INF.
1919 W.W. II 1944

No towering, impressive monument stands here for the eye and mind to ponder. There is no great epitaph carved in stone. On his left lay his mother and father, and to the right rests a younger brother, Curt.

The sojourn into the life of an uncle I knew only by anecdotes over the past thirty years or so has begun.

His life up to now, an old frayed, but cherished box of letters, memorabilia stashed away in a forgotten corner of the attic, and memories...........

May God help me!

Chapter I

The Beginning

Matilda with Myrtle, Jean, Mary and Alfred

My mother, her brother Alfred and the rest of their siblings grew up in a small white house that sat almost on the last curve before the last bridge going into the rural mining town of Fairchance, Pennsylvania. When they'd moved, their parents Jesse and Matilda (Tillie) Wilson thought their new two story home, with two bedrooms, a nice sized parlor, and a big kitchen, had plenty of room.

However, on regular basis, one of the upstairs bedrooms became a favorite rendezvous spot for the stork and Tillie. By 1931 there were five boys and five girls making sure that any chance of the yard turning into a luxuriant green carpet was nonexistent.

With ten kids, the four rooms of the house were filled with babies crying and the laughter and play of children, but my Grandma Tillie filled it with the one ingredient that held it all together, love.

The Depression didn't make it easy on big families back in the 1920's. My Grandpap Jesse usually only had work two days a week in the mines and for most of those early years, they had no electricity or running water. Grandma Tillie, a resourceful woman, became adept at standing between the ogre of hard times and the lives of her offspring with everything she had and at times, some things she didn't have. My Uncle Harold once said, "We were poor, but we

1

never knew it. As kids, we were having too much fun." Parenting has always been a challenge whether it's been at the beginning of a century or at the end of one.

Several times a week no matter what time of year, Tillie would reach into the oven of the big black coal stove and pull out a half dozen golden brown loaves of bread and set them to cool on a sideboard while their warm tantalizing aroma wafted into the noses of the kids hanging around at the time. Longingly they would watch and wait for them to be cool enough so that Mom could slice off a piece of the still warm bread, spread a layer of thick yellow butter across the soft white surface, and then, lay the whole thing into their grubby little outstretched hands. There was never much said while they ate their treat and they never tired of the taste and smell of it.

Using a washboard, it would almost take a whole day for Tillie and her helpers (my mother and her sisters) to rub all the clothes across its hard surface with a few raw knuckles thrown in. There was always a baby in the house, so if you thought there was nothing to do, forget it. Invariably, Tillie could always put a pair of hands to work washing the tub of dirty diapers that always sat waiting.

Tillie sat two tables at mealtime. While visiting relatives one day, my Uncle Harold abruptly got up and started to leave and was asked where he had to go in such a hurry. Harold replied, "I've got to be going or I'll miss first table." If it was humanly possible, a family member made it to the first sitting with Jesse and the little ones. If you couldn't make it till the second table, you made do with what was left over. You knew the meat would be gone so you put an extra piece of bread on your plate and covered every inch of it and your potatoes with gravy. There was always lots of gravy. There were always lots of potatoes. A cousin, Augusta Decker, jokingly said, "I know Tillie peeled about a peck of potatoes for a meal." Thank goodness for spuds.

What really amazed me was when my Uncle Harold told me how they would sleep. You'd normally think of them sleeping long ways in the bed. But they didn't. Tillie would get them cleaned up and ready for bed, march everyone up the narrow stairway, down the hall and into their bedroom. Then, because it allowed them more room to sleep, they all found a place to sleep sideways on two beds. Aside from the two baby beds set up in their parents room for the wee ones, and before the oldest boys were old enough to sleep downstairs on a roll out couch, all the rest of the kids had to sleep in the same room on two double beds.

In recent years, my Uncle Harold, a fun loving soul, told me about all the laughter the family shared in those early days. History, over the past four years of research, has taught me about all the specialness of their love, courage, and the tenacity embraced by one and all. The close family environment shaped their lives and caused one of them to be long remembered by many, immortalized by some, and receive our nations's highest military award, The Medal of Honor. While in office, Harry Truman once said that he would rather have that medal than to be president.

It is this uncle, Alfred L. Wilson, who I have come to admire and love beyond all scope of understanding, whose biography you are about to read.

While I was growing up, my mother Myrtle, who was the oldest daughter and ever the pessimist, was always regaling me with tales of all the work associated with her growing up. I certainly never viewed those anecdotes with much enthusiasm or interest, especially when her first words were, "When I was your age..." I could never figure out what her having to work for a whole week for a head of cabbage had to do with me needing a new dress for Easter or why I couldn't read a book before I finished cleaning the house.

And then there were my days of youth. When my mother wasn't raising me the way she had been raised, I was busy trading in my real world for the fantasy life of the characters in my Zane Grey books. At other times, in my imagined world, I would travel to far off places or rapturously streak horseback across my ranch in Colorado.

My mother and father were always very close to their families and they regularly took my brother and me over the mountain to visit all the relatives in Fairchance. We enjoyed visiting with Grandpap Wilson and, until his passing in 1958, my Uncle Curt. With those visits is the faint recollection of a picture of Alfred in the living room on a stand beside the couch. Many of the things that I took for granted in the fifties and sixties, are now stored up memories that I am more than grateful for.

As a "baby boomer," and with the predictability of the ocean tides, my youthful dreams were left behind on the saddle of my horse "Lucky," and I got swept along by the busyness of living. After marrying in 1966, my husband and I started raising our own brood of four children. Our comfortable little niche was close enough to walk to work and go visiting the grandparents. Home, family, and friends made up our sphere of being. During those hectic days, I expressed little interest in my forefathers or anything they did or didn't do.

Thinking back on how things were, I have to admit that the whole process of meeting life's daily needs left me with little time to think about such deep subjects as who we are, or why we are, or where we've been, much less to take the initiative to think about where we were going. With four kids, I didn't have the energy.

Still, contrary to my lifestyle and for some unfathomable reason, I would think of Uncle Alfred at times. I had always felt a strange affinity toward Alfred, once, even dreaming about him. In the dream I was approaching the gate going into heaven. Looking straight ahead, beyond the gate, I could see someone waiting for me. As I got nearer, this man kept looking at me and smiling. I knew it was my Uncle Alfred and he was waiting for me to come to him. I remember walking right up to him and knowing who he was. He put his arms around me, and when I woke up, I remembered everything vividly and thought right away that the man in the dream was Alfred. I hadn't seen a picture of Alfred for at least fifteen years, so a few days later I asked my mom if she had one. When she retrieved the picture from a drawer and I looked at it, it was the same man. I always thought it was some kind of premonition. An intangible thread seemed to bind me to the memory of my uncle.

There were other subtle ways that my past was trying to work its way into my conscious mind, and even though I never acknowledged the ideas, I nevertheless believed them to be true.

Deep inside me I knew that existing somewhere inside all of us in the need to picture ourselves in the scheme of time and motion. To feel that we are not merely bodies existing for the sake of existence. I always felt that it was far too easy to feel lost in the labyrinth of technology and a mobile society. Somehow, somewhere, and someway we needed to know we were persons of immeasurable worth in the things we could accomplish, and with a reasonable hope that we could become anything we dared to believe in and strive for. Time has given us the luxury of looking at things in retrospect. It has also given us the benefit of its wisdom. We are an accumulation of what has gone on before us. Our validation for who we are comes from the past and our present. It certainly can't come from the future. It's just a little hard to see and comprehend unless you look for it, and I wasn't looking in the right place yet.

So, my interest in anything past had definitely not been piqued by anyone or anything special yet. Anyway, I couldn't quite see what relevance had to do with me today. The present was about all I had time for. And the future....well, it would definitely have to take care of itself. I was very happy and content in my comfort zone and anyway, if I wanted to delve into my past, it was a mere two hundred yards up the road at my parents'.

Luckily, a few of us can still step out our back doors and parade our emotions back to the days of skipping rope or wriggling a hula hoop around our waists. If we care to ask questions, parents or grandparents are wind up toys, just waiting for their string to be pulled so they can release the memories containing such fun as cleaning the globes of their kerosene lamps, or the art of banking a fire in the big black kitchen stove, or scrubbing clothes on a washboard till your knuckles hurt.

The truth is that distance is irrelevant when there is no time to dream dreams or see visions. No time to listen to the voices from the past or no inclination to do so. That was certainly my state of mind.

But those voices were out there, screaming from deep inside our souls, or from the old house sitting along the side of the road that you've passed a hundred times and found yourself wondering about. They're out there, we just have to take the time to stop, open our hearts, and listen for an opportunity to present itself.

For me, understanding the past was right in front of my face, intertwined with the obscureness of the daily grind, and hidden by the fading memories of my Grandfather, my Uncle Curt, and a picture of a uniformed soldier that set in the good living room on an old end table. Then there were the bits and pieces of stories my mother had shared with me over the washing of dishes. With the mention of a medal, though, there was a turned away head and unshed tears glistening in her eyes.

Then came that fateful day in May of 1989 designated by my mother as attic cleaning day when the focus of my whole life would be changed to include the past in one simple act. If I would have had a crystal ball and could have known how one single day would change the rest of my life, I can't say I would have had it any other way.

My mother's theory has always been to save everything. "You might need it someday," she'd say. I call it the Depression Era Syndrome. So every year we move and clean and go through most of the things she's saved for all of her married life.

In all honesty, I must admit that attic cleaning has never rated high on my to do list, but it's a fact of life. So, one absolutely gorgeous morning in May of 1989, I was helping my Mom clean her attic. Now I hate to admit this, but I was actually enjoying going through those old boxes and trunks. I felt somewhat like a prospector searching for gold. Excitement and anticipation gripped me every time a box was opened which yielded some artifact.

As I was sitting in an old rocker, having just put a box of goodies on the floor, my Mother approached me with a frayed candy box clutched in her hands. She asked me if I knew what was in it. To this day I have no real explanation of how I knew the contents of that box, but some instinct told me that they were letters from my Uncle Alfred. He had written incessantly to my Mother while in the Army during World War II and she had kept every page. As my Mother laid the box in my lap, I felt as if she had just handed me a priceless jewel, and I carefully and eagerly lifted the lid to see the faded letters piled inside. Letters written with hope and love to a beloved sister at a time when their world seemed to be turning upside down.

My fingers gently lifted an envelope out of the box bearing a 1943 postmark. Carefully pulling the handwritten letter from its faded cocoon of 47 years, I read the first letter of many that Alfred wrote to my mother.

As I read the letters, his vitality, humor, compassion and dedication to family leaped at me.

I was awed at the kind of man he must have been. His Army Chaplain had written a letter that impressed me. It was addressed to his pastor back at his home church in Fairchance. It read, "I have come to admire this young man and have observed his integrity. I am enjoying his friendship very much." He also gave me an intimate look at the state of Alfred's heart toward God. Alfred has come to him in repentance over some sins he said he had committed in the past. As to the nature of the transgressions we will say that it is best left between Alfred and God. Perhaps it was a small thing that loomed large on his conscience, but whatever it was, it is remembered no more. They discussed the matter and prayed together. Alfred left knowing God's forgiveness and that nothing stood between himself and God. Alfred seemed to have found a profoundly deep relationship with God. In a few months from the time the letter was written, that relationship was to be put to the ultimate test.

As the sun started to set beyond the hill in front of the house and the time to leave off house cleaning for the day approached, I sat enthralled in my rocking chair. With a letter still in my hand, I stared out the window and wondered what was transpiring inside me. The ghostlike apparition that Alfred had always evoked for me in the past now seemed very much alive. It was almost as if he had walked up to me and introduced himself, sat down in a rocking chair and chatted away. In a few short minutes I had come to know that I had a wonderful man for an uncle and had never known it. From what I had read, I was sure that he was a finer person than I had been led to believe. The realization that this man was part of our heritage and that my children knew nothing about him made me sit bolt upright in my rocker. All that this man was could not be lost to myself or my children. I had to find out more about him. What a shame and loss for all of us if Alfred's story were lost with the passing of his closest family. Were we never to know what had made him the kind of man that commanded the respect and admiration of those who knew him?

Like a dormant seed that suddenly and impetuously explodes open with a tiny shoot, I felt something inside me take hold and start to grow. Sitting there, I remembered thinking that Alfred's life should be recorded somehow, written, preserved, published, or whatever. I wanted my kids to feel the pride in this Great-Uncle or theirs that I had felt sitting in that chair. Besides, not every kid can lay claim to having a relative who was awarded the Medal of Honor.

The birthing process for Alfred's biography had inextricably begun and I wasn't even aware that anything special was happening except for this funny feeling in the pit of my stomach. It was like finding out I was going to have a baby. I was simultaneously excited, scared and full of anticipation.

I knew it wasn't a coincidence that those letters had laid up in that attic for forty some years of my life and I had never known about them. Then, to have my mother choose that day to drop the box of letters into my lap. There was definitely a plan and purpose here. Something in the back of my mind told me that things were happening that I had no control over. I really wasn't ready for this!

Decisions don't come easy for me. But I knew that God's gentle voice was urging me to seriously consider writing the biography of my uncle. Thus ensued for some nine months my own personal struggle with the destiny that God and Uncle Alfred was directing me toward, and my own feelings of inadequacy.

I vacillated between the heights of courage one day and the pits of discouragement the next.

Inexorably, as the days passed I could not find any peace within myself. Alfred's story was never very far away from my thoughts in a haunting sort of way. The struggle between mind and heart became my constant companion until slowly the pendulum swung in favor of writing Alfred's biography. It was time to face my fears and put my faith in myself and God into action. Deep down I was longing to embrace the intrigue and challenge that was beyond my own small circle of attainment.

Finally, on a cold, windy day in February of 1990 I drove resolutely over the mountain to Fairchance and made my way to the graveyard on the outskirts of town. After parking the car, a few steps took me directly to the small granite stone in the ground with Uncle Alfred's name engraved on it.

Bending down I let my fingers trace the outline of the Medal of Honor standing out in relief on the tombstone. Tears spilled down my cheeks with love and admiration for the uncle I had never had the privilege to know.

Kneeling on the brown grass next to his grave, I whispered a commitment to write his biography.

Later, it was here, standing over Alfred's grave, that I penned the prelude to this book. I felt God had given me a mission and I could not escape the destiny that was entwining my future with the past of a simple coal miner who had neither sought nor cared about fame of immortality. My uncaring attitude had disintegrated - it was time to look back at my roots.

With the cloak of skepticism and fear thrown off, I eagerly undertook the incredible task of researching Alfred's life.

In March of 1990, I visited my Uncle Melvin Wilson in Fairchance and told him of my intention to record his brother's life. Later on as I sat on the floor of his living room surrounded by pictures of Alfred, old letters, commemorative plaques, and faded newspapers that my grandfather had saved, I was overwhelmed by sadness, tears, and pride. I opened up a gray folded envelope on which he had written the 1933 dates of the passing of Wallace and my Grandmother, and held in my hand a lock of her long red hair.

As if that wasn't enough, Melvin pulled out a video that the army had sent the family of the rededication of Wilson Barracks in Landstuhl, Germany in 1984. Sadly, no family had been present to enjoy it first-hand. I watched as a military band played "Ruffles and Flourishes" and as a chaplain acknowledged Alfred's certain inspiration by a loving God. Then came the reading of Alfred's Medal of Honor citation, which a Major started by saying "It was a dreary, overcast cold day with rain intermittently on that November 8th in "44." He ended with, "Corporal Wilson through distinguished devotion to duty and personal sacrifice helped save the lives of at least ten wounded men."

The ceremony ended with the video camera catching the somber mechanical movements of a squad of soldiers as they fired a twenty-one gun salute. I have never sat up straighter nor been prouder.

Talk about being proud. Later on after meeting the men of the 328th Infantry, to my way of thinking, they are heroes who, like my uncle, had their lives torn asunder by men who thought to set themselves above the world. The voicing of their deeds, thoughts, and emotions, profoundly struck my soul and has become an intrinsic part of my being. It has changed me irreparably. I owe a debt of gratitude to those who knew or have been touched by Alfred's gentle spirit and zeal to do good, and their willingness to share them with a stranger. Thanks guys!

One naturally expects family members to stand by their own, but the loyalty I encountered when I met with Alfred's fellow World War II buddies caught me off guard. A picture emerged of intimate friendships bonded together by tragedy and circumstance so closely that not even time could eradicate them. They referred to Alfred by his nicknames. To them, he was still "Big Al," "Pappy," or "Big Stoop."

One of my first interviews was with Alfred's best friend, Bill Walls and his Wife, Ann. He had gone into the construction business after the war and still resided in Fairchance. Unannounced, I knocked on their front door. In the old days you could drop in on folks on the spur of the moment, but these days, everyone is so busy. As I waited for someone to answer the door, hoping my impetuosity had not led me into an embarrassing scene, Ann opened the door.

After telling her who I was and why I was there, she told me Bill was home and graciously invited me in. They made me feel as if I had known them all my life, and sitting around their kitchen table, we wound up talking for a couple of hours. With a tape recorder silently humming away, Bill told me of his remembrances of Alfred.

That first interview with Bill raised the burning question of why Alfred refused to allow himself to be taken in for treatment. After I started delving into the facts surrounding his actions, I was haunted by the outcome of his decision in Bezange La Petite. It could have ended differently.

Bill has been a valuable source of information about the training camp days and the details of a soldier's life. I carry a load of indebtedness to both of them for the support and encouragement they have given me from this biography's inception and throughout the whole process of writing. From my perspective, they don't come any finer or more decent than this couple.

From the Walls I learned that Alfred's outfit, the 328ᵗʰ Infantry 26ᵗʰ Division, held an annual reunion. These were Alfred's army buddies and if there was a chance that I could be there and meet some of them, I was going to take it.

Bill gave me the address of the secretary for the 328th Combat Team Association, a Robert Clapp, and we started corresponding. I asked to be able to attend a reunion in Alfred's memory and an invitation was extended to me and I danced around my kitchen table when it arrived in the mail. The big weekend was being held at a resort in the state of New York and I was looking forward to the event with great anticipation.

From this point on, life took on a special excitement when the telephone rang. The big reason for this came about because Mr. Clapp put a small article in the *"Yankee Doings"* stating that Cpl. Alfred Wilson's niece was looking for anyone who had known him during the war.

From that simple notice, I started to receive telephone calls from all over the United States from men who had trained or been overseas with Alfred. When the calls started, I remember getting so excited it was hard to talk at first. These men had actually walked and talked with Alfred. Their memories suddenly became a precious link between me, them and Alfred.

One such call came from New Yorker, Ed Kuligowski.

He had been the commander of Alfred's C Company. After a few preliminary words, his first statement was, "We all loved him." Hanging up the phone after talking to Ed, I couldn't get over the fact that after forty-six years, the first thing he would say about my uncle was that they loved him.

With each call, Alfred loomed closer and more real.

Paul Yee called from California. He and Alfred had been good friends during training, and in France, had worked out of the same aid station. James C. Mayfield, another medic said, "Al was a fine, loving fellow and I still think of him often."

By this time, mid-October had lazily floated in on an orange and red carpet of foliage from the maple trees that dominated the landscape here in Western Pennsylvania, and the weekend of the 328th reunion had arrived.

My husband David went with me, and after placing a grandma at home as chaperon for our teenagers, we headed out for the great state of New York and a resort hotel set in the mountains.

At dinner that evening, I finally met Robert Clapp in person.

After corresponding with Bob for several months, it was a genuine pleasure to finally meet this gentleman. My memory banks really buzzed trying to store up all the names of the men I was introduced to who had been medics in the war or who in some way had known Alfred.

The meeting of Robert T. Marshall and his wife Ann, a super couple, was especially significant for a myriad of reasons, one of which I never fully appreciated until I was driving in rural France. Robert had been on the evacuation jeep that had taken Alfred to the aid station in Richicourt. His eyewitness account was priceless in piecing together the course of events as they had occurred in France. He also supplied me with many documents such as casualty lists, World War II maps of France, and details that I would never have gleaned from anyone else.

Paul Yee was there and filled my ears with all sorts of information about camp life. My mind had trouble comprehending that a soldier could buy a carton of cigarettes for 50 cents. No wonder so many men took up smoking. It was a cheap way to pass the time and helped keep the hands busy.

These men amazed me by remembering the smallest detail of their "war" days. As one guy put it, "If you asked me what happened last year, I couldn't do it. But if you ask me something about over there, I can remember it like yesterday." Places, events and emotions had been seared into their memories. Some of them could recall the temperature on a certain day, while one guy recounted perfectly when a buddy was looking to find a new pair of boots outside of an aid station: "He found this pair that looked to be about the right size, and he pulled one of his old boots off and decided to stick his foot into the new one to see if it would fit. Well, when he started to put his foot into the boot he sure got a big surprise. There was an amputated foot still in there." After almost fifty years, he laughed, recalling how his friend sort of went white, wretched the boot off, threw it down and stuck his old one back on.

The silent whirring sound of my tape recorder caught the voice of John Flynn as we sat and talked. "I admired him very much," he said of Alfred, "am very proud of him." John was a big man himself and perched on the edge of his chair, he leaned toward me and spoke about how A and C Companies had been parallel to each other that November day. They had taken heavy casualties and again, he voiced the same question that Bill Walls had raised about why Alfred wasn't evacuated earlier. That part was starting to bother me a great deal too, and I was going to look for some answers.

Al "Zoot" Zottola knew Alfred well and remarked how he was always happy and smiling, and pretty well known around the companies. Al said, "This was the military and thousands of men coming and going. If you said my name to someone in another company, they'd say, 'Who the hell is he?' No one knew anyone else, but when you said the 'Big Stoop,' everyone knew who he was." A gentle giant, his height and bigness were respected, although he was kidded about it. As a matter of fact, they looked at him in awe a bit because he was so big, but yet so mild mannered. Anyone could say anything to him and he never got mad. He could become irate at a situation, but never at an individual. He shared with everyone. Ironically, the family back in Pennsylvania probably helped him gain part of his reputation. If they hadn't been such good cooks.....

Sitting side by side with these men, listening to their voices and watching their faces was like a camera into the past. Months later as I started to meticulously go through Alfred's letters, my perception of their army days and the order of events was much clearer. An added bonus for me was that I had a whole batch of great new friends. My Christmas card list had magically grown longer.

The story of my uncle is theirs as well.

Only one obstacle faced me. The act of putting pen to paper. I didn't know where to begin. So, I went to the one place where inspiration comes naturally to me, the Rocky Mountains of Colorado.

I first pilgrimaged to Denver to visit with Alfred's oldest brother Harold and his wife Winifred. I spent hours listening as he relived life in the Wilson family during the early nineteen-hundreds. It wasn't hard to get him to talk and I was more than a keen listener. During that visit, my cousin Esther Winters and I would ride horseback through the mountains and get caught in a storm, change a tire on a horse trailer and hunt down old ghost towns along with their abandoned graveyards. I was in heaven.

It was a few days later on a beautiful summer's day in July, that I would be on the outskirts of Leadville, Colorado, sitting at the edge of a vast mountain scene. Before me stretched the brilliant blue water of Turquoise Lake.

This fisherman's paradise nestled perfectly in a valley edged by the splendor of tall pines. Towering behind them in relief against a deep blue sky were the stark gray peaks of the awesome range of the Rockies.

Waves beat against the rock strewn shoreline. Above this din was the wind. It seemed to roar through the forest of pines, bending and swaying them like coral fans on an ocean floor. It was a scene I could have watched forever without being tired or bored.

This is where I had come to begin my new adventure as a writer of a biography. But I was not alone. I concluded that the God of the universe had been orchestrating, to a great degree, the thoughts, feelings and events of my life. It was also a succumbing to the spirit and voice of my Uncle Alfred, for at times it seemed that he reached out to me. It was as if he stood by my side, watching, waiting, and guiding me.

Existing within me now is a deep yearning to know and to share the life of my uncle. In reliving the past, I am finding who I am here in the present. But it is not without apprehension. Scripture implies that we see through a glass darkly, that we can only now know in part. A sense of that pervades my spirit when I try to look at the whole picture, past, present and future.

But thank God I have been blessed with a confidence, that for those who knew Alfred, for myself in coming to know this hero, and for the family whose generations will follow him, we can take some measure of comfort in the fact that a destiny that was started in a rural mining town of Fairchance and bravely continued on a hillside in France, will now be brought to fruition in a biography written by a niece, who wished it could have been otherwise.

Chapter II

The Early Days

Alfred, Curt, Mary, Melvin, Lloyd, Bernie and Ellen

The four-room white clapboard house that Jesse and Matilda raised their family in sat along what the Indians called the Old Catawba Trail. When the pioneers pushed west from Virginia, crossing the Blue Ridge Mountains in their wagons, they wound their way through the foothills following the same path which the Indians had used, and which they named the Mountain Road. A lot of folks still call it that today, but if you're asking for directions, they'll tell you to take the Fairchance-Hopwood road into town. But be prepared. Indians and wagons never followed a straight line, so you'll travel around some pretty sharp curves.

Those men and women were adept trailblazers, though, and finally settled down, bringing their white civilization to what is now Fayette County, in Southwestern Pennsylvania. They must have figured they had a pretty fair chance of surviving this wilderness because the town was called Fairchance.

Alfred's forefathers, the Wilsons and the Mitchells, helped the new borderland grow.

The town grew into the 19th Century, becoming a booming

15

industrial hub in those early days. Iron, brick and coke ovens, a powder mill, and a glass factory sprang up around the developing railroad. Every kind of entrepreneur gravitated to the growing metropolis.

Adding to the color and spirit of this one-time frontier town was a nefarious gang of rogues called the "Cooley Gang," and if you know who to talk to, you can still get an old Fairchancer to spin you a yarn about their now famous antics.

Mostly at night and with a little locally made moonshine for courage, members of the band would set about to rob the local citizenry.

According to the old-timers, they used a cave located in the mountains as a hideout, which might indicate that robbery wasn't a very lucrative business. Delaney's Cave, as it was called, had an extensive labyrinth of passages and was almost inaccessible located among the rocks along a mountain cliff. Few people even knew how to find the hole, so gang members felt pretty safe from the law. Their little paradise was only intruded upon once in a while by a few would-be cave explorers.

Reportedly, their carousing came to an end when one area farmer, determined to defend his milk house, kept a loaded shotgun handy by the door. When the raiders decided to appropriate a little refreshment, the farmer was ready for them with a reception committee. Their purported leader, Jack Cooley, was killed in the melee, and the gang broke up soon after.

With the fear of being held up by the Cooley Gang put to rest, Delaney's cave could once again be explored by the curious and the brave. In modern times spelunkers can still descend into the earth's depths at the cave, now known as Laurel Caverns, the site of a thriving tourist business.

In the early days, coal mining was a big industry. It was said that a man could always get a job mining if he had a strong back.

The life of a miner was filled with danger, the immutable black dust, and fear. He pushed his body to the limits of physical endurance. A constant struggle existed between the miner and Mother Earth to wrest the hard black ore from her clutches. She has been known to jealously guard her domain and the miner knew well how dear the price could be in exchange for her booty.

But these were tough men. Not because they wanted to be or tried to be, but because they had been molded by their environment. Generations of men were forged by fear, death, poverty, and hard work. They did it with courage, fortitude and skill. This was the legacy that produced men such as Alfred Wilson.

It was always understood in those early days that a coal miner would never be rich. For the most part, the best a miner could hope for was to provide his family a decent place to live, all the food they needed, and fairly suitable clothing. No piano lessons or ribbons in the hair. That was for the mine owners and their families. The important thing, though, was that it was a living. They were grateful for what they had.

For large families such as the Wilsons and the Mitchells, it meant that their cooks had to find imaginative ways to fix up beans and potatoes. It also meant that a young man had better fall in love with a young woman who knew how to cook, and especially how to bake that wonderfully aromatic home-made bread. Matilda Mitchell did both.

Matilda (Mitchell) Wilson and Jesse Wilson

Alfred's mother was a Mitchell and some said that a Mitchell wasn't good enough for a Wilson. But the brash young Jesse Wilson didn't put any faith in what folks said, and fell in love with her red hair, smile and all. They married in 1913.

In early photographs, Jesse always looked a little stern, whereas Tillie had a softer look. She always had long red hair and a sweet round face. When she smiled, her eyes laughed and danced.

Matilda's parents were Samuel (Chaf) and Mary B. Mitchell. After she had married, her parents went through a stormy divorce. Despite this, the older grandchildren loved the grandfather who came to stay with them from time to time. Chaf worked for the mine owners in one way or another, his last job being a sub-station operator. Grandma Mitchell, outspoken and independent, was to remain a strong influence in everyone's life for many years to come.

George and Anna Wilson, Aunt Zilla Fields (left), and Agusta Fields

Tillie's in-laws were George and Anna Wilson. George was a miner. In his prime he stood well over six feet tall and never did carry too much meat on his bones. Anna Rodgers married both George and the coal dirt. After three girls, they named their first boy Jesse. They were a close knit family and very religious. George sported a handle-bar mustache which the kids all loved. He smoked a pipe, and when a grandchild crawled up onto his lap, the smell of tobacco wrapped itself around them as close as the big arms of their grandfather did.

According to family genealogy, the role of the oldest son in the family was to maintain a strong tie with his mother. It certainly explained the especially close relationship Jesse had with Anna and a sister, Ella, who escaped spinsterhood by marrying at the age of thirty-three.

George had passed away and Anna, described by a grandchild as, "a feisty little old lady" and Ella, priming herself to rule the clan someday, were with Jesse many a Saturday night. He would crank up the Model T, pull up in front of their house and hand them both into the car, squiring them about town to do some shopping or visiting. There was always a lot of coming and going to the homes of Aunts and Uncles.

Matilda and Jesse had come from large families. The Mitchells had eight children and the Wilson's had ten. They both had a clear stubborn streak that many of us contend still runs in the family.

Jesse and Tillie moved several times in the first few years of marriage and it wasn't long before they were blessed with their first boy Harold, born March 3, 1914. Two more girls followed rather close together, Myrtle in 1916, and Jean in 1917.

In the 1800's, Fairchance's Main Street was called the Cherokee or Old Catawba Trail. Alfred's Grandma Mitchell owned a medium sized house along the well known street which she rented out. The house had two bedrooms upstairs and a hallway that was great for running along, and downstairs, the parlor was on one side with the kitchen sprawled the length of the other.

Tillie was pregnant again, and everyone told her it was a boy. Grandma Mitchell thought so too and asked for the privilege of naming him. In exchange, she would give them the house along the Fairchance-Hopwood Road. Well, Tillie was getting pretty tired of moving all the time, and with only three kids, they thought there was plenty of room. They talked it over a little, smiled at each other and later Harold said, "That's how they got the house and Grandma got to name Alfred." The family moved for the last time. Life was sweet and the future stretched securely out in front of them.

After they'd settled into the new house on the Fairchance-Hopwood road, Tillie knew she was pregnant again. She hoped this would be another boy. As Alfred would have said, "The stork shore was busy."

The long-beaked bird and Tillie were becoming well acquainted with each other. The bundle he and she collaborated on this time was not a disappointment to Tillie. But when the time came, she did have to put in a little extra work.

Early in the evening on September 17, 1919, Jesse sent the little ones to their Grandma Mitchell's and had a message delivered to the doctor that they might be needing him. Doc Patterson arrived some time after midnight and was pretty sure that it was going to be a big baby, so he stayed to see Tillie through. In the early morning hours of the 18th of September, Tillie gave birth to their fourth child, and the first one born in their new house. The baby boy made his entrance at 4:00 a.m., and as Doc said, "He's a big'in." The next evening she and Jess contemplated their new "big baby," whom Grandma Mitchell had named Alfred Leonard, after an uncle.

The young family was growing rapidly and more babies arrived in the upstairs bedroom: Curt 1921, Mary 1923, Melvin 1925, Lloyd 1927, Bernice 1929, and Ellen in 1931.

By then a total of ten children clamored for the attention of their parents.

There wasn't plenty of room anymore or plenty of anything, except babies, work, love and laughter.

The sound of children bubbled and flowed from every room, every porch, and overflowed into the dirt of the yard. Patches of green grass had to fight with bare toes for survival.

For Jesse and Tillie, the joy was tempered by the woes of feeding and clothing a large growing family. As one of my uncle's put it, "They were poor in worldly goods but rich in the things that counted the most."

Some weeks Jesse only worked two days. The times were hard. The Depression saw to that. Sometimes breakfast was as simple as a slice of bread sprinkled with sugar and coffee poured over the top.

A big black coal stove sat along one wall and a long kitchen table with a bench behind it sat on the other. Open shelves from floor to ceiling and a sideboard helped Tillie keep things in order. If she would have counted the hours spent bent over that hot stove cooking or standing while kneading batch after batch of bread for her family, well, the time would have been considerable. Myrtle laughingly said of her brother Alfred especially, "He was always hungry." Years later her niece said, "Why, Aunt Tillie spent most of her day just getting meals on the table. Everything was made from scratch, bread, pancake batter, butter, the only thing you bought much of was sugar, flour and coffee."

Everybody had a job and the kids picked dew berries and strawberries for pies. The family kept a good-sized garden in which they took their turn at weeding. When it came harvest time, Tillie canned everything she could put into a jar.

The Wilsons didn't farm for a living like their neighbors, Sam and Chat Woods, but they did raise chickens for meat and eggs, and kept a cow that Tillie milked twice a day. Like a lot of folks back then, a couple pigs were growing fat to be butchered at Thanksgiving. That meant sausage and bacon for breakfast at least until spring.

Jesse was an avid rabbit hunter. He never failed to bag his prey. This wasn't any reflection on Jesse's prowess as a hunter, but rabbit was about the only thing he seemed to be able to bring back for Tillie to work her magic on. Everything else eluded him or maybe it was because he had a good rabbit dog and there wasn't any fun in hunting anything else. But to be fair, Uncle Harold did tell me that once in a while other wild game was added to the larder, especially when he and Alfred started to get older.

The company store sold the Wilsons their beef, called leg meat or shank meat. Uncle Harold said they bought thousands of pounds of the stuff to feed a growing family of that size. To go with the meat, they mashed potatoes by the bushel, almost. Tillie also made a lot of different soups from her garden produce including everyone's favorite, vegetable soup. There were a lot of tummies that needed filling up and a bowl of soup and a slice of bread was a meal.

Sunday dinner was always a big affair and they very often had some relative or another sharing the feast. Combined with the smell of freshly baked pies (Alfred's favorite), and bread from Saturday, the aroma of roasting meat and potatoes could be sensed as soon as feet touched the yard.

When church let out, the kids would head home as fast as they could, arriving breathless and all talking at once. It was a mad race with Alfred in the lead to change out of their good clothes and clamber down to the kitchen to be the first to plop into a chair. The older girls tied on apron's and helped their Mom.

After dinner each Sunday the kids were sent into raptures when their Dad handed out a once a week allotment of candy. After receiving their goodies everyone scattered to promptly devour the sweet treats a fast as humanly possible.

That is everyone except Alfred's sister, Myrtle, who would try and save her candy to be eaten whenever she chose. Like a squirrel hiding a nut, she hid her cache of goodies. In such a small house and with so many kids, she often had a hard time finding a place to do so. Someone was always watching, and Myrtle said, "Alfred was right in there leading, he was the worst one." They'd scour the house till they found where the candy was stashed. Invariably, a riotous scene exploded among them when Alfred and the other kids found it and tried to do away with it before they were caught. Myrtle never took it kindly when she discovered the theft and was mad at everyone for days.

Then there were the sleeping arrangements for ten kids. Jesse and Tillie had one bedroom and there was always two baby beds in there for the little ones. As an adult, one family member told me they would sleep three or four, not long ways as is usual, but sideways, in two beds in the other bedroom. No wonder this family was so close. Anyhow, it was one good reason to soap up real good in the old washtub. As they got older, a couch in the living room opened up and the bigger boys grabbed it for the night.

The family would gather to pop popcorn and make their own potato chips on the top of the coal stove. Apples could be sliced and baked in the oven or fried. There was always much laughter, joking, and good times. Augusta Decker, a cousin, smiled widely when she told how they would walk over to Jesse and Matilda's quite often. With all the kids and goings on, it was like one big party all the time for those visiting. Aunt Tillie always had room for one more with a smile and an extra plate.

When Harold was seven and Alfred about one, Dad bought their first Model T for one-hundred dollars. The sedan was a crank model and only had two seats front and back. Jesse never had to ask twice if anyone wanted to go with him after that. Although they seldom traveled as a family because there simply wasn't enough room, the whole bunch of them would pile in for special occasions like picnics.

Matilda lived for her children. For Tillie, Saturday night entertainment was to gather her brood around her rocking chair on the front porch. There she would rest and rock, waving to acquaintances going to and from Uniontown.

There was always a cherub-faced baby to care for. Of course, everyone pitched in and helped. Myrtle recalls, "I always hated when we had to wash the clothes. You couldn't use the excuse you were too little either. Mom just pulled out a stool and you stood on it and scrubbed clothes." She couldn't remember life without a tub of dirty diapers. The best job seemed to be that of watching a baby, especially if he went to sleep!

Matilda was a woman with deep religious convictions. Sundays were always special. On Saturday night everyone would get his weekly bath in a tub set up in the kitchen. On Sunday morning, Jesse would flip everyone a pancake, and Matilda dressed her brood in their Sunday best, and off they went to church. Surprisingly, Tillie never went herself. Maybe it was because she thought her clothes weren't right or good enough for Sunday meeting, or maybe the plain truth was that by the time she had all the kids ready to go, there wasn't time or strength left for herself. Then too, she was usually breast-feeding a baby. A good reason to stay home. Jesse never went with them either, but that changed later on.

The kids always regularly attended church. Early on it was to a Methodist church, and then when Alfred was about ten, Harold started taking them to the Church of the Brethren. It was at least a mile walk and Alfred liked going to the new church, especially enjoying Sunday School. The next year on January 31, 1931, Alfred was baptized and his name was added to the roll.

From then on this unpretentious building on Gallatin Avenue would be like a second home and family. It was upon this foundation of faith that Alfred would draw upon later in adulthood.

Life was a kaleidoscope of daily simple pleasures. A song was written a few years ago about an old lamplighter. In their day he probably wasn't old at all. It was just a job. My Uncle Harold said, "Me and Alfred used to try to follow the lamplighter as he propped his ladder against a gas light post and with his torch, light each lamp along their road. After a while we'd get tired of looking at him and stop and watch the glow of the lights as they wound a path in the dark."

Then there were times when things weren't so simple, when one crisis followed another. In large families, there was always a financial crisis, and with so many kids anything could happen.

At about the age of two, Melvin came down with a high fever and was quite sick. Tillie tried everything to bring his fever down but nothing would work. Doc Patterson did what he could, and finally diagnosed him with polio. As a result of his bout with the disease, the toddler was left with a permanent physical disability. As fate would have it, Jonas Salk was still a child and the cure for polio was some thirty years away.

Then there was the time when Alfred was about eight, that he and Harold were playing in the woodbox a little too close to the stove. Mother ordered them out immediately. Alfred clambered out first and picked up the fire-shaker and proceeded to hit the woodbox with Harold still inside. Harold was hit in the head and rendered almost unconscious while Alfred stood sobbing out the words, "I didn't mean to hurt him." Besides a knot on the head and a headache, Harold recovered from the blow and within a short time they were up to their usual antics.

The other kids had great fun with Alfred because he was always sleepy, and when he'd doze off, they would get him to talk by asking him questions. Most of the time he'd just mumble a reply, but they had a ball.

Alfred always seemed big for his age. In school he towered over the kids in his class and sometimes was even bigger than his teacher. Although Alfred got along well with his classmates and teachers, he struggled with his schoolwork. School was never easy. Alfred liked to do things with his hands. Book learning just wasn't his forte. With times as they were, in all probability, Alfred never expected to graduate from high school anyway.

With most of the kids in school, the Wilson family was feeling pressure economically and four teenagers now helped their Mother in keeping track of the rest of the 'kiddies' as Alfred used to call them. Ellen, born in 1931 was the baby still in diapers. Myrtle sadly commented, "I never had the chance to finish school, Harold either. Mom and Dad needed us to make a little extra money. At fifteen I was working in Uniontown for a lady. I'd take the streetcar on Monday morning and stay all week, getting back home on Friday night with one of her old dresses or a head of cabbage as my pay for the week." She went on, "There were a lot of kids to feed and shoes to buy, we did what we could to help."

In 1933, Tillie was pregnant once again. She'd had some rather serious conversations with other members of the family who were concerned about her having so many children. One Aunt had commented to her, "You can't keep having babies Tillie. It's going to be too much for you one of these days." Tillie and Jesse however, didn't seem to be too concerned. With ten already, one more wasn't going to make any difference. Besides, times would get better and there was lots of love to go around. Birthing babies had become as natural as breathing. The parents knew what roles to play by now. They could handle it.

But a different script would play out this time, and the curtain would drop on a pregnancy that was to end in tragedy.

Her mother never complained Myrtle said, "but she was having some problems with a tooth. It just wouldn't get any better no matter what remedies she tried. Finally, a little before she had the baby, she had to go and have the tooth pulled." Everything should have been okay, but the infectious bacteria had already started to insidiously weave its way through her system, and, as they found, in the baby's as well. A short time later, on Monday evening, the sixth of November, Matilda gave birth to another boy with waves of red hair, just like his mother. They named him Wallace.

My own Mother relived her Mother's death so many times to me that the story is seared into my memory. My Grandma never recuperated from her ordeal of giving birth to her eleventh child. She remained very ill and laid in bed with severe headaches. One worry nagged away at what little strength she had left and she called my Mother to her bedside one day. She explained, "Myrtle, the life insurance policy is due and your Dad doesn't have enough to pay it. We need six dollars. I hate to ask you, but I know you have some money saved. If you'd put it in an envelope and mail it to Uniontown, it would be paid up." Grandma knew my Mother had been saving her money to buy a coat. My Mother told her not to worry, that she would take care of it, and she did. The new coat would have to wait.

My mother said, "We had been walking softly and trying to keep the kids quiet for weeks. Mom just didn't have any strength. It was all she could do sometimes to nurse the baby." Mrs. Wright the local pastor's wife, visited Matilda a few weeks after Wallace was born. She was deeply distressed when she saw how sick Matilda was and tried to persuaded Tillie to go to the hospital. The eternal mother, Tillie refused to go unless they allowed her to take the baby with her. She told Mrs. Wright, "I'll go, but let me take Wallace with me so I can nurse him." So Mrs. Wright made all the arrangements and returned a few hours later with her car.

By this time, the family knew that mom was leaving, and a great ache tugged at the hearts of everyone gathered. After nestling the infant in her arms, Mrs. Wright helped her down the steps to the front door.

Tillie's sister, Virginia Smith came to stay with the kids. There wasn't much time for goodbyes. Ellen pouted for her mother, and tried to reach for her, while some extended a hand to touch her or gently kiss her cheek. Tillie murmured "Mama loves you." An older child replies, "We love you Mom." Virginia patted Tillie's shoulder. She and Wallace were escorted through the door. The light and life of the house had suddenly dimmed.

For most of the kiddies, this was the last time they were ever to see their mother alive. Wide-eyed and frightened the family looked on as Mrs. Wright got Tillie and the new baby in the car and headed off for Uniontown. The older kids held the little ones close in their arms, while a toddler clung to the sides of his brother and Aunt. Amid the emptiness they feel, the only thing left to do was to hang on to each other and pray.

My mother has always lamented, "What a difference a shot of penicillin would have made back then. If she could just have had a shot of Penicillin." But in 1933, Alexander Fleming had stopped work on the mold that seemed to retard the growth of bacteria, and it would not be taken up by others until 1939.

There was nothing to stop the infection that remorselessly sped through her veins. At the hospital, she was put in isolation because they thought the infection was contagious, and the doctors administered Mercurochrome into her blood to try and stop the infection. There was little hope that she would recover though, and family members who tried to visit had to put on a protective gown and wear a mask over their mouths.

Matilda had always told Harold she didn't want him to be a miner, "I never want to see you with your face black with that coal dust" she had told him. But after she went to the hospital, Harold got a job in the mines. Hurrying home at night, he cleaned up extra good before he went to visit his mom, and she never knew that he was a miner.

The police notified Jesse on a Sunday night that he needed to go to the hospital, and his oldest son went with him. Dad and I were with her when she died," Harold said. "Someone had brushed her red hair out, and it laid out across her shoulders and the white pillow. She was just beautiful. She knew she was dying and talked to us. Mom looked at me and said, 'I just wish I could leave the others as well as you are.'" She closed her eyes, and Matilda Wilson, wife and mother, departed from this life into eternity.

The undertaker prepared her body. They brought her back home to be laid out in the living room of the white house along the road. A niece remembered, "They puffed Aunt Tillie's hair out from around her face and with her red hair and white skin, she was a beautiful corpse." There were a lot of tears as friends and family came to pay their respects. Cousin Augusta and Ora Mae remembered Alfred crying behind the door of the room in which his mother lay.

Matilda Mitchell Wilson was buried November 29, 1933, the day before Thanksgiving, with services being conducted from the Presbyterian Church because it had more room than the Brethren Church. Jesse would always say years later, "When I think of Thanksgiving, I always feel sad."

Their neighbors brought a lot of food to the house, and on Thanksgiving Day, Aunt Virginia cooked dinner for the family.

The lethal infection had also attacked the frail body of baby Wallace, via his mother, and he too died a few weeks later on December 12th. He never had much of a chance. They laid him to rest beside his mother on a windy, cold winter's day in Union Cemetery.

Alfred, tall and broad-shouldered already, had turned fourteen in September. Baby Ellen was two years old. All ten children were still at home. It would be a long time before the little house would reverberate with any real joy.

Jesse took the passing of Tillie especially hard. He started going with the kids to church after their mother died. He told his oldest daughter, "I promised God that whether he took Tillie home or allowed her to stay with us a little longer, I would serve him and go to church the rest of my life." Until he suffered a stroke in his seventies, he attended the Church of the Brethren every Sunday and served the church in many capacities. He had made good on his promise.

*Harold, Jean,
Alfred, Myrtle*

Chapter III

Boy to Manhood

Christmas of '33 came and went and it was hard to remember what presents they had gotten. They had put up a tree with colored lights in the corner of the living room.

Everyone said that time healed all wounds, but it did not ease the pain of holding a grieving child who asked why God took his Mother away. There was little solace for the family as they learned to go about a life devoid of the maternal love and guidance that they had depended upon for so long.

Grandma Wilson and Aunt Ella tried to help out by coming over regularly and doing some of the washing. They'd mix and knead the dough for a batch of bread, make the loaves and set it to rise. The girls would bake it later on in the day. Sometimes they'd take baby Ellen home with them for the night.

But, even with help, the struggle of day-to-day living, cooking, washing, baking and packing lunches for the five kids going to school, was heavy for Jesse and the older kids. They couldn't ask Mother how many sandwiches to make, or how to keep the starter for flapjacks fresh, or how to take the full responsibility for having everyone's shirts and dresses ironed.

Reminiscing of those days, Myrtle's voice takes on a note of sadness, "I think it was the darkest days of my life after Mother died. We were all numb yet, but there was so much to do. She wanted the best for us. I wish she could have seen how we all turned out."

She had been the epitome of motherhood and the mainstay of her husband and children. Her nurturing influence both spiritually and physically, had taken deep root in the older children's lives and especially in Alfred. As an adult and years after her death, Alfred would say, "I always remember Mother," or "I was thinking of Mother yesterday."

Her passion for love and goodness were a bequeath that he

clutched to his heart and let them shape the attitudes and convictions that would become the very fibre of his heart and soul. He had sat at her knee and that of God during those years when he was a child. They had taught, and he had listened. He had already acquired the ability to live out one of life's greatest principles: It is more blessed to give than to receive.

Going back to their days as kids with Alfred and the other cousins, Augusta said, "There was just something different about him. He always had this grin on his face and his eyes weren't real big, but they sparkled and danced like. As kids, he never aggravated or fought with us. He was always the peacemaker."

Alfred also had a natural propensity toward helping others and his extreme good nature. In the coming years, he felt more than the rest, the weight of keeping the family going. It wasn't mere coincidence that he willingly took up more than was his share of the family burdens. His brothers and sisters started to depend on him almost as much as they did on their Dad. As time went on, even Jesse counted on Alfred for many things that needed doing. The boy was growing into a man.

The human spirit is indomitable, and as the days went by, the Wilson family laughed a little more, cried a little less, and the great ache in their hearts healed. With help from the extended family and their own self-determination, Jesse and the kids kept the home going. Within the next year, Myrtle would marry William Cunningham (Bill), a grand fellow from up on the hill, and life settled into a predictable rhythm once again, at least as far as problems were concerned.

Alfred's nature was gravitating more and more toward protecting his younger siblings and helping wherever he could. In a family photo, five of the younger kids look like stepping stones until Curt and Alfred. Curt is about the same height as Mary, who is two years younger, then Alfred, who stands more than a foot taller than his little brother next to him. But Curt made up for the shortness in spunk. The new trouble had started with the nights that Curt had complained about his knee and leg hurting him.

It seemed like it hurt worse at night, so in the late nocturnal hours, a brother or sister would get up, get the alcohol and rub his leg for him. Pretty soon it seemed like his knee was hurting all the time. Myrtle said, "He was in a lot of pain, but he just kept going." They doctored, but there was never much improvement. Hobbling around on crutches the next few years, Curt's condition gradually worsened. He was finally diagnosed as suffering from a crippling form of rheumatoid arthritis. From then on Curt was almost an invalid.

Curt had an engaging smile and a keen sense of wit. The boys could always find something to laugh and joke about. Those attributes would be put to the test in the coming months and years.

When Alfred took to carrying his little brother around, it became a brotherly indulgence for them both. Sometimes it was where Curt needed or wanted to go or just where Alfred wanted to take him. One thing is certain, Curt never let his disability get the better of him, even when at one point, in order to help stop the onslaught of the disease and be free of some of the pain, part of Curt's leg was amputated.

But even this could not daunt the intrepid spirit of the Wilson boys.

Harold and Myrtle had quit school in order to help out at home. Alfred, "Big Al," as he was starting to be called around town, was impatient to do what he could for the family.

Whether he made the choice to end his formal education to stay at home or just because the life at school had become too tedious for him, Alfred's last year must have been interesting. Even though he tried in his subjects, he just couldn't measure up academically. His heart wasn't in it. One day, he and a teacher, Miss Carr, had a little to-do about something he thought he was too big for, and she thought that she couldn't let a big boy like him undermine her authority in the classroom. Going into the cloakroom, she picked up an old flagpole and hit Alfred over the shoulders with it while he sat reading. Alfred took the flagpole incident very personally and told his sister later that day, "I never did anything to her to deserve getting hit like that." Alfred was stunned by the incident and that year, the ninth grade, was his last in the classroom.

Before school started the next fall, Myrtle remembers her brother saying, "I'm not going back," and he never did. Besides, he was old enough to get a job and help out at home. God knew they could use some extra money.

These were still Depression days and money was scarce. There were kids always needing a bigger pair of shoes or a new dress with a hem in it. Myrtle walked back home several days a week and did what she could by washing and helping with the baking and cooking. Miraculously, they always had what they needed. Cousin Augusta said "They never really wanted for anything." Nevertheless, the older kids were willing to work at anything, but there weren't many jobs to be had because no one had any money to pay a worker. Nevertheless, odd jobs could be found for those willing to work. Sometimes one didn't even have to ask.

Chat Woods, a neighbor woman, would holler at Alfred from across the road, "Hey Alfred! Come here a minute!" Good old Alfred would plod on over, already knowing what she wanted. Looking up at Alfred she'd say, "Would you go on down to Harts and get me a sack of flour?" to which Alfred would reply with a grin, "Sure, Chat!" He'd get the twenty-five pound bag of flour usually charging it to Chat's tab, then sling it across his shoulder and walk the goodly distance with it to her back porch. A word of gratitude was the only payment he accepted.

When he was seventeen years old, his brother Harold recalls, "Alfred needed something good to wear to church. What he'd been wearing didn't fit anymore, so I bought him his first real suit." Harold remembered exactly what it had cost, twelve dollars and seventy-five cents and he wore it proudly to church until he grew out of it and it too became a hand-me down.

In those days, there was nothing Alfred liked better than after a breakfast of coffee-bread, to head for Grandma Wilson's home, or to a neighbor's, Mrs. Dora Albright. There he would help paper, lend a hand with spring house cleaning, do some painting or any chore the ladies had for him. A big jar filled with fat sugar or raisin cookies provided all the payment he required. For Alfred, food rated real high on his priority list. It was just as good as money.

As Harold said, "Alfred just didn't sit down and eat a piece of chicken. Heck, he'd eat the whole chicken!" His reputation as a voracious eater was widely known. His sister Myrtle said, "He always ate good. I baked as much for him as I did for Bill and the boys."

His physical size wasn't the only part of him that was taking on maturity, however.

At about eighteen, Alfred was already man-sized both physically and mentally. Along with his family he had known the pangs of deep suffering, borne responsibility earlier than most, and endured the rigors of hard work. As heat tempers steel into a perfect hardness so had adversity fired the reckless nature of his youth into the mature composure of a man who knew exactly who he was and what he wanted. Alfred L. Wilson wouldn't stand back in the shadows if there was something that needed doing or a cause that needed a supporter.

It was this nature, or some folks might say "that Wilson stubborn streak," that led to a little fracas between Alfred and his older brother Harold on a summer afternoon.

It seemed that Alfred had set his younger brother Lloyd working in the garden and mowing the lawn. The sun might have been hot, Lloyd might have thought he'd worked long enough, or there might have been other circumstances, but for some reason Harold took up for Lloyd against Alfred.

Alfred rarely backed down from anything, not even a brother he loved dearly who was five years older, and pretty well muscled too. Both men stood for what they thought was right, and neither one gave in. Harold said of that time when he was young, "Alfred was too big to lick. I never thought we'd have a fight like that. But we sure did." The next thing they knew, the two brothers went about settling the argument with their fists.

It's unclear as to who landed the first blow. But according to Uncle Harold, "We sure went at it." They started exchanging blows in the bean patch, and before long, their battle was tearing up the whole garden. With no thought of giving up, they moved the action into the yard and even onto the porch of the house. With two men of goodly size throwing each other around, it wasn't surprising that something had to give. Their clash of wills broke off part of the railing that surrounded the back porch, causing a temporary lull to the fight.

Both of them had plenty of muscle and tenacity. They'd probably have taken things into the house and torn it apart, too, if exhaustion hadn't taken its toll. But a glance at the scared faces of the kids watching their two brothers with shirts torn half off, bodies bloody and dirty, made them realize to what extent their actions had taken them. The fight ended abruptly and nobody admitted to anything, so my Uncle Harold said.

The Wilson's had spirit and they sure proved it occasionally. After tempers had cooled off and everyone started talking, Curt openly expressed his opinion, "Alfred sure has growed up. He ain't a kid no more."

It is worthy to note that this is the only story of a difference of opinion that resulted in a physical altercation. One rhubarb like that was enough for everyone.

After turning eighteen, Alfred was eligible to enroll in the C.C.C. program. Officially it was the Civilian Conservation Corps. Part of the "New Deal," this was a national work relief agency set up by President Franklin D. Roosevelt. There were so many without jobs that this plan was put into effect to provide employment and vocational training for young men for a limited period of two years.

They built roads and dams, erected telephone lines and planted trees. They carved hundreds of State Parks from wilderness areas, some of which we still enjoy today. There were those who found themselves dismantling a whole town after the Army Corps of Engineers had moved out or fighting a forest fire in the West. Alfred worked most of his stint near Somerset, PA., in Somerset County, building Laurel Hill State Park.

The men who signed up worked a regular work week for about a dollar a day and housing was available in a camp atmosphere. To get to work, he rode a truck provided by the C.C.C. If he missed it, he hitched a ride with someone who was driving. To get home when the truck wasn't running he stuck out his thumb and hoped for the best. "One time," Harold stated, "Alfred had a fellow give him a ride from where he was working clear to Hopwood. He was sure tickled." Alfred hitched many rides from Somerset County back over the mountains to Uniontown. From there to Fairchance he had it made. Alfred never liked it when they had to stay in camp for weeks and never made it home for a weekend.

The guys in the C.C.C. had the reputation of being a pretty wild bunch. The story was told that at meal times they blew a whistle and everybody grabbed a chair and sat down to the table. Manners were left at home with Mama. Here it was pass the dish, grab the food and eat. The name of the game was "Don't leave much for the next fellow." Alfred was still a little new and when he did manage to get a serving dish, it was about empty. For this guy, it was as near starvation as he was about to put up with. So Alfred, always polite and not wanting to set a bad example, put up with the slim pickings for a while. But patience and an empty stomach didn't sleep too well, so he tried the diplomatic route and registered a complaint with the cook, who proved to be quite unsympathetic with Alfred's plight.

One night Alfred decided to deal with the matter in his own inimitable way. He was going to be first in the picking line. The menu happened to be hot dogs. When the whistle blew, Alfred was first. He stabbed at a couple of the hot dogs, which incidentally happened to be linked together. As a result, his plate was heaped up with a goodly portion of the meat for the evening. The cook, seeing that one guy had taken a lion's share of the hot dogs, yelled at Alfred, demanding to know what he thought he was doing. In reply Alfred simply stood up a yelled back, "What do'ya want?" When the cook looked at the size of the man standing, he hollered back, "Hell, sit down!" Not too many guys wanted to argue with Alfred Wilson. Alfred always had plenty to eat after that.

Alfred's physical size was pretty formidable. He stood well over six feet tall and weighed over two hundred pounds. To those who knew him though, he was really a great big teddy bear with a giant soft spot inside. Everyone who knew him said how Alfred was always joking and laughing with friends and family. He could also laugh at himself. Some said that he could talk and laugh at the same time.

There were times when he didn't talk much, but let his actions speak for him. Once Alfred told Melvin to jump in the car. Melvin didn't know where they were going or what they were going to do. Alfred pulled up alongside the road and Melvin said that he couldn't see anything but brush and pine trees. Telling his brother to stay in the car, Alfred jumped out and slammed the door. As Melvin watched, Alfred took two steps and disappeared into a growth of leaves and vines. My uncle related how he'll never forget Alfred bursting through the boughs of the trees with Charlie Collins, a friend, cradled in his arms. Charlie suffered from arthritis and couldn't walk from his house down to the road, so along with Curt, Alfred took them to Uniontown once a week for therapy treatments.

Alfred's vulnerability showed up especially where his family was concerned. His sisters Mary and Jean tell how Alfred would stop at the store every night, get cakes, bananas and boiled ham or whatever they needed for the next day. In the morning, whether he was working or not, he was always the first one up. He had the fire going and the house warm for everyone else. He'd pack their lunches including Jesse's, lay out his dad's work clothes, set the table, then start on breakfast. Usually someone else was up by this time. When Grandpap was ready to head out for work, Alfred already had the car parked out in front all warmed up and ready to go. I heard it mentioned that Alfred might have had his Father a little bit spoiled by anticipating his every need. It was just that Alfred couldn't do enough for the family he loved.

As the father and son grew closer, Jesse relied more heavily on Alfred to help out at home. When one of the kids needed new shoes, Alfred always took them to the store.

While he was still in the C.C.C., Alfred took on the job of janitor at the church. Saturday would find him sweeping, dusting, and getting things in shape for Sunday's service. In the winter, on Sunday morning, he'd be up early and on his way to the church to fire up the furnace so that the sanctuary would be nice and cozy for the worshipers. He never took any money for the job, looking at it as a privilege to be doing something for the Lord.

Myrtle said of Alfred, "Life was never dull with him around. We were mostly serious, but he'd joke and tease with almost everyone else." Myrtle recalled, "Billy had this big wart on his finger and Alfred picked him up and took him the sink and rubbed it real hard with soap and said some special words." She didn't know what he had said to his nephew, but, "the wart disappeared in about a week or so."

When he wasn't working or doing something for someone, he found time to enjoy himself. He was an avid baseball fan. There were always some fellows ready for a game of baseball in summer or a little football in the fall on the corner lot. When his turn at bat came, everyone started falling back from their original positions, because the ball sure would go a sailing.

Playing marbles was a pastime that he liked to do also, even as he got older. Then there was swimming in Zap's old swimmin' hole in the summer.

Alfred got a kick out of joking and kidding around. The ultimate high, though, was to get the best of other jokesters. As Uncle Harold told it, one day a couple guys poked an old tire through some hedges out on the Morgantown road. In the middle of the tire they left a pocketbook. The idea was when someone stopped to try to get the pocketbook, the guys on the other side would pull tire and all through the hedge before the pocketbook could be grabbed. Of course, it was all amid hilarious laughter when someone attempted to grab the purse, only to come up empty-handed. Well, Alfred and Harold got their heads together and Alfred, with a twinkle in his eye looked at Harold and told him, "Let's get that pocketbook." A daring plan was devised to get it using speed, agility and nerve. Harold would drive the car and Alfred was going to nab the purse.

The plan kicked into gear as Harold drove, maintaining a fast speed, and just as they neared the tire he suddenly slammed on the brakes and slowed down, just enough for Alfred to yank open the door, lean his huge body out, and extend his long arm toward the booty. In a flash he had grabbed not only the pocketbook but the tire as well. "Alfred got the pocketbook and we laughed like crazy with him trying to hold onto that tire through the window till I got far enough down the road to stop," Harold chuckled. The guys behind the hedge were left wondering what in the world had happened to their farcical scheme.

Everything wasn't all fun. There were things they took quite seriously.

Fairchance is a rural community and a few minutes out of town is rugged mountain terrain. Alfred was a typical country boy with the challenge of the outdoors close by. He and some of his brothers would always be tramping the woods hiking and exploring the mountains. He reveled in tramping about, splashing through streams and climbing over the rocky hillsides. Often he and his brothers or some friends would go camping. He always took Curt along.

Jesse had instilled in his son a love for hunting. In the fall and winter he would often go with his brothers or take up his rifle, call the hound dog to his side, and trek out by himself into the hills. Heading out for small game was his favorite hunting trip, but the boys would roam about for anything that was in season.

Raccoon hunting was a favorite pastime. Alfred would show up at Bill and Myrtle's place, eat a couple of cookies, and ask his brother-in-law, "Doing anything tonight Bill?" If he wasn't, "Thought maybe we'd head out and catch us a coon or two." Bill had a good coonhound and he was never adverse to any suggestions of strapping on a carbide light to go hunting.

After a summer of feasting on field corn and furring up in the cold of the late fall, raccoon pelts were thick and could be sold, and some brave souls would even venture to stuff and eat the bandit-eyed critters. But mostly, Bill and Alfred went for the fun of it.

Bill and Myrtle's two boys, Dick and Billy, always begged to go along and most times the men let them, even though they slowed things down some. One night they'd headed out into the mountain by themselves, let the dog go, and the hunt was on. Bill always had a silent trailer (a dog that wouldn't bark on the trail) so they sat and waited till they heard the dog barking at the tree where he had put the coon. They hadn't waited too long when the dog started to bark and they got up and high-tailed it after him. When they arrived at the huge oak where the dog and coon were, they couldn't make out the little bandit because of all the leaves on the tree. Alfred volunteered to climb the tree and chase the coon down to where Bill could get a shot at it. Well, it turned out that the coon was a big old wily fellow who was pretty wise in the ways of coonhunters, and after Alfred had started up the tree, the coon decided to start down, and the two met mid-tree. Bill said he didn't know what happened up there, but he heard a lot of noise and hollering and the next thing he knew, the coon came tearing down the tree, used the top of Bill's head as a runway and was off into the woods with the dog right behind him. When Alfred got back on the ground he asked Bill, "Where'd the coon get to?" Bill spun a wild tale about what he recollected had happened and they both sat down on the ground and laughed till they cried.

Alfred liked simple activities like coon hunting and going with family and friends. During tranquil times at home he listened to music or hymns, his favorite one being "Onward Christian Soldiers," or he'd read one of his favorite books, the **Bible**.

Jesse's second son never ran around much. There was a bunch of local guys that Alfred liked being with. "Punjab," as he was called by his friends, would drop in at the local eating place, the Dairy Bar, and usually some friends would also have the same idea. They'd nurse a five cent bottle of coke and catch up on each other's news.

His vices were few. He never drank, smoked, or cursed. He really never even cared much for tea or coffee, but he did drink coffee with his meals, or when out visiting he would indulge in a cup with a piece of pie. At Myrtle's house, his weakness was her filled cookies. Whether it was pineapple, apricot, or raisin, he loved them all and she made the best.

There was another thing he loved: Girls! Females just naturally seemed susceptible to the tall, dark, handsome, virile type, and Alfred pretty much fit the bill.

He had the same eyes as his mother. The turned up corners and white teeth of his smile could melt hearts. His charm and sexuality were quite natural and unconscious. Still, he knew that girls were attracted to him and he made the most of the situation.

Reading some of the love letters written to him in the late thirties and forties, it was very interesting to note what values Alfred's girlfriends held in high esteem. A familiar thread throughout the letters was that they wanted to be morally good. They wanted to be good wives. They wanted a husband of good character. One young woman expressed her desire to be treated with respect. The basic premise of their relationships were based on respect for themselves and a deep concern for the future. They wanted to have fun and enjoy themselves, but they were more aware of making right decisions. They weren't perfect, but they tried.

Alfred enjoyed the company of quite a number of females. They shared a mutual attraction. It was understood what each wanted from the other. Grace Smiley, one of Bill's sisters, tells the story of a date that she had with Alfred. She was a widow with small children and Alfred asked her to go to the movies with him. He wanted someone to enjoy the movie with and she needed a break. Grace quickly pointed out that it was just a friendly time together. Alfred liked lots of fun.

Sometimes a crowd of young people would go up to the caves exploring. In the evening some of them would gather up on Cunningham hill and sit on the porch, sing songs, tell stories and laugh.

When he was cleaning the church, it wasn't unusual for a girl to drop by just to see what he was doing. In those days, one of the best places to get to know the opposite sex was in church. More than one letter states that they would be seeing him in a Sunday evening service or at a Bible study meeting. He even corresponded with several girls, one of them in Washington, D.C. He was looking for that special girl. They were looking for that special guy. More than one of them thought Alfred was the one they were waiting for. I've found evidence of a least two engagements, both official and unofficial.

Alfred's admirers could be found almost anywhere. His brother Harold had taken a job doing some wall-papering in the home of a local Jewish family in the late thirties. As he was walking through the house a familiar picture caught his eye. In one of the bedrooms a framed 8 x 10 picture of Alfred reposed on a bureau. As Harold stood gazing at the picture, the girl's mother quietly came up and stood beside him. The next thing he knew she posed a question to him. "Is it all right for a Jewish girl to marry a Gentile boy?" Harold was surprised at the question but managed to answer that he felt that it wouldn't be a problem. The Lord Jesus had been a Jew.

There was one other girl. At one time Harold and his wife, Winifred, were living at Rummell, PA., while he was working on a farm. They attended a Church of the Brethren in the vicinity and made the acquaintance of a girl named Alice Mock. Alfred, always ready to light out anywhere, would go over the mountain to visit them. At church one evening, the two were introduced to each other and a friendship developed. Another conquest for his entourage?

Chapter IV

Mining Black Gold and Waiting for War

During the late 1930's and into the 40's, our country was starting to emerge from the dark days of the Great Depression, via government programs, time, and the sheer guts of the American people. But its tenacious grip still could be felt in the hearts, minds, and pocketbooks of families from every walk of life. At least now there seemed to be some sense of hope for the future.

Miraculously, after Alfred's stint in the C.C.C., coal mining jobs started opening up slowly. Jesse Wilson was one of the first men to get work with the A.C. Frick Coal Company. He then helped those who were married and with families to find employment. Still single, Alfred was among the last to get work mining the black gold.

Years later, Ora Mae, Uncle Ott's daughter, sat amid her antiques and thought back to when they all worked the mines, "It wasn't an easy decision to send Alfred into the mines. Uncle Jesse and Dad (Ott) had already lost one brother in a coal mining accident years before." But, they reasoned, mines were safer now. Things weren't like they were in the old days. So Alfred became another generation of Fairchance men to follow the shadow of his kinfolks and trudge into the murky, dark hole of a coal mine.

Superbly built, this son of a miner stood 6 feet 3 inches tall and weighed around the 230. Lithely proportioned and finely muscled in the shoulders and arms, his physique was perfect for the job of timberman. His stamina and strength were considered to be unique among his counterparts. Mentally, the job suited him. This guy didn't know the meaning of the word "fear." According to family and friends, there wasn't much he would shirk, even if it was difficult, and timbering in a mine was not only hard, but dangerous. "You couldn't just walk in there and get a job," Ora Mae would continue, "You had to have an experienced miner take you in and he was responsible for you and saw to it that you learned how to conduct yourself. My dad took Alfred in, but they all worked together."

New men in the mines wore a helmet that had been painted white. A "white cap," Alfred would not be alone as he donned his dark shirt and trousers that was the unofficial uniform of the miner. Adjusting his hard hat with a carbide light attached, Alfred, his Father, and his Uncle Ott, would descend down an elevator to their assigned work level.

Timbering was one of the first jobs performed in a tunnel after blasting. In order to make the passages safe, the walls and ceiling were secured with wooden beams. The timbermen usually worked with a family member or a close friend. With their lives on the line, they wanted someone dependable to work with. After working their shift "down under," they emerged black faced and be-grimed with coal soot and would head home for their daily bath.

This ritual was not a luxury, but a necessity. Augusta recalled her father's daily washing, "You had to be particular, especially when it came to getting the coal dirt out of your ears and around the eyes and eyelids. If you didn't you looked like a raccoon." Alfred once remarked that "miners were the cleanest fellows on earth."

"Big Al," a nickname Alfred picked up in the mines, was well-liked by his fellow miners. The men found him easy to get along with and he never got mad at the jokes that were pulled on him. As the saying went, "he could hold his own" in the mines. If he ever had a problem or was taken advantage of by someone, it only ever happened once. Nobody tried anything with Alfred the second time. They either respected him on sight, or learned to.

The year 1940 was a pretty good one. Myrtle emphatically confirmed it. The style of living was changing. The fast pace of technology was affecting everyday life dramatically. Women were ecstatic to be able to wash clothes without having to boil them in a copper kettle over a hot stove.

The Wilson family was doing alright. With all the men working most of the time now, there seemed to be enough money to buy what they needed. Jesse Wilson was now earning the grand sum of $52 a week. The house was a little less crowded as three of the children found spouses and left to make a new home of their own.

Alfred's sister and brother-in-law, Myrtle and Bill, along with their two boys, Billie and Dick, had bought land and were building a house a stones throw from Bill's home place "on the hill." On the 4th of July, while Bill was working the night shift in the mines, Alfred came up home to see Myrtle. Walking over to the partially dug foundation he found her digging away with pick and shovel. With hands on his hips he exclaimed, "Myrtle! What do you think you're doing down there?" She replied, "What do you think I'm doing?" Alfred then proceeded to order her out of the dirt by tersely saying, "Myrtle, now get yourself out of there and go back to the house where you belong. This ain't no kind of thing for you to be doing." Seeing Myrtle struggling at such a task went against the grain of Alfred's sense of femininity. This was the age of chivalry. Men took pride in their masculinity and tried their best to protect the essence of womanhood. So, it was like him to relieve her of her task.

After ordering her out, he jumped down into the hole, grabbed up the tools and picked and shoveled at the dirt until late in the night. All heart, Alfred would dig by hand most of the foundation for the house himself.

While Alfred worked away in America, 1941 rolled in, and the Nazis were sweeping though Europe. France was no longer free, and German troops tramped on Russian soil. President Roosevelt and Congress were talking peace and working to keep America out of the mess. Newspapers were carrying the events of the European war almost every day. After all, many Americans still had close family ties across the ocean. As much as we didn't want any part of what was happening over there, the storm clouds of war were gathering momentum and hanging over our heads like am ominous black mass.

Young men and women were living the lifestyle of a nation on the precipice of turbulent history. Their philosophy still parallels our own society's feelings as depicted in some of our television commercials. Take all the gusto from life you can, while you can, for tomorrow can disappear like a morning frost in the rising sun.

It was as if America was waiting for the onslaught of a raging hurricane, knowing by experience that storms of this nature are usually fraught with pain, uncertainty, and grief. With the winds of Germany, Italy and Japan setting a course for world power and conquest, a path would be cut where whole nations would be changed forever.

Everyone waited and watched. And while we did, the European community staggered under the harsh brutality of their invading conquerors. Could hope ever exist again in the midst of such cruelty and deprivation?

While Americans prayed and hoped, our nation's waiting game came to an end in one cataclysmic event on a far away shore.

The place was Pearl Harbor, Hawaii, December 7, 1941.

When Japanese planes took off from their carriers on a Sunday morning, there would be no turning back. Besides, the Axis powers had presumed that even if America entered the fray, she could not sustain a war on multiple fronts. It was that military estimation that led Japan to carry out the daring raid on U.S. Naval and Air Force Corps installations based in Hawaii. Killing thousands and sinking ships with their crews still sleeping below decks, the Japanese sunk four battleships, and damaged four more. Our Pacific fleet had been severely decimated.

America was at war.

Practically everyone remembers where they were and what they were doing when they heard the news. Myrtle had been sitting at her kitchen table. She too remembers that morning, "When I heard it on the radio, I felt really bad. It was a terrible feeling. I just felt bad. I sat there holding a cup of coffee and staring at the wall till Billy came in. I didn't want to believe it."

In preparation for the advent of the howling mass of destruction, we had already set up draft boards and printed rationing coupons. America's war machine started clicking into place before the smoke had cleared off the U.S.S. Arizona's watery grave.

A young man's eighteenth birthday wasn't as joyous an occasion as it used to be because in all probability, it meant leaving home. Men were being inducted into the service as fast as the paperwork would allow. Combat training camps for all branches of the service were springing up like desert mirages, except these images were very real. There was a place for everyone from the combat soldier and pilot to the file clerk, truck driver and surgeon. In every town across our country men kissed their sweethearts and families goodbye and were put on a bus, streetcar, or train.

Induction centers became beehives of activity.

Fairchance gave up its share of native sons. As each month passed, more were drafted and the age limit was raised. Married men with children who once thought they wouldn't be needed were called up.

Throughout the period from December of '41 until December of '42, Alfred worked the mines and watched his buddies leave home and learn the art of warfare. Here and there around town, stars in windows denoted a boy in the service. Gold stars were starting to appear in windows of some homes signifying the sacrifice of a loved one to the war.

Jobs were plentiful now. But the male work force was severely depleted. So we women donned a pair of pants, tied up our hair and went to work in the ship building plants and steel mills. They did what they had to, and welded and worked alongside the men who couldn't pass their physical, were too old, or worked in a job that was rated essential.

Then there were the whispers that reached Jesse Wilson's ears. Families with men dead, wounded or still fighting in some far-off corner of the world questioned why a big, strapping man like Alfred should still languish amid the comfort of home and hearth. Some folks said it wasn't fair. Some folks even intimated that Grandpap had pulled some strings to keep him home. The truth was that Alfred hadn't been drafted because miners were considered exempt from the draft. The country needed coal to send to the steel mills so mining had been declared an essential industry for the boys on the front lines.

As the months rolled by, Alfred would remark to a friend, "You know, it don't feel right, me being here at home yet and working, with George Wilson and some of the other boys signing upon being drafted. Just don't feel right." Soon, it would be a matter of pride.

These were times when sound thinking became blurred by the emptiness everyone felt at having a loved one in a dangerous situation. Now the rationale was, "If my boy has to be over there, everyone else's son ought to be there too." The war raged on and they were soon to get their wish.

In the meantime, Alfred worked, waited and carried on with

life as well as any man could. Their first car had joined the ranks of the obsolete and the Wilsons had moved on to bigger and better. Reposing now beside the old white clapboard homestead was a six passenger Model A. Indeed it must have been a welcome replacement for the family. Alfred loved to put as many kiddies that he could into the car and take them for a ride to the top of Summit Mountain. It also came in handy if you had a date for Friday night.

Date or not, Alfred found ways to keep in touch with the girls. Correspondence was regularly flowing between Alfred and several girls. Wanda, from Ephrata, PA., seemed to be ahead in the race for Alfred's affections at the time. In a letter, ironically dated December 7, 1942, she was bold enough to address him as darling, and ended by saying she remained his, "as ever, love Wanda." Things were heating up with this one. She was in love! It oozed from every page. She had sent him a Christmas present and knew that he was sending her something special. He didn't let her down. After Christmas she wrote him a letter thanking him for the beautiful blue housecoat that just happened to go with her new blue slippers. She figured there had been a little bit of collusion with her Mother on Alfred's part, especially when her mother just happened to find this present at the end of the day. Anyway, she was very happy and hoped to hear from him soon. She ended this letter with, "your wife to-be, Wanda."

A Washington, D.C. postmark was still showing up from time to time. It came from a little hometown turned big city girl by the name of Janice. She was sort of like an old friend of the family and everyone knew she had a thing for Alfred. She was hanging in there even though it sounded like she wasn't getting much encouragement. Hope dies hard in matters of the heart.

Then there was Francis, another hopeless cause. But she tried.

Once in a while a postmark from Windber, PA. crossed the post office window. Another one still in the running. But that rapturous feeling called love hadn't found its way into Alfred's heart yet. Love is a powerful potion, particularly during wartime. Emotions and feelings run hotter and stronger. She was out there waiting. It was only a matter of time. Except time was a luxury a lot of forks didn't have and they knew it.

As 1943 was welcomed in by "Auld Lang Syne" and the

Tommy Dorsey band, young people jitterbugged away the night and greeted the dawn of a new year. However, by now the grim reaper of war had plunged a nation into darker days more than even the Depression had. Sons were being killed in catastrophic numbers and the news from the warfront wasn't at all encouraging.

War wasn't just hard on the soldier. At home, every man, woman, and child was chaffing under the coupon rationing system. Sugar was rationed. Homemakers learned to substitute it with anything even resembling sweet, but molasses and maple syrup worked best in most recipes. Anything needed for the war effort was in short supply. Families in Fairchance would travel miles over the mountain to try and buy a couple pounds of meat. Going out just for a ride was an unheard of thing. Gasoline was as precious as water in the Sahara. For the ladies, vanity was even to be sacrificed. Nylon hosiery became almost impossible to buy. If you had a pair, you saved them for a special occasion because nylon was used in making parachutes.

The new year found Alfred in a state of mental turmoil. On the one hand he loved his country and wanted to join up, thereby ending the rumors and talk around town. On the other hand, he was adamantly opposed to killing a human being. He not only didn't have it in him, but he believed it to be morally wrong.

A distant cousin and friend of Alfred's, J. W. Goldsboro, now a local funeral director, said of Alfred, "I considered Alfred to be the only true conscientious objector that I ever knew. I know he wasn't, but he had the convictions to go that way if he would have wanted to." He had known Jesse and his family quite well and had attended the same school as Alfred. He was well acquainted with Alfred's upbringing in the Brethren faith.

The Church of the Brethren, long known as a pacifist church, maintains to this day the basic tenet of peace and opposition to war and killing in any way. These were the principles that Alfred was raised on as a young man. He believed in the Brethren order of ethics that literally took the Bible at its word, when it stated in the Ten Commandments that "Thou shalt not kill."

J. W. and I agreed that sane and rational people have trouble with the taking of human life. But most of us accept that there are extenuating circumstances that might require us to have to do something we wouldn't ordinarily consider. The protection of self, family and war comes under this heading. But the true mark of a man is when he finds himself aligned on a certain path by his convictions, he will allow himself to bend and act in an appropriate manner according to the situation. To borrow a popular phrase from the eighties, Alfred really was made of "the right stuff."

J. W. continued, "I believe that Alfred's decision wasn't a spur of the moment one in order to save his skin. He'd made up his mind before he was drafted that he wouldn't kill anyone." But his country was at war, and he would serve his country, in the capacity that befitted his nature, the saving of lives. It is ironic that he never got the chance to carry through on his decision.

Sitting a fence between war and peace was never a comfortable position. Alfred's exempt status had allowed him to stay true to his strong religious convictions and gentle-spirited nature. But somehow there had to be a way to work it out.

Nobody will ever know the true facts on how Alfred came to be called up, considering the fact that miners were supposed to be exempt. The fact remains that he received the call from Uncle Sam who was depicted during World War II, with his flowing, long white beard and dressed in red, white, and blue, pointing a finger straight at the reader that read, "I WANT YOU." I guess being subtle wasn't one of the war department's strong points.

Alfred's impending departure into the army affected his father and the rest of the family and friends deeply. One girlfriend, Wanda, hearing he was leaving for the army in February, penned these lines in a letter dated February 15, 1943. "I hope you will see my side and not let me say goodbye without being engaged to my future husband. All I can talk about is love because that's what I feel. Please make me a happy girl before you go, dear." She practically moved heaven and earth to get to Fairchance to see him the day before he was to leave.

Myrtle was particularly sad at the news. The brother and sister shared a strong bond and they promised to write each other. Myrtle promised to send cookies.

On a Monday around the middle of February, 1943, hundreds of selectees from Fayette County Draft Boards took their final examinations at Greensburg, PA. A few of the men to pass that day were: Patrick J. Caruso, Edgar A. Pope, John Cipoletti, William M. Walls, and Alfred L. Wilson.

Alfred passed his physical, but the family has always shaken their heads as to how he did it. As Melvin recounts, "Alfred really had high blood pressure. When he came home Alfred said that the first time the Doctor took it, it was extremely high, so he told him to take a seat and they kept retaking his blood pressure until they got a suitable reading." By this time the army needed bodies and pursued any soldier it could get. It is probable that standards became a little lax.

My Aunt, Mabel Bowers, told me how my Uncle Milt was running the streetcar on that cold 22nd of February from Fairchance to Uniontown. The draftees and families gathered for the last tearful farewell at the terminal before boarding the streetcar that would take them to the B & O Railroad Station in Connelsville.

Later that night they boarded the train heading for Fort Meade, MD.

My Uncle Melvin recalled those last moments with nostalgic sadness when his Father took Alfred aside and told him, "Serve your country son, but take care of yourself." He remembers his father throwing his arms around Alfred and saying, "You can't win the war by yourself, you can't save everybody." But Alfred would sure give it his best shot.

ORIGINAL DRAFT ORDERS
SO#39, US Army Recruiting & Induction Station, Greensburg, PA., Feb. 15/43

2. Each of the following named enlisted men, inducted into the ARMY OF THE UNITED STATES this date, is released from active duty this date, is transferred to the Enlisted Reserve Corps, and will proceed to Uniontown, PA.

Wood, Elmer W., 33429519	Yasochki. Joseph R., Jr. 33429520
Wilson, Alfred L., 33429521	Kozosky, William M., 33429522
Karwatske, John C., 33429523	Hummell, Leonard, 33429524
Leonard, Ray S., 33429525	Walls, William M., 33429526
Provance, Amadee H., Jr., 33429527	Kaifes, Charles M., 33429529
Labin, Richard, Jr., 33429528	Savage, Robert J., 33429530

McCormick, Edwin C., 33429531
Kissinger, Owen J., 33429532
Wilkins, Lloyd H., 33429533
Bean, Donald "J.", 33429534
Dennis, Ray E., 33429535
Lehman, John W., Jr., 33429536
Balchak, Frank A., 33429537
Sesler, Phil O., 33429538
Stewart, Lloyd F., Jr., 33429539
Wiland, William R., 33429540
Goisse, James E., 33429541
Marker, George E., 33429542
Hollen, Robert R., 33429543
Wise, Robert W., 33429544
Hoone, Harold O., 33429545
Miller, Robert D., 334259546
Blasinger, James W., 33429545
Plevelich, Charles G., 33429548
Burnsworth, James L., 33429549

Effective February 22, 1943, each of the above named enlisted men of the Enlisted Reserve Corps is called to active duty, and will proceed from Uniontown, PA., at approximately 11:30PM (2/22/43), arriving at Fort George G. Meade, MD., at approximately 8:00 AM (2/23/43). Upon arrival thereat, they will report to the Commanding Officer for duty.

It being impracticable for the government to furnish rations in kind, while travelling, meals for the above named men will be furnished on U.S. Army meal tickets under the provision of Par. 2, AR30-2215, for one (1) meal at the rate of $1.00 per meal per man when served in dining cars, and at the rate of $0.75 per meal per man when served elsewhere. The quartermaster Corps will furnish the necessary transportation, and charge rations and transportation to FD31P431-02A0425-23. The travel directed is necessary in the military service.

Because of Alfred's age and size, he was appointed Acting Corporal and given temporary responsibility of enlisted men until they reported to Ft. Meade.

Chapter V

Fort Jackson, South Carolina

For Alfred and the rest of the green recruits from up north, that first train ride south catapulted them on to a brand new stage of endeavor. Alfred was "in the army now."

The Letters Begin

For the reactivated 26th Infantry Division and the men who had just been inducted into the army from Greensburg, PA., their first camp was Fort Jackson, South Carolina.

Alfred L. Wilson

February 26, 1943
Fort Jackson, S.C.

Alfred's first letter to Myrtle was filled with optimism of sorts. They had a good meal of fried chicken, had traveled by train almost 900 miles, gone through four states, and he hoped to see more states. He seemed awed by the immense forests of pine trees that stretched along their route and even estimated their towering size at about 80 feet into the sky.

He was finally in a camp and while he wrote, Bill Walls was sitting next to him writing a letter to Ann. He was not overly optimistic about getting home very soon as he had been talking to some of the other guys already in training and some of them had not been home for a year and a half.

Alfred did not engage in any of the usual vices that most of the men fell prey to. He neither smoked, drank, used foul language or gambled. He wrote, "Boy, is there a lot of card play and playing of dice. There is a dice game going on now in our barracks, but I haven't played a game yet and am not going to. They also sell beer here. I went to church today and how nice it was."

As social creatures, we gravitate toward those whose likes and dislikes are similar to our own. Paul Yee told me that was probably why he and Alfred were close during most of their training and stateside days. Neither one of them was partial to the fast crowd so they hung around with each other a lot. Mostly they would watch movies, go to the P X for a Coke, write letters and otherwise try to stay out of trouble.

Alfred was personable, fun loving, and always pulling a trick on a fellow soldier. To be around Alfred was to be in the middle of laughter and some kind of fun or another. Paul recalled, "We would play football quite a lot. When I would see Alfred coming at me, it was always wise to duck the other way or else he would grab a fellow in his huge arms and give him a bear hug." Everything was done in great fun and the men grew to metaphorically regard Alfred as a great big teddy bear or a gentle giant. Alfred stated that he felt that he was getting along well with the boys and was having a good time. But he would be glad when basic training was over.

A soldier's days were filled with maneuvers, training sessions, and learning how to put a pack together. In the evenings, he had a few hours that he could call his own. A half hour was needed just to shower and clean up.

In the midst of army life, Alfred didn't forget who he was or what he stood for. I read this in a letter of March 11, 1943.

"Myrtle, I have gone to Church every Sunday and am reading at least 3 chapters every night and saying a prayer too, in silence. Tell everyone that I am just the same as I left. I haven't done anything wrong and I said I would not do anything that I did not do at home. I still think about Mother so don't worry about me."

Every letter without exception inquired how things were going at the church. How he hoped this or that was okay or asked if Reverend Jones had gotten a house yet.

Just a few weeks into basic training Alfred hinted at his vulnerability when he laments to my mom about not getting any letters from Wanda. Army life is hard on the romantic aspirations of a soldier. She had practically begged Alfred to be engaged to her before he left and had almost broken her neck to get to Fairchance to see him. But absence was evidently not making the heart grow fonder. Alfred was disappointed that she was not sticking by him, so he put up a brave front by saying he had received a letter from a Thelma and had felt better after reading it. She sounded like a nice girl and he had almost decided to write her and ask her to be his girlfriend. He wanted to know that he had someone to write to and to like. That basic need to love and be loved existed in the best of times and the worst of times.

The life of a soldier never stood still for long in wartime. By mid-April, the new recruits were breaking camp in South Carolina. They had to sleep in pup tents for a couple of nights, and on the last night while it was pouring down rain, a peg broke loose and the front part of Alfred and his buddy's tent collapsed. In the melee everyone and everything managed to get soaking wet. Nobody said it would be easy or dry.

The next day, big trucks soon rolled in and the men and equipment were loaded up and headed south for more southern hospitality and a new camp.

Chapter VI

Camp Gordon, Georgia

Marches and Sweat

For the northern boys, the spring of '43 would be memorable. Instead of being greeted by April's leftover snow banks, they sped by green grass, spring flowers, and through a steady downpour of rain as they made the trip from North Carolina to Camp Gordon, Georgia.

"The trucks have brought us 6 miles from Augusta, Georgia," Alfred wrote to his dear sister Myrtle from their new camp. With all the rain and just getting his things dried out, he appreciated the new barracks and being dry again. Besides, this one had running water, showers and toilets in the same building. "It sure is nice," he said.

He wrote of being uncomfortable with having to sleep on the bottom of a double bunk bed. He didn't like the idea of a fellow sleeping over top of him.

Basic was over and they were anticipating their real training, or, as the officers called it, advance training. Now they would be separated into the areas they were specializing in.

From the first, Alfred had said that he didn't want to kill anyone and had requested to train as a medic. There were other options open to him that would have allowed him to refrain from being in a combat position. J. W. Goldsboro stated the opinion, with Alfred's aversion against the taking of a human life, he would have had a legitimate case for deferment." John Flynn, now a Pittsburgh resident, echoed the same thought, "With Alfred's state of mind regarding killing, it would have been logical for him to seek a conscientious deferment."

During World War II, many men who would not carry a weapon, received a conscientious objector deferment and served their country working in hospitals, as aid men, and also helping in the training camps. This was an honorable way to peacefully serve ones country with a clear conscience. An added bonus was that in most of the situations, one was out of harm's way. Alfred chose no such route, and the army granted his training request.

Without wanting to doubt the wisdom of Alfred's decision to serve as a medic, the question arises if he fully understood the extremely vulnerable positions that medics served in. Maybe he did. By this time the country had been in the war long enough for the guys to know what the score was in a combat zone. There were too many gold stars in the windows back in Fairchance.

And then again, maybe he didn't. His access to the records of the 1st Battalion Aid Station would have listed the simple garden variety of fatigue, blisters, and a few casualties. Another copy, retyped from the original dated May 8, 1945, read somewhat differently.

Scanning the roster of aid-men in the original Normandy position and comparing it to the list made up at its final position in Oberhaid, Czechoslovakia, out of the twelve medics, serving four infantry companies, only a third of the names appeared as still alive at the end of the campaign, and only one of them was still a medic. "It was a very vulnerable position," one of the guys called it. Walking into the fire with no odds-on favorite would be another way of putting it. Every one of those guys was a hero.

Medics were on the front lines with their company in the action. They dug a foxhole alongside the fighting soldier and shared his tent with him. They ate the same mud as he did after three solid days of rain. They prayed through the night with him, and the next morning they all tried to clean up as best they could using their helmets as a wash basin.

To the infantry man in time of trouble, a medic represented safety and help. As Al Zotolla told it, "The medic patched them up and arranged with the litter bearer to get them evacuated." The medic carried two bags of supplies containing scissors, bandages, tape and a few other items. A medic could give a shot of morphine if a soldier was in extreme pain. The Syrette looked like a travel size toothpaste tube with a needle on the end. The medic jammed the needle into an arm and did one of two things. He either taped the empty Syrette to the soldier or threw it away and put a tag on the soldier saying he had received a shot of morphine. This was to prevent someone else from administering another shot that might prove fatal. Also in the kit were sulphur tablets and yellow sulphur powder. The powder acted as a disinfectant and also cauterized the wound. For those who suffered from a concussion, they also gave them medication similar to aspirin.

The medic was someone who would be there no matter what. As the occasion warranted, he was also the soldier's psychiatrist and friend. It was part of his job to help everyone be cool.

Here's the situation. There you are, flat on you back in the middle of a field somewhere in a country you don't want to be in, and this schrapnel someone talked about on a training film has attached itself to your body in a dozen places totally uninvited. You're bleeding like a sieve, and you didn't know it was going to hurt this bad. Trying not to flip out, you tell yourself to stay calm. Your eyes look up into the face of the medic as he leans over you, sweat pouring off him as he desperately tries to stop you from bleeding to death, and all the while he's saying, "You're gonna be allright, you're gonna make it." You know this guy. Wasn't it just yesterday that he was giving you a cookie that his sister had sent him. He wouldn't tell a lie if his life depended on it. But this is your life, and your blood soak'in the ground, and he wouldn't let you down. Somehow, you believe him.

By this time, these guys knew each other and their medics well. The names of girlfriends and family, likes and dislikes, fears and strengths, were common knowledge. The medic epitomized everything fine and decent to his men. As Ron Still, a Regimental Historian for the U.S. Army Medical Department at Fort Sam Houston told me, "The medic took his job more seriously than most. He was ever cognizant that he was a bridge between life and death to the wounded." Depending on circumstances, the ministrations of the medic on a gravely injured man made the difference between making it out alive or having his name appear on the casualty list as a Killed in Action (KIA).

The medic was a succor of hope to the officer and the soldier alike. Bullets don't have any respect for those in command. When pain and possible death are sitting on one's chest, there was only one name to holler. Well, actually there were two, but you didn't have to say the other one out loud. If a wounded soldier was in a tactical position where he thought he might not get help quickly, and he had the physical strength, he turned his gun upside down and pushed the muzzle end into the ground and left it standing there. It became an unspoken sign that someone was alive and needed help, badly.

Medics were not allowed to carry a weapon. Off the record, I was told that a lot of the medical personnel managed to carry some kind of concealed weapon, even if it was only a knife. The idea being that anything was better than being at the mercy of your enemy. When asked if Alfred carried any weapon, the men who knew him answered, "No, no Alfred never did carry any weapon." He would not compromise his own ethics or a rule.

The reality of World War II and its medics was that they became targets for the enemy, and each company tried to protect their medic as much as possible. Because of their training and ability to save the fighting soldier, the enemy considered them a prime target. In the early days of the war, medics wore a red cross on an arm band. Later on in the war so as not to be recognized, they tore off all medical insignia, even though the red cross was a sign of medical personnel and they were not to be fired upon. So much for the Geneva Convention rules. All is fair in love and war.

Camp Gordon, Georgia
April 20, '43
Dear Sister Myrtle,

They say we will be here for 2 to 3 months. I hope things are well at home. How are Curt's chickens doing. Make sure he has feed for them. I am sending some money for you to help pay some of the bills out home and buy then some groceries. Tell the boys to do all they can for their Dad and I will get them something when I come home.

Sure am hungry for some of your chicken how you do it. Camp cooking just doesn't measure up to yours.

Could you do me a favor and get a pair of plain brown shoes, size 11 1/2. Also I need stamps.

Some of the guys in the outfit have been asking if

I am getting anymore of my sisters cookies. If you could spare some, I'd sure appreciate a box of them. It doesn't matter what kind. Write soon.

So long. Alfred

May 5, '43
Dear Myrtle,

Just a few lines to let you know I am well and hope you are the same. I am having a good time here. Went to town. It is the second time since we have been here. The fellows I went with got me a big spaghetti supper and was it good. The people here seem to be friendly. But would rather be home any day.

The boys ask me when I was going to get some more of those good cookies. I said I hope to get some a little later on after I write this letter. That's why I haven't wrote thinking you was waiting till you bake.

Myrtle, I tried to get Easter cards when I went to town, but couldn't. So I couldn't send anybody one. We weren't allowed to go to town till our basic training was over. And they said if they caught anyone it would be too bad. So I didn't go. But am glad to hear that you had at least something good to eat. It was just an ordinary Sunday with just what we always had.

Myrtle, you ought to be here. The sun is shining and it is really hot. We haven't had a cold day yet since I been here. People have stuff up in their gardens already, even cabbage. So you know it is good for things to grow.

Hope it soon breaks up so you can get your garden in.

Myrtle, with the $30 that is in this letter I want to see that some of Dad's bills are paid. So they won't be behind so much. I will be sending some every month. We will get paid on the last day of every month, so you will be expecting it. I shore am sorry to hear Chip Collins shot himself. I shore hate to hear that. When will he be buried? I shore would like to see him.

Sometime during this period, Wanda had finally written him and sent some cookies. But, it may have been too little, too late. Alfred was thinking that this was not the girl for him and perhaps he wasn't going to write her anymore. She should know how he feels so as to be free to do as she pleases.

Even though Alfred was having girl troubles, it never affected his appetite. The fellows have taken Alfred to town and bought him a spaghetti supper. They took him along with them on occasion to make sure that everyone got back to base safe and sound. You can look at it this way. He was their little piece of the rock. Insurance against anything that might befall a young soldier on a pass to town. They knew they could depend on Alfred.

The fellows have nicknamed him "Pappy." Drafted at 23, he was a bit older than most of the other men. Like a mother hen gathering her chicks, he shouldered the responsibility and role of protector. Bob Walls remembers Alfred one night, "The barracks door banged open and here come Alfred with a fellow slung over his shoulder, and I thought he was just dragging a jacket in the other hand, but here he had some guy passed out and he had him by the back of his coat just dragging him along." Drunk or sober, walking or carried over a shoulder, he got them all back to camp on time and even put some of them to bed.

According to their fun loving nature, the medical detachment and the men of the companies they were assigned to were always pulling pranks on each other. One stands out in my memory that Alfred told Myrtle while on leave.

He and some friends were in town and went into a bar. Alfred was drinking his usual bottle of red pop while the other guys were soaking up something a little stronger. They waited for an opportune time when Alfred wasn't nursing his pop and managed to substitute it with some whiskey. Alfred would tell Myrtle, "I didn't know they'd went and put that whiskey in there. It shore made me cough, and I almost choked on the stuff. I'd wanted to laugh at the fellows, but figured I better be serious or they'd do it again."

He set the bottle down, looked around the table and never said a word to his buddies about what they had done. The bottom line was that they never pulled that stunt on Alfred again. By this time they had a healthy respect for Alfred's size, and they had tried it once. They didn't want to stretch their luck to see what would happen if they tried it twice.

A big part of army life then consisted of drilling, marching, First Aid courses and naturally, lots of bandaging. "But," he wrote in one letter, "it is worthwhile work and I like it better than the times with the rifle company. The day shore goes by. We see a show every day, but can't tell you anything about it."

The army has started taking the men out on maneuvers. Bone weary, Alfred and his company lay around on their bunks after having just come off of twelve days of night maneuvers.

May 6, '43
Dear Myrtle,

I received your letter and was very glad to hear from you. Myrtle, when you buy my shoes get plain, brown, not with holes like mine before I left. I will send you money next pay day. Myrtle, I will tell you a lot of things when I come home. That is when they let us come home. But it will not be for a while yet. But as soon as I get a chance, I'm coming home. We are going to start a 12 week of night problems. That is where you go out in the night marching, digging foxholes, slit trenches, and sleeping out in our pup tents so you know it will be a while before I will get to come home.

How is everyone? Hope they get the strike settled. I got a letter from Harold today and was shore glad.

Give Dad as much money as you can and forget about my shoes. They need it worse than I do. I kept $15 because we have to get a hair cut and get soap and other things so I think I will keep a little but just spend what I have to.

Myrtle, it is a least 98 here and does it make me sweat. You talk about sand. That is all there is here and does it make your feet burn.

We had a good supper tonight. But would rather be home eating. They don't cook like you do at home. Because they have to cook so much and it doesn't get as done as I like it, but still I have gained weight. I am remembering Mother.

Went to town with a buddy a couple of days ago. He stopped and ordered some flowers to be sent back home to his mother for Mother's Day. It near broke my heart because I sure wished I could have done the same, but I know that someday I will see her again "on high."

Myrtle, this is all I can think of now, so I will say so long. Till I see you or hear from you.

With love, Alfred

Alfred thought a great deal of his mother. It was this deep feeling and respect for her that prompted his "Mother's Day Speech." One of the men in his unit remembered how on that Sunday morning Alfred got up early, spit and polished his outfit and dressed in his best uniform. His bunkmates railed at him from under their blankets, "What are you bucking up for, Pappy, there's no inspection today." They didn't know of any special occasion unless he was going out to find himself a girl.

It was then that Alfred would begin to tell them how he had lost his mother when he was a boy and how much he had honored and loved her. He continued, "Now I don't know about you fellows, but I'm going to church on Mother's Day, and you can do as you please." Later on that morning the Chaplain was shocked and surprised when it came time for the Mother's Day service. His Chapel was filled to capacity and I think it worthy to note that Alfred's barracks was conspicuously devoid of soldiers.

May 17, '43
Dear Myrtle,

Just a few lines to let you know I am well and hope you are the same. Today was a very hot day and we did have to do some hard work. We had close order drill. The afternoon we had to dig a foxhole and does it take a lot of work. I had to dig mine 5 1/2 feet deep and had to make it so nobody could see it. Then an officer came around and inspected it. Out of 45, only 3 passed and one was mine. They said it really was good and I got a good grade out of it. Then we had to fill them in. We carried the dirt away, then we had to carry it back. We couldn't leave it around the foxhole. I could wring water out of my undershirt. It's been really hot. It's 105 last Friday.

We went out on a two day and night problem. And did we have a time too. I was in the 2nd B HDQ, C. There were at least 200 men in it and two of us had to take care of them and what a job. We had to carry 70 pound packs like all the rest. When they gave them a 10 minute rest, we didn't get to rest. We had to take care of the other men. When we stopped the first time, I had to take care of lots of blisters. On the way back there were lots of them to take care of. You could hear them ask where was an aid man. We were shore busy. We were there till 4:00 in the morning. But before we got to our barracks, they let us eat all the cake and drink all the coffee we wanted.

My Mom had ignored his earlier entreaty and had bought him shoes. He sure liked them and they couldn't fit any better.

Glad to hear the mines were back to work. How is S.S. (Sunday School) going. Boy, you ought to see how the fellows carry on down here. Do we have lots of fun. We have several fellows from the South and are they comical. I laughed sometimes my side hurts. Some of them are writing, some singing, some are just laying on their bunks. The fellow just came from the kitchen and they brought some apples with them and do they taste good now.

We had a good supper tonight of baked beans, all we could eat sauerkraut, green beans, jello, apples, cocoa, crackers and bread. I called that a good supper, but it could have been better. We had ham and eggs for breakfast.

Myrtle, I wish I could see you now. Boy do I miss home. But it wears off and I forget about it. For someone is after you or it is time to go eat, or start out to wash or it is time for the light to go out. That is 10:00 and up at 5:25.

Some of the fellows are getting ready to go on a hike tomorrow but I don't have to go and are some of them hollerin about haven to go. But I have learned to keep my mouth shut and I don't have to go out so I will get to sleep a little later. They will get up at 4:30 tomorrow

We have a radio here and it shore does go except if you get itchy feet to dance, you either have to dance with another fellow, which is funny, or tap your feet real loud.

Tell everyone I said hello at home and hope everything is all right at home. I will have to say so long.

Your brother, Alfred.

May 21, '43
Dear Sister Myrtle,

We just got back from a problem (maneuver). We were gone overnight. Will go out again Monday and stay the whole week. Don't know if allowed to take writing paper, but I will try. Boy, do I feel good now. I just got through taking a shower and put on clean clothes.

I heard about Chip killing himself. Did he do it with a gun? I never thought he would do anything like that. It was a shock.

First I hear the mines are going back to work and then someone writes and says that they are coming out on strike. Boy, why don't they get it settled.

I am glad you and Dad got those potatoes because the kids really like them. So do I. I wish we would get that farm. But I guess you will have to get it yourself, because one of these days we won't even be here. But hope to get a leave before we have to go. I hate to hear Aunt Ella is sick.

I'm surprised of Ora May (a cousin). Archy will shore crow. Hope she will come through alright and the baby lives too.

I will say so long.

Alfred

Chip Collins had been one of his buddies back in Fairchance. The farm mentioned was part of a dream that he had shared with Bill and Myrtle. They had hoped to buy some land and work it together on the other side of the mountain in Somerset county.

Alfred's cousin was pregnant and his fear that he expressed about the baby living was due to his memory of Wallace dying as an infant. But, mother and the baby boy they named Arch Harry came through fine.

May 25, '43
Dear Myrtle,

Here I am sitting in my tent waiting to be called out to do something. But while I am waiting I will tell you all that happened. We left camp Monday morning to hike 11 miles. It started to rain before we left and it rained all day. We were like drowned rats. To make matters worse we had to go through a crick up over our knees. And beside that we had to sleep on the wet ground. But I didn't. I got a litter and layed on it. It was off the ground and I slept very good.

We had fried hamburg and eggs for breakfast, also milk, coffee, grapefruit and bread. It was good, but I could have eaten a little bit more.

Myrtle, I got your cookies? They were shore good too! How are the kids? How is everybody at home? I can't think of anything more.

I will say so long.

Alfred

P.S. You ought to see our tents, you can hardly see them. They are canvas logs and it is still raining.

May 29, '43
Dear Myrtle,

Maneuvers again! We marched for days in the rain, even the officers. It rained so hard you couldn't hardly see ahead of yourself. And to make matters worse, we had to cross a crick and it was over my knees. Everyone had to go through it, even the officers. You ought to have seen us. We had to sleep in our wet clothes. Went on canned rationing out there. We each got 5 cans of food. Two cans of pork and beans. Two cans of vegetable stew, and 1 can hard biscuits called bread.

I was shore tired when we got back. It seems as if that pack got heavier every time we walked at first. But I don't mind it now for I am getting used to it. But would rather be back home working in the mines.

Corn here is about a foot high!

Wish I was at your place when you were ready to get those chickens cleaned. To be able to put two in a pot and have everything that you always have with chicken. Boy, do I miss the meals I had when I was at home. Has anything been changed at home?

I got a letter from Thelma. She said she hasn't given very much thought about being a steady girlfriend. But she said she will always write to me. If it wasn't for the War, I would be her boyfriend. But the way things are, she said that she thinks to be a friend and let time tell the rest. She shore does write me good letters. When I get one, you don't know how good it makes me feel. Wanda has been writing to me quite often now. I just don't know which one I like the most. But there will be lots of time to think about that.

We been hearing that we are going to move soon but don't know just where we are supposed to go.

I bet the Jones are tickled pink when they will be Granddad and Mother again. I hope she gets along well and hope it will live.

Myrtle, don't put your sugar into cookies for me. You will need it worse than I do. So, if you can't spare it, don't bake for me. Tell me if Bill and Dad are working or not.

Your Brother, Alfred

Sometime around the end of May and first of June, Bill Walls and Odie made it home on their first leave. The Army let so many go at a time. Alfred's turn was coming.

Sugar came in five pound bags and each family had a rationing coupon for one bag per month. One batch of cookies took at least two cups of sugar.

June 1, '43
Dear Sister,

I received your letter yesterday, but couldn't answer it. I was out on the shooting range as a first aid man.

I hope you get your housecleaning done. I always hated it when I was at home. But it won't take you long to get it done.

The only way and best way to send chicken or anything else, is to put them in a jar. If you send chicken, take it off the bone, put it in any jar and seal it real tight. Then put it in a tight box. That is what Harold did and it got here alright.

I know Lawrence Firestone had to go, bet his mother hated to see him go.

I heard about Tommy flying over. But one of these days, there will be something happen when he is flying that low. But hope it doesn't.

Yes, Myrtle, I got your cookies. They were very good and thanks for them. I ate almost all them myself. They shore did taste good at bedtime.

I hope S.S. is keeping up. I go to S.S. and church every Sunday. The Chaplain shore gave a good sermon.

We had a good dinner, but would rather be home eating instead of here. But I guess I will have to stay.

Tell all at home I said hello and hope you get your garden in. I got a letter from Winifred and was I glad to hear from her.

So long, your brother, Alfred.

June 3, '43
Dear Myrtle,

Just a few lines to let you know I am well and hope you are the same. Well, how is everyone at home. I bet Dick and Billie are wanting to go swimming by now.

We missed going out with a Company by half an hour. I didn't know where they were so we went out to the Kitchen truck and ate dinner. Then laid around for two hours and come back and our day was done. It was the easiest day we had.

But we will have to go with a different company and sleep, eat, and march with them all the time.

Myrtle, I am sending this money order and I want you to use it to the best advantage for Dad. I am told I will be a P.F.C. soon. But I haven't been told by an officer. But it will give me $4.00 on the month. Is everyone working? How is S.S. keeping up? I was talking to Odie and he said he might have gotten what you was going to sent broken so he wouldn't try it.

Well, that is all I can think of.

So long, Alfred.

The medics had not been assigned a company yet, but were starting to spend more time getting used to company routine.

June 6, '43
Dear Sister Myrtle,

I just received your letter fifteen minutes ago. I just come home from a range detail. I am glad I went. I don't believe I could be treated any better than I was today. The fellows were swell and so were the officers. I would like to go with them all the time.

We had ham sandwiches for dinner and they weren't afraid to put ham on them. I ate seven and boy was I full. We had all the cold drinks we wanted and all the apples too.

We ate supper with them too. We had ham, potato salad, corn, jello, bread and we had all we wanted.

Boy is the weather hot. 110 yesterday and today. To make matters worse, we had to walk three miles or parade to be interviewed by a one star General. It only took 5 minutes to do that. I don't see why they wanted the men to do that. You ought to see how the men were fainting or having sun stroke.

Myrtle, don't skimp for me for I know how hard it is to get sugar. So don't worry if you can't send me any. I will think of you just the same. I heard they had a nice program on Decoration Day. Uncle Ott wrote and sent me the names of the fellows they read off.

Till I see or hear from you,

So long, your brother Alfred.

June 14, '43

Dear Myrtle,

I received your letter today just before supper so I am answering it now. Myrtle, when I wrote Saturday your cookies hadn't got to me. But I got them Sunday afternoon. Oh! how they tasted to me. They were shorely good and the other fellows that ate some of them said the same thing. They shore did taste good at bedtime. I always save some for that time.

Myrtle, I always tell you when I get something from you. I thank you for sending them to me. I will try to do something for you whenever I can. I also think about you and will say you are the best. I don't know when I or Dad will be able to pay you back for what you have done for us. Do as much as you can and I will see what I can give or do for you when I am out of the army.

Myrtle, I would like to see your yard when you get it done. I know it will look nice. But I don't know when I will get home.

Tell Billie just keep on doing what he can for his mother in going to the store and mailing your letters. I will close for now. So I will say so long. By now.

Alfred

June 23, '43

Dear Myrtle,

I received your letter just about five minutes ago. So while I haven't anything to do I am answering it. We are here in the woods now. We will be here till Saturday morning. We are 14 miles from camp and boy do I have it easy. I haven't done anything but eat and sleep. I am in the aid station for sick call, but there isn't very many comes.

I got my picture taken in a studio so when they come back I will send them home. I will get some made from the negatives.

No Myrtle, I don't get tired of cookies. They really taste good. Myrtle, can you bake some drop cakes. Or make a flat cake in a pan and put icing on it if you can. but if not send those cookies.

Myrtle, am I glad to hear that Ray Woods isn't dead. I hope the Japs don't kill him. I bet Clara feels better now. I hope something happens that he will get back alive.

Well Myrtle, I hope Lloyd and the rest make out good. What did Dad say when Lloyd asked him to let him go? I hope he does good. It is a lot different out in the world alone than when you are at home.

I am glad to hear your garden is doing good. It will help you out this summer and winter, at least you won't have to buy the things you grow.

It really is a shame that Maggie Nemcina baby died. But I think it is better off than to be like it was, don't you think so. I bet she hated to see it go. But I wouldn't give up if I were her.

Yes Myrtle, Bill Walls and I run together. He is shore a good sport. I do things for him and he does the same for me. I keep his money for him. He tells me when he comes to me for money for me not to give it to him. He has thanked me several times because I had his money. He said if he would have had it he would spend it.

Till I see you or hear from you, I will say so long.

Answer as soon as you can.

Your brother, Alfred.

June 26, '43

Dear Sister Myrtle,

Just a few lines to let you know I am well and hope you are the same. I just came back from weeks out in the woods. What a week it was. If I had to stay out another day, I would have went crazy. All we had to eat was K-rations. I am going to send you what we had to eat for 2 days. You will be surprised. Only one accident. One fellow shot himself in the foot.

Accidents of this kind were not a rarity. During training many of the men had never handled a firearm before, and adding clumsiness and nervousness together, a gun going off in the wrong direction was not a strange occurrence. At the 26th's reunion one of the men told me that after they went overseas, whether due to plain fear and a word I hate to mention, cowardice, there were those who purposely blew a hole in their own foot as a way out of combat.

Veterans explained what a K-Ration pack consisted of: gourmet item number one was a can of something that qualified as hash or whatever name you wanted to put on it. The C-Ration packet consisted of biscuits or crackers and some kind of cheese, a piece of hard chocolate, some instant coffee. As one guy put it, rations were enough to keep you alive. With Alfred's appetite, he probably thought he was near his end.

The GIs in the European theater were sometimes besieged all for the sake of a chocolate bar. It wasn't unusual when Americans went through a town to have children surround them and their vehicles begging for chocolate. It was the first thing they asked for.

One soldier told me that while giving the chocolate away it was done so with a warning to either a child or a mother that it was to be eaten very slowly. One GI said, "I'd give them a little piece at a time, if you didn't, they'd get sick." For the most part these children were starving and eating very little food. If the chocolate was eaten all at once, it would make them ill. Knowing the nature of kids, it is doubtful that too many heeded the American advice.

Also included in the C-ration packet were a few cigarettes and matches. It was a subtle way to encourage smoking.

Myrtle, I can thank you a million times for those cookies you sent me. I ate them yesterday just when we were tearing down the aid station. And boy, was I hungry too. When I ate the first one, I felt a million times better. Those cookies really filled me up. I was really starved. Myrtle, they were all good. None of them were moldy. So you don't have to worry about sending those kind of cookies.

How is everyone doing? And up on the hill? Is Dad working even if they are out? I read in the paper that the mines are out. I hope they won't be out long. How are the gardens doing?

How is everyone at home. I wrote the other day last week, but haven't gotten any answer. How is Curtis and his chickens doing? Tell me how they are getting along. I suppose everything in Fairchance is just the same. Tell me the news around there.

How is the S.S. (Sunday School) getting along. Tell them to keep on the way they are. I really like to hear they are having good attendance.

Myrtle, I am going to a show tonight. They have a pool table, but I don't like to play. I don't gamble so this is what I do for my past time. I go to Church every Sunday when I can. Sometimes I have other work I have to do and don't get to go then.

They are supposed to give us a party for the 4th but don't just know if they are going to have it for shore or not. I hope you and the rest of the family have a good 4th. I don't know when I will get to come home. I don't know if we are even going to move or not, for they change everything now.

Well this is all I can think of now. I will close saying, so long. Answer soon.

So long, Alfred.

July 6, '43

Dear Myrtle,

I received your letter a couple of days ago. But was waiting till I saw Major Vernin, the C. Commander, but he wasn't in just then. Then we had to leave and come out here in the woods.

But as soon as I get back, I will see him and they will do it for me. So you can expect to receive it or rather Dad, but it won't come till next month because it will take some time to get it ready. But will be able to get it next month. I will try and get as much for Dad as I can.

Myrtle, just save $15 for me or $10 if it is less.

We will be out in the woods all this month. We will only get to go to camp over the weekends. We will leave Sunday for the range. That is where we will get lots of hard and dangerous training.

I also hope Bill will make out better at Kyle than he did at Ralph. I know what it is when you try to change jobs. But hope he makes it alright.

Yes, Myrtle, I heard from Jean that Lloyd left for Washington.

It rained last night, but I didn't get wet even if I am sleeping in a little tent. But today the sun has come out and it is starting to get hot. It always get hot down here after a rain.

I can't hardly wait to see how things are at your place and home. I bet the house looks good now. I shore thank you for what you have done for us. Some of these days I'll try and do something to repay you for what you have done for us.

Yes Myrtle, I got your cookies and no, they didn't spoil. They shore were good. Thanks a million for them.

Myrtle, wasn't that a shame about Loretta. I wish it would have lived, don't you. At least it would have made her feel better. I bet when they tell Marshal about it, he will be sad, thinking he had a baby, but don't.

I wish I could have seen Sam Woods. But I guess I will have to wait. I don't know when I will get to come home. But hope it won't be too long. For I can't hardly wait to come home.

Jean told me about Ab getting a new car. I guess he needed one.

Oh yes! I forgot I got a raise. I am a P.fc. I will get 4 dollars extra this month or next. So put Pfc instead of Pvt on my letters.

I will close now, love Alfred.

Alfred had signed up for an allotment to be paid to his Dad. Part of it would be automatically taken out of his pay. Another sister, Jean had written Alfred and passed along the information that brother Lloyd went to Washington for a job. Jean's husband was Ab Beatty.

Sam Woods was a neighbor kid across the road who had been drafted.

July 18, '43

Dear Sister Myrtle,

Just got back from three weeks of rougher training yesterday and was I glad. I got tired of sleeping on the ground. I wish they would stop for a little while. They keep us on the go. We get to sleep one night on our bunks and then we will go out again.

I hope we don't have to walk anymore, but I guess we will always walk. It really makes my legs tired when we first start, but I am getting used to it now.

Myrtle, I applied for an allotment for Dad. The clerk said I could, so he will be getting it next month. They will take $22 out of my pay and the government will send him $28. In all he will get $50 at the end of every month. Save me $15 out of every pay. I don't know when I might need some money. Don't know when I can come home, but will have enough money to come home on, so don't worry about me.

Answer when you can, Alfred

Alfred did get used to the long marches, enough so that his tremendous strength became part of his reputation. Several of the medics and aid men including John Flynn, quite a big fellow himself, recounted those long hikes during the summers of '43 and '44. "He had long muscular legs that just ate up the miles." Those hikes were hot, muggy, and frustrating, especially with seventy pound packs and an officer constantly hollering. John continued, "Some of them couldn't quite make it and Alfred would pull up alongside a fellow and relieve him of his gear, carrying the extra pack and gun until he could regain his composure enough to get back in the act again."

More often than not, he would walk faster than everyone else and make it to the rest area before the bulk of the troops got there, rested up and ready to give aid to those who had limped in with blisters, or collapsed upon arrival from the heat. John recalled, "One time Alfred amazed us by arriving at the rest area loaded down with three extra packs and rifles." Only a former timberman with hands twice as big as anyone elses could have accomplished such a feat. No wonder everybody loved him.

August 16, '43
Dear Myrtle,

Just a few lines to let you know I got back safely. I arrived in camp at 8 o'clock Sunday.

Myrtle, you ought to have seen the two girls I rode with to D.C. One was beautiful. She had red hair, blue eyes and fair complexion. She wore a black dress. And did she like to talk. She got so sleepy she laid her head on my shoulder and went to sleep. But she wasn't the only one who went to sleep. I did myself.

The cookies were all moldy, so the fellows had to throw them out. They were all disappointed.

You ought to read the letter Thelma wrote. It was a real letter too. I always feel good reading her letters. Don't forget to send me those pictures. I will look at them and send them back. I just want to see them. We are to go to Kentucky at the end of the month.

Just as soon as we get there, I will call you up and tell you the new address. I bet it was at least 120 degrees today. And did it go hard with me. And the first thing, we went on a 13 mile hike. I just made it too. I was soaking wet when I got back and my feet hurt a little. But I will be allright in a couple of days.

I will get to come home a lot more when we get to Kentucky. I will be able to make it on a three day pass.

Myrtle, there are some ratings to be given out and I think I will get one.

Tell Dick and Billie, I will get them caps when I go to town on Saturday. I must close for now.

I'll say so long, your brother, Alfred.

Alfred had finally made it home, and he did it his way. Setting a pattern that he was to follow from then on: He only let Myrtle know he was coming, then walked in and surprised his Dad and the rest of the kiddies. As he told Myrtle later, "I just love to watch their faces light up and everyone being so happy."

As soon as Alfred had rested up for a while at home, he hitched a ride up the hill to Myrtle's house. She was ready for him too. She'd fixed chicken, noodles, corn on the cob out of the garden, and baked his favorite, cherry pie.

She and Bill, with Dick and Billy hanging onto Alfred's khaki pants, showed Alfred the yard they'd finished and the garden he had pictured all the way from Georgia. Myrtle said, "A lot of nights, Alfred came up late and we'd sit around the table sipping coffee, eating pie, and talking."

That first leave they had a big family reunion up at Aunt Ella's where they always had their get-togethers. Everyone was there and really happy to see Alfred.

For most leaves, Alfred usually stuck pretty close to home. He made the rounds of all the aunts, uncles and grandparents, and visited a few close friends like George Roupe. Augusta remembered, "Alfred always visited Dad. He and Alfred had been real close and especially since they'd worked together in the mines. Dad though a lot of Alfred."

When asked if Alfred ran around with girls when he came home, Augusta didn't have to even think about it, "Alfred was family oriented. When it came to family or something else, he chose his family. He never brought any girls around. I don't remember any girls, but I knew Janice and him were good friends."

He'd most always stop at the Dairy Bar to see who was there, but the chance of seeing any of his friends wasn't real good.

August 27, '43

Dear Sister Myrtle,

Just a few lines to let you know I am well and hope you are the same. I guess the boys will have to wait for their caps until I get enough money to get them.

I suppose Dick can't wait to go to school. Write and tell me when they go and how he gets along.

Tell me if Dad is getting the money that I signed for him to get. Tell all to write yet to this address or until they hear from me. I shore has been hot here for the last few days. How are things up there. Write for letters shore do mean a lot to a fellow.

This is all I have to say. So I will close.

So long, Alfred.

Chapter VII

Camp Campbell, Kentucky

Somewhere in Tennessee

September 7, '43

Dear Myrtle,

Myrtle, we are on our way to our new camp. And what a time we are having. It has rained every day since we left at the end of Aug. Last night, Sept. 6, and where we are now. I don't think even the officers care anymore. It rained about 6 miles out from where we are camping. It rained so hard you couldn't see where you were going. But we had to get off just the same and pitch our tents. Boy was I wet, too. And you ought to see the mud. I thought I was walking on stilts. We ate supper in the dark. Boy what a mess we had. We didn't know what we were eating. It's a good thing too.

But the sun has come out and is drying the mud up. Some of the trucks got stuck and haven't got out. Boy, have gotten tired of riding. We have gone about 400 miles and have some more to go.

I can't tell you where we are going, only that we are somewhere in Tennessee now. I shore have seen a lot of country I hadn't seen before. Tell the rest to write, but I won't answer till we get to our new camp.

Your Brother, Alfred

September 12, '43

Dear Myrtle,

We are here at our new camp. I don't know what's here yet. But will in just a few weeks. After we camped at that mudhole, we rode another 120 miles to our main camp. We saw lots of beautiful towns. You ought to see how we looked and hollered to the girls along the road. We didn't go through any big towns, just the skirts of them. It is colder here than in Georgia. The last time we camped my toes got so cold, I thought I didn't have any. I even wore a field jacket and have been using two blankets since we left Georgia.

I wished I could have been at the church picnic, but didn't I know you would have a good time. I just thought of you and could almost taste the food there.

I just knew Dick would get in a fight. I said to Bill Walls, I bet he would. When I get to town I will send them something. It might not be what they want, but at least or hope it will please them.

I hated to hear Eleanor Hughes had died. And as it is a shame to think she had to leave a baby behind. But, I hope his sister takes good care of it.

I bet the colored people liked the singing and the preaching Jones did. I hope he keeps on preaching like he does. And hope our church keeps on growing good.

Myrtle, will you try and send me some cookies when you can. Take some of my money and buy the stuff. See if you can get some paper for me. But don't deny yourself for me. See if Mary got those two pens for me yet. They are for two good pals and I don't want to let them down.

Boy, I have been in a lot of states since I been in the army. Of all I like old PA. the best. The next one is Kentucky.

I shore have lots of letters to answer. I just got a letter from Janice now.

Wishing you the best of luck, your brother,
Alfred.

September 18, '43
Dear Sister Myrtle,

I received your letter on my birthday. Was glad to hear from you. I was wondering why you didn't write. Or maybe I was just wanting a letter too much. I found out that it takes from 4 to 5 days for a letter to get here.

I received those cards and they were very fine. They shore did make me feel good. I wish I could have been home on my birthday and to be there for Dad's too. I hope he gets some nice gifts. I am sorry I didn't send him anything. I didn't get to town because of the inspection we had today. I shore was tired. We were on the go since 4:30 in the morning. We had a lot to do and I was shore glad when it was over. I was asked one question in all that time. He asked me if I had everything. I said, "Yes Sir!" and he walked on. I was glad he didn't ask me anymore.

I am glad that Dick and Billie are getting along good in school. Wasn't he smart to say he would sneak out if he didn't like it. I hope he gets along fine.

I shore would like to be at the picnic that Aunt Ella is going to have. but I guess I won't be able to make it. But just think of me while you are eating and having a good time.

I will say so long and I always think of you,
Alfred.

P.S. Myrtle, I might get my tonsils taken out while I am here. Right now they are hurting. I have had the sore throat for the week. I have been on sick call. Trying to get them well. I also got all my teeth fixed. I have them all filled with silver. They are as good as new. I feel much better now. After I get my tonsils taken out I will be in good shape.

Would you go out home and get the print of me in my plain suit and get three pictures taken for me. Lloyd wanted one and also Francis. Get one more made in case someone else wants one and send them to me. Myrtle, I might be home in a few weeks. I found out it only takes 17 hours to come home and it won't cost much. It will only be $15.15 to come home. What do you think? Should I try it. I am going to try to get a 4 day pass to come home on. I will be able to be home two days or more. So write and tell me what you think about it.

Tell Dad I am thinking about him today on his birthday and wish I could have been there also. I shore am glad I have a good Dad like him. And hope he has many more to come. Myrtle, I am going to close now, so long, your brother Alfred.

September 23, '43
Dear Myrtle,

Just a few lines to let you know I received your letter today and was glad to hear from you. I am well only for a little cold I got. After I get well enough, I am going to get my tonsils taken out. The captain said he will see to get them out.

I got several birthday cards and one box of candy. The candy was from Ellen Walls and was it good. Myrtle, get some shirts for Melvin and Curtis and try to get the girls some too. Get the kids some warm clothing for winter.

Don't let Dad keep Bernie home. You see that she goes to school. For she is too young to do all the work at home. Sometimes I lay awake at night and think what will happen to everyone at home. Who will help Dad. I worry about Mary. I hope she has not gotten married and will stay at home. I would hate to see someone strange come in the house again.

Tell the rest of our relations to put Cpl on my next letters instead of Pfc.

We are to get our barracks fumigated tomorrow. So we will move out in the field in back of our place. Boy, no one is glad to see that. For it will be plenty cold sleeping out now. I hate the idea, but guess I will.

Thanks a million for the birthday cards,
                              Your brother, Alfred

September 27, '43
Dear Sister Myrtle,

Just a few lines to let you know I am well and hope you are the same. Myrtle, when I get to come home it won't be on a furlough. I will be on a three day pass. I have a furlough coming up the 20th of January.

The captain said if there wasn't anyone that goes over the hill, he will try and get us a weekend pass, and a Saturday and Sunday pass. That will be 5 days. If I can get it, I will come home. Bill Walls thinks he is going to get a 5 day pass too. Whatever they give me, I will be satisfied with it and try to make the best of it.

Myrtle, I hope you can get things straightened out for Dad so he can get the money for the kids. I shore would like to hear he has gotten it. Tell Dad to use it for anything he wants to. I would rather see Curtis have something to do and to get some money from what he does. Don't worry about me now. For I will be able to take care of myself. For I got a raise. I will get $66. I am now a Corporal T/5. It is two stripes with a T underneath the stripes. So don't worry about me. I will send $5 this month for a payment of Dad's teeth. And don't let him talk you out of it either. Make him get them.

I will be looking for the box you are sending me. Don't worry about me not liking it. Anything will suit me. I am going to see about getting my tonsils taken out next week. For I am over my cold and am feeling fine.

I will have to close for the lights are going out now. So I will say so long,

Your brother, Alfred

As Alfred mentions his friend Bill Walls in his letter, it is a reminder of an anecdote that Bill recounted. A bunch of them were on furloughs to go home, Bill and Alfred included. Alfred had packed all his stuff into one small suitcase, while everyone else was lugging two big cases. The men arrived at the station and were milling about on the platform waiting for the train to arrive. All of their bags were sitting on the pavement in front of the tracks ready to be thrown on board when the train pulled in. It wasn't long until they heard the whistle of the northbound passenger train and it slowed down to a stop in front of the soldiers. They didn't have much time to board, so Bill said, "One of us grabbed Al's little bag and they all climbed onto the train, leaving Alfred to struggle alone with the rest of the huge suitcases." Bill chuckled over that one as he said, "You know, Alfred was just so darn big, that we just naturally left that kind of stuff to him. We knew he could handle it. Why, one of his hands would made two of mine. He took everything easy, never took offense at anything we did."

October 2, '43
Dear Myrtle,

Myrtle, that box you sent me was the best one I received yet. Even though you send good cookies. I think that cake was and is better than cookies. The cake was in good shape. Just one side was smashed a little, but for that it was fine. I ate most all of the cake. I gave a couple of the fellows a piece.

Don't deprive yourself for me. For I know how hard it is to get things and how many points it takes away out of your rationing book. So don't do anything that will keep you from having things for the kids.

I will thank you and Bill a million times. Hoping to be able to do something for you in time to come.

Dad should get more money. The clerk told me he would. If he doesn't, tell me and I will find out why he didn't get more.

I know I haven't done all I could have done at home, but now I am trying all I can to help Dad and the kiddies at home. Sometimes I wonder just what war does to us that makes us think of the things we should have done.

I know I spent more and done things Dad didn't like. But I see it now and will do all I can for him. I hope he doesn't hold it against me.

I am glad to hear that Dad got the chicken pen built. Hope Curtis does good with them.

I come home in November. I will be home from the 9 till the 21. Don't tell them I am coming home. For I want to see their faces when I surprise them like I did before.

Myrtle, would it be too much to have our Thanksgiving then, for I won't be home on the 25th. Tell me what you think. Anything will suit me. So don't go to extremes just only for me. But just have a nice dinner, that's all I ask. I will give you some money when I get home to help pay the bills.

I am glad to hear Ralph C.'s (Cunningham) baby is better and is home. I bet they are glad. Boy, the stork is shore busy. You better watch out, he might see you. Ha! Ha!

The weather is changing down here. It is warmer now. We also are changing into woolen or O.D. now. For it gets really cool at night. And it's the Army's woolen time.

I hope things will be different when I come home from what they are now. Do all you can for Dad's sake and the kiddies. So long till I hear from you,

your brother, Alfred.

P.S.

Thanks a million for the writing paper for I was just about out. Get me one more writing tablet with lines. I bet you are saying, what does he think I am. But I can depend on you better than anyone. Myrtle, you are a really good sister to me. At least I can talk to you and know you really try and do what you can for both me and for home.

October 4, '43

Dear Myrtle,

I received your letter and was glad to hear from you. No matter how often I get a letter, I always enjoy them. For there is always something new happening.

I am always glad to receive anything you send me. I don't blame the kids or Bill a bit for eating the cookies.

I will be home for Thanksgiving. There has been a change in the furlough here. Now I will be coming back after the 25th. Boy, was I glad of that too. But I better not count the chickens before they hatch.

Just came back from supper. We had a fair one, I guess. I will close for I have to go to a Non-Com. (Non-Commissioned Officers) meeting. I will say so long and wishing you the best of luck in the world. Write when you can.

So long dear sister, Alfred.

Myrtle baked Alfred a batch of his favorite cookies, and before they had cooled enough to pack, she had to leave to go out home. After she left, Bill and the boys returned home hungry to find fresh cookies on the counter. As you might expect, they did more than observe the soft round objects. Bill got out the milk, sat the boys down at the table and they stuffed themselves till they were full.

Myrtle came home later in the afternoon to fix supper, opened the kitchen door and the first thing she noticed was that Alfred's cookies were gone. Myrtle recalls, "I was so mad. I screamed at them, 'why did you eat those cookies,' they should have known they were for Alfred. I was put out because there wasn't enough sugar to make anymore." In a choked voice she continued, "I was disappointed because I couldn't send Alfred those cookies. They meant a lot to him. I was really mad at your Daddy."

October 14, '43
Dear Sister Myrtle,

I am on fire guard all night. Nothing to do, so while I am on it, I will be able to catch up with my letters.

I got back alright and was on time also. I shore had a good time coming back for I met up with some other fellows and we joked and talked of home. There is one place along the train station that gives coffee, cakes, gum, apples, sandwiches and other things to just only the soldier boys. And does that place come in handy. For it is about halfway between home and camp. I know the boys thank those folks for doing that. I also went into the USO club in Pittsburgh and got a free meal. It shore is a fine thing to do.

I got back to camp about 3:00. I just had 2 hours sleep when they called me again to get up. Boy was I

84

sleepy.

How did Dick and Billie like their overseas caps? I bet they liked them. Tell Bill that I hope his dog does fine, for I might want him to go hunting sometime. I think a lot of the things I would like to do if I were back home.

We shore have had a lot of fun since I come back. I have been deviling Bill a lot. I shore get a kick out of it.

Closing with love, your brother Alfred

One of the men who came to know Alfred at Camp Campbell, still resides at Providence, Rhode Island. George and Rose Trabucco raised their family within a mile of his New England home place. In France, he had been a litter-bearer working at Alfred's aid station.

An animated look came over George's face when he told how he would bounce up to Alfred with a fighter's stance and throw a few punches. Then he would turn and run like hell with Alfred running behind him, chasing him. As George put it, "I was into boxing a little, you know, sort of feather weight. I'm 5 feet 7, and weighed maybe 135 pounds. I'd take a couple jabs at him and then run as fast as I could. I mean, here I was this little guy and he was so big. If he got me in them arms, he'd crushed me to death."

The camaraderie that existed between these men was phenomenal. Such relationships could never have formed under any circumstances other than the capriciousness of war.

These men came from every different social and economic background known to society. In civilian life, a lot of these men wouldn't have even spoken to one another. Now irrelevant to the social ladder, in wartime, they tell each other their dreams.

Some were mature men well into their twenties. While others, like George Trabucco, received a tap on the shoulder from Uncle Sam two weeks after his eighteenth birthday. For George, it was almost a birthday present. He was ready to explore the world beyond his New England home town. But as George puts it, "I was just a kid," and sometimes life slaps us in the face with more than we'd bargained for when we are too eager to embrace it with youth's impetuosity.

What they found in the camps was another kind of family. A

niche where water became just as thick as blood. Where friendship was counted on for more than a movie, dinner or a game of pool. If the situation arose, and they hoped it didn't, they knew they might have to count on a friend to save their lives.

Everyone was in the same fraternity. These guys lived and ate together for almost a year and a half before they went overseas. They sweated blood and groaned their way over 25 mile hikes. Unobtrusively, what developed with time were caring and intimate relationships. When mail call came and a buddy didn't get a letter from his girl back home and came in and threw himself down on his bunk to stare at the ceiling, a friend was there. He'd go over, sit down on his bunk, get him talking, share in the disappointment, and suggest a shower and a game of pool or anything to cheer him up.

These were friendships forged by living, loneliness, and the will to survive anything the army dished out. The bottom line was you always hoped that you would never be put to the test.

Your buddies meant everything to you and after the first of November, when their greatest fear had come to pass, the committing of the 26ᵗʰ Division to Combat, these comrades in arms faced the inevitableness of a swift decimation in their ranks.

With a voice cracking with emotion, a former soldier related how close and special those friendships were. "When you had to watch them die one by one, it just hurt too darn much," he said, "It was like a part of you died each time a friend got it. That was why, later on in the war, you learned not to let yourself get too close to the guys coming in as replacements. You backed off from asking where they were from or how many kids they had. You tried to keep things impersonal. That way, there was less chance of being hurt. Having to say goodbye to a corpse was just too painful."

Fifty years later at a reunion of the 26ᵗʰ Division, I wondered if even the wives and then sweethearts, could understand the ties that bind these men to one another and motivates them to keep in touch year after year. Only men, who had walked the same paths of life and death, could truly empathize with each other.

They say that the eyes are the windows of the soul. I have come to believe it. I remember in several interviews, when the guys were telling of the horrors of war, that after looking into their eyes for a few minutes, I had to look away and find something else to focus on while they talked. It was as if looking into their eyes I could see the ghosts of pain and memories that I had no right to intrude upon. Perhaps there are times when it is better for some things to remain in the mind and wind up buried in the grave.

October 23, '43

Dear Myrtle,

Just a few lines to let you know I am feeling fine after having my tonsils taken out. They only gave me a local anesthetic. In other words they just yanked them out like a dentist does when he is going to pull a tooth. I didn't even know when he had them out. Only way I knew was when I looked at them afterwards. I have been in the hospital ever since and will be here till Wednesday or Thursday of next week. I wouldn't care if they left me here for it is really nice here.

I have been getting a lot of milk, bread pudding, and soft foods. I shore have been treated good. What gets a guy is when the nurse comes to take your pulse and temperature. She holds your hand to take your pulse. I don't mind them doing it a bit as it sort of makes a person feel good. Too bad my throat is getting better fast.

How is Ralph C's baby. Has it been given anymore blood lately. How is Curtis getting along. I bet he is pleased with his chickens by now. Has he been getting lots of eggs.

How did things go at church after I left. I got a letter from Janice and she said there wasn't very many at church when she was.

Have you heard anymore of Sam Woods (neighbor)? Is he better or just the same? It shore is a shame. I hate to see anybody sick. Sometimes I can't hardly get them off my mind. You don't know how helpless it makes me feel. I wish I could be able to help them.

Boy I can't hardly wait to come home. It will only be about 20 more days until I will be home. I am going to try and get a three day pass with my furlough. If I get it, I will be home a day before it starts. Other fellows have got it and I am too. Boy, if they don't give it to me, they will wish they had. For someone is going to hear from me.

So long now, but not for long, your brother, Alfred.

Ralph and Betty Cunningham, Myrtle's brother and sister-in-law, have a baby girl named Judy who was born without a spleen. Alfred usually inquires about the health of the baby.

Alfred had even found the strength to charm a few nurses at the hospital.

October 29, '43
Dear Sister Myrtle,

I received your letter a few days ago. It caught up to me from being in the hospital. I am out now and am feeling fine. Don't think I forgot you sister, because I can never forget you. You have been a real sister to me. Thanks to you for everything my dearest sister.

Myrtle, I was almost caught when I came back. We were just outside of Cincinnati when some M.P.'s got on the train and started to check passes. But when he came to me, he looked at it for a long time, but handed it back without saying anything. But was I scared. I got back from there allright. I will never do that again. I will stay at home from now on.

Your brother, Alfred

Myrtle related how one time Alfred thought he would use his travel pass and visit an Aunt and Uncle who lived in Ohio on his way back to camp. Travel passes were only to go home on and not to travel all over the country. It sounds like Alfred decided not to do much visiting very far from home again.

November 1, '43
Dear Sister Myrtle,

I am out of the hospital and in good health. I can eat real good now. I will be in good shape when I come home. It is good to think I will be home for Thanksgiving.

I am going to ask you to do something for me. That is if you can. But if not, it will be allright just the same. This is it. Will you send me $10 to come home on. I got paid today, but only got $30. I owed Bill Walls $10 when I came on that 3 day pass. And I told him I would pay him today and I did. When I tell anyone anything, I mean to do it. So I paid him. And I am even with everyone now. I have just $20 and some change. But there is something I have to get, then I won't have enough to come home on. If you can spare it, I would appreciate it a lot. But please don't tell Dad about it. Then when I get my pay in November, I will send it back to you. Please don't tell Dad! For if he hears about it, he will give me the devil. He will say I spent my money foolish. I rather owe you than anyone here, because they ask you for it sometimes when you really don't have it.

I hated to hear Dick hurt his arm and hope it isn't too bad. But I would watch him so nothing will set in and make him a cripple.

I would have liked to see the boys all dressed up for the Halloween party. I bet they really looked good too.

I hope Ralph's baby gets well. I also am glad to hear Sam is better too.

Hope Curtis chickens does good. At least he can have some spending money and something to do.

I heard Odie was drunk while he was home. When he tried to sneak in a window and got stuck, I think they ought to have left him there the whole night. That would be a fine place to sober up. I heard Mabel has to send him money. But you know what he does with it. I don't think he will ever do any good. Mabel would be better off if they would send him across.

How is Sunday School going? How is the water in the dam holding up? Does Dad have the car running yet? From what you said it doesn't sound like he has yet. Hope he gets it going soon, so I can go over to Ables (neighbor). I got a letter from Mildred Milket, you know Dad's sister. It was the first one I had got from her. Hope all are allright at home.

Closing with loads of love to your house and family.

Alfred

November 7, '43

Dear Myrtle,

It is raining. I will start writing till it is time to go to church. It starts at 10:00. We shore have a good chaplain.

We have been going out on over-night problems. We started at 4:00 and will be going till 4:00 the next day. Boy, was the night cold. We couldn't sleep because we were on the go all night. We did get a couple of hours, but what is that. Was I tired when we got back to camp. Some of the fellows had to have a smoke before they went to sleep, but I just laid down on my bunk and went to sleep without taking my clothes off.

Dad has not got his money yet. The clerk keeps saying it takes time. I know how much red tape a person has to go through to get money. But hope you and Dad will keep it up even if it is a job. A little money is better than none at all.

I am glad that Bill has got some game. He shore does like to hunt. Did Dad get a license. Hope he did. So when I come home I will be able to eat some game he kills. Remember how Mom used to fix rabbit for us.

I am going to thank you for the cookies. They were appreciated because we won't be here this coming week. We will be out in the woods. So, if you don't get a letter right away, you will know why. It is because I can't write. But will answer as soon as we come back in. And maybe we won't even go out. A person don't know till the last moment what you are going to do.

Listen Myrtle, don't rob yourself to send me cookies or cakes. Because I know how hard things are to get. So don't worry about me. I will love you just the same. So don't send me anything that you can give to the kiddies.

Myrtle, I am glad to hear they are going to go back

to work. But to me, they didn't get much of a raise by the way the paper talks. I have been reading and hearing it over the radio. They gave them a little more money, but put more hours on them. I don't see where they made much on the deal. But it is better than nothing.

Myrtle, you are like me. I can talk faster and can tell you more than I can write. And I have a lot to tell you too.

I am glad Dad is getting the car fixed, because I will be able to go over at Ables.

I can guess how Odie was at home. He is better off here than at home. At least he can't be drunk all the time.

I am glad to hear the Rev. Banchi got that much money. The way I got it, he didn't get much. But at least he got more than I thought. I wrote to him, but haven't got an answer back as yet.

I am also glad to hear that Ralph's baby is a lot better and also Sam Woods. It shore is a shame.

Myrtle, I got a letter from Lloyd and he said he might be home for Thanksgiving. But don't say anything to anybody. For he might not be able to get there on time and everyone will be expecting him. So just leave it go and see if he does come.

Tell everyone to write. I haven't got a letter from any of them since I came back. Tell them I want them to write because I don't know how they are. So tell them to write to me or you tell me how they are.

Myrtle, I am glad you found those negatives. For Lloyd wants one, Thelma Roupe wants one, Mildred Bailey wants one, Janice wants one. But wait till I come home before you get any made.

I will send you some money when I come back so you can get some more made. I can't give you any now because I just have enough to come home on. But will have some more when I come back. It will be over payday and I am going to get a fellow to get my pay and hold it for me. I know he is a good fellow and I can trust him. He won't lend anybody any money.

This is all I can think of now and it is church time.

So I will close with loads of love and good wishes. Answer soon.

Your brother, Alfred.

Speaking of holding someone's money, Alfred was known to be banker for a number of fellows who had trouble hanging onto any of their pay for one reason or another. As Myrtle told it, one acquaintance of Alfred's, and a pretty steady drinker, asked Alfred to keep his money for him and no matter what he said or did, Alfred wasn't to give him a red cent.

It so happened that one day this guy started on a drinking binge a little earlier than usual, and what with buying drinks for all his buddies, the spigot ran dry before he was quite ready. But, no problem. He'd go to Alfred and get some of the green stuff to keep the flow going, or so he thought.

Approaching Alfred in a state of inebriation, he demanded that Alfred give him some of his money. Alfred refused, reminding the guy that he had given his word that he would save it for him, and that was what he intended to do.

Unfortunately for the guy, he did not take no for an answer graciously. After a little pushing and shoving and a few more demands, the guy finally told Alfred that if he didn't give him the money, he'd punch him out and take it. Alfred's reply to him was, "If you feel you want to try it, go ahead." With alcohol in his brain instead of common sense, he hauled off and hit Alfred with his fist. With his customary cool style, Alfred never said a word but swung his own big fist and laid the fellow out with one blow. The poor fellow didn't need anymore money that night and got a good night's sleep without even half trying.

The next morning, Alfred received a sober apology from the fellow for the embarrassing scene he had caused the night before and promised that it wouldn't happen again.

When Alfred gave his word, it was a bonding agreement, and he rarely broke it.

Camp Campbell, Kentucky
November 9, '43

Dear Myrtle,

I received your letter and box today and did the box of cookies come in time too. We were out all day Monday and Tuesday. It was shore cold sleeping on the ground. I almost froze last night. We didn't have anything to eat till 10:00 Monday night and the next morning we missed breakfast. The reason was we didn't hear the kitchen come in. They parked about 30 feet down the road and then carried the food in and we didn't hear them. Then when we did hear them, it was too late. Because they were all done eating and were carrying the food containers back to the trucks. And as soon as I got to the barracks, the mail clerk said I had a box and it didn't take very long getting it opened! Boy they shore did taste good. Myrtle, thanks a million for them.

While we were out, I kicked out two rabbits and a black squirrel. I could have killed those rabbits if I would had a stick.

Myrtle, I am glad you sent the money. I will send the money back, so you can keep it for further use. I am going to start sending some home so you can save some for me.

I am glad Dad got the car running because it shore will be cold walking around to everywhere I want to go. But I am not going to run it very much because I am going to stay at home a little more than I did before. Besides, it is too cold to be going all the time.

I am glad to hear Dick is getting better now. I can imagine how it hurts him when someone bumps him. I hope you are well and hope you will always keep that way.

I will be glad to know how the weather is when I come home so I can get prepared for it. I will watch everything so no one will get it.

I hope Bill and the rest get lots of game so I can eat some when I come home.

I read about the raise they got at the mines. It shore

is a shame. But hope it soon comes to an end.

I bet Dick and Billie can't get over going coon hunting. They will be like Bill, always in the mountain.

I am glad to hear Sunday School is going good and hope it always will be that way.

It shore is cold here tonight and boy, I am shore glad I am here to sleep in a good bed. But have to go out tomorrow. And do I hate it. We will be doing it all this month and next. But don't know what will be next. They are shore making a lot of changes here. So you can be ready to hear almost anything now. Some of the guys think we will be going across pretty soon. But things always change here. But don't say anything to Dad. I will let you know what takes place. Don't worry too much just yet. Just think of me coming home in one week. It will be soon now. Just one more week and I will be home.

The lights are soon to go out, so I will close. Closing with loads of love to you sister.

Your brother, Alfred

"Think of me coming home," he had told his sister. Despite the severity of the war across the Atlantic, our holidays continued to be observed unabated, and families clung to the traditions they represented.

Alfred had made it home on furlough for Thanksgiving. His furlough was an excuse for everyone to have him over for a meal, Aunt Ella, Uncle Ott, the Grandmothers, and of course, Myrtle. On Thanksgiving Day at home, they put all the leaves in the table and everyone gathered around for roasted turkey, stuffing and a prayer of Thanksgiving by their father. Alfred looked around the table and wondered if this might be his last Thanksgiving. He'd told Myrtle, "I sure enjoyed Dad and all the kids and everyone being there, but I thought that a fellow never knows."

Contrary to his plan, he had taken the car and run around to those who were pretty far away until the gas was about all gone, and then he was down to his favorite pastime, walking.

He'd seen a few friends, mostly girls, and they'd come to see the men off with a few hugs and kisses when they left to go back.

December 7, '43

Dear Myrtle,

Well, got back safe and as yet nothing was said about being a little late. I haven't been called in by my C O, so I guess it is allright.

We are out in the woods and having it easy. I haven't done anything since I have been here, but eat and sleep. It is really nice and it isn't too cold. But it is a little damp. Have to watch that stuff doesn't mildew. The meals are pretty good here.

When I left, some of the girls saw us off and I bet they will get some teasing. I really hated to leave. And Bill's mother shore hated to see him leave.

Tell Aunt Ella her cookies tasted real good. I didn't spend any money on the way back. We are to go back to camp soon. And when I do, I will write you a better letter.

With love, Alfred

A small faded envelope, dated *December 15, 1943*, contains a lone Christmas greeting.

> "At Christmas time and through the year,
> Someone thinks of you,
> And wished that the Season's Cheer,
> Will glow thru all you do."

For some reason, Alfred never signed the Christmas card.

December 22, '43

Dear Sister Myrtle,

I just got off from watch and we had mail call. But I didn't get any. I am writing asking why I haven't received a letter from you. Is there anything wrong at your house. I mean, is anyone sick? I haven't received a letter from you since I came back. The last one I wrote was Dec. 7. Please write to me. For I need to hear from you. I am wondering and thinking something has gone wrong. It is terrible when you think something might be wrong and you don't know. So write as soon as you can.

The weather down here has been very cold. And I guess it has been cold up there too. We have been out in the cold most of the time. And after Christmas we will be out for two weeks. And do I dread it. These California fellows are having a hard time of it too.

Myrtle, we shore had a terrible thing happen yesterday, I mean Monday. Two fellows got hurt and one got killed by a mortar shell. I helped dress them up. They were hurt really bad. I was 300 yards from them up on a hill. But was getting to go where they were. I shore was lucky by not going with them. It makes me think what we are in for when we ever go across. I don't think I have ever been afraid yet, but when I think of what it means, I get to feeling I will. But, I will do the best I can knowing you and the rest are keeping me in prayer.

Don't be surprised if you get a letter with a new address. But just don't know when it will be. But this one thing I do know. They are getting ready to do something with us. We are transferring a lot to the second army. And getting new men. Our general was down at Washington and he was there for something. He said we were getting ready to go somewhere. But don't tell anybody else until I tell you different. But still put my address the same. Some of the boys say they are ready to go and fight the Germans. I say to be happy that we have not gone already.

How is everyone at home. I am glad to hear Mary left. Now the kiddies will have some peace. And you can do things a lot better too. I know it is lots better. Bernie said so in her letter. I bet she could eat me for what I said, but I don't care. It is the truth. I still hope things work out for the best for her.

Well, how is Sunday School doing? Hope better now than before. Has Billie and Dick been asking for things for Christmas? I bet they want lots of things. As soon as I get my pay, I will send them something. So don't think I forgot them, for I haven't.

I have gotten several boxes already. And the other day I received a fine fruit cake from Eleanor Walls. I haven't cut it and won't till Christmas.

Hope everyone is well and don't forget to write soon. I was going to write sooner, but we have been out most of the time. My letters will be a little late next week, and the following week because we will be out.

Have to close for it is time for Retreat, so I will say so long and wishing you and the rest of the family a Merry Christmas.

With all my love, Alfred

The general Alfred refers to is General William S. Paul.

December 26, '43
Dear Myrtle,

Just a few lines to let you know I received your letter and was very glad to hear from you. I was hoping all of you are well and that you had a very nice Christmas. Hoping Dad and rest had a good one too. I shore had a fine Christmas dinner. I and another fellow went to town at Hopkensville and went to the U.S.O. club. We had no more than got there when the hostess asked us if we had a place to eat dinner. I said no. She said if there was an empty place, we could go.

So at 12:00 they called up and got a place for us to eat. So the people came in a very nice car and took us to their home. And what a home. They were old maids. But what fine people and home. And what a dinner. They had a 20 lb turkey and everything that went with it. We also had nuts and candy, cakes, anything we wanted then. And what a plate she gave us. It shore was a fine dinner. We stayed and helped to clean up and sat around and talked till 6:00. Then we went to the Club and watched a dance. And was there a lot of beautiful girls. They would talk to you and even asked you to dance. I danced with a couple of them and managed not to step on their feet too bad. I'm not much of a good dancer. They really were an entertaining bunch of girls and did I enjoy myself. But it was Christmas. I rather be home but just couldn't make it.

I am glad what happened out home. Now the house will look lots better than before. I told him before that he would get home sick, but he tried to make out he came home account of me. I didn't care, but hope he will do right at home.

I still am giving some money to help get Dad teeth. Just find out how much it will cost. Then I will know how much I have to send to help get them for him.

I only hope Dad and the rest do good where they are now. Hope Ab got his car going so to not make it inconvenient for Tom Appleby. I know the stork was to visit out at his place. Because I was told by the one that is to have it visit. She told me, but said not to tell anyone. So don't tell anyone I said what I did to you. Boy the stork is going. Shore is busy after he gets around to all them in the hollow. I guess it all will be that way. You better watch out before he catches up with you! Ha! Ha!

I am glad to hear that they are treating at the church. But hope only the people would keep on going instead of just coming one day because they will get something. I hate to hear that there were only a few at prayer meeting. Hope the attendance will come up again. I heard Alvin Lewis left. I bet his mother hated to see him go. I wish things would get settled so that we all could come back home and this would be over.

I don't know, but I don't think Odie is going to get home, at least not for a while yet. But don't tell anyone. I saw him the other night and he was flying high then too. He didn't hardly know who I was. I helped him get back to his barracks.

I am glad you took Ellen and Bernice to town and got them those things. Did Curtis get a letter with a money order in it? Did he give any to the kids and Dad? If he didn't let me know? Tell him to write to me.

I know toys are dear, but hope the kids like what

they got. Myrtle, don't worry because they didn't say anything about me going late. Yes, Bill went to school. He said it is really tough. But getting along fine. I don't know if I will get to go or not. We are to go out in the field for two weeks starting Thursday. And what time it is going to be. It has rained for three days already and it is still raining and getting colder. Boy, talk about dreading something. I hope we don't go through all this for nothing. Or maybe I hope it is all for nothing and we get to come home. Anyway, I guess I will have to go.

I hope no one is sick at home. The flu is bad down here. Let me know if anyone at home has it, and hoping they don't.

How is everyone on the Hill? Hoping Bill's family are all well. I am glad you are doing all you can for Dad out home. I just can't give you very much now. But hope some day in the coming future to give you something.

I can't think of anything else. But, oh yes, Dad sent me a five pound cake and I got one from Eleanor too. Boy, they shore taste good.

I will close now and say so long till I see you or hear from you, if I am still here. So long dear sister and good wishes to you all.

Your brother, Alfred

As the days and months go by, every time Alfred hears of someone else having to go into the service, he is saddened. The really sad part is that the soldiers are either getting older or younger.

December 31, '43
Dear Myrtle,

Just a few lines to let you know I am well and hope you are the same. I received your letter today and also the other one you wrote. I have answered the other letter and so here I am answering the last one you sent.

I am glad to hear that Dad and the kiddies had a good dinner. I knew you would see that they got a good dinner. I hope they always think of you. I am sorry to hear that Dad hurt his foot again. But am glad to hear they have gotten over the flu. Hoping that everyone who has it will get over it so that they can enjoy life. Hope Dad can get his glasses so that he will be able to see better in the mines. That is no place to be if you can't see. I hope you don't get the flu or anyone else.

I am glad to hear that you and the rest had a good Christmas. I shore had a good one as I told you. I am glad your kiddies liked what they got. I know things were hard to get.

You know I said that I got a fruit cake from Dad and Elna Walls and I got one from you. Mildred, Dad's sister, sent me one and someone else, but I can't think who it was. I got a gift from Harold. It was writing paper and pen. It shore does write good. I am writing with it now.

I am glad to hear that the Program went over good. I knew the church wouldn't have enough candy. It is always that way. But what makes the difference. If people could only know.

The weather here was just like what you had at home. It rained three days here and the last day we went to the field. It rained all that day and I got all wet and everything else. I bet there was two feet of mud. And we had to walk in it too. What a time we had. The ground was soaked. But still we had to sleep on it. Boy was it miserable. The fellows didn't joke any too much that day and night. Some were shore short in tempers.

But we are back in barracks now. We only stayed for one week. But we are going to do something else soon. We are to have a couple overnight problems next month. Don't tell anyone what I am going to write. We are to leave here some time next month. To go on maneuvers for two months starting about the first of Feb. We will move to where we are to have them, then when we get to them we are to go to a P.O.E. That means before or in April or the last of April or the last of March we will be going across. But don't tell Dad or anyone else. I will tell you more about it a little later on. But if

I have to go before I get to tell you more, it will be okay, because they are taking so many out of here. You don't know when you are next. They even have taken some from different places already. This is what I am going to do.

I will get my money put into bonds and send them to you so you can hold them for me. But if anything happens, take what you need for them and do the best you can with it.

I don't know if I will get to come home again or not, because they have stopped all furloughs till a later time. But even if they do start up again, I won't get home till April. So don't look for me till I see what will happen to us. But if I get a chance I will come home even if I don't get to stay long. Just to see everyone is all I want. I couldn't make it this week. But hope to next week or the following one. But don't worry about me for I will get along allright. Please don't leave Dad or anyone else read this letter. The General said we are going and that soon too. But don't want the people to know I told you, so that they can't say I told when we are going. I just don't know when we are going as yet. But we have heard some rumors. I won't say when till I really know. But if I do go, and don't come home to tell you we are going across, you will find an A in the top left hand corner, meaning we are going across. If we go to England, it will be a B. Or if we go to the South Pacific, it will be a C. So don't forget what these letters mean. But hope to get home before we do anything or go anyplace. So don't worry about me for I am coming back if we go overseas.

Hoping everything goes well at your home and mine. Hoping all will get well so to enjoy life. Tell everyone I am thinking of them and will try to see them as soon as I get a chance. So till then I will say so long and may God watch over everyone of us. I told you about C.J. Taylor who was burned when we were home and who went with Bill to get married. He left today for overseas. I will close now so don't forget what I have written and don't tell anyone please.

Your brother, Alfred

P.S. Please don't cry because if you do they will know something is going to happen or something is wrong and they will be asking what it is.

January 12, '44

Dear Myrtle,

Just a few lines to let you know I am well and hope you are the same. We were out Tuesday and came in Wednesday morning. We walked about 12 miles, but didn't do a thing. Just laid around. It was a good night. It wasn't too cold and I slept like a log. We always have the afternoon off when we come off a problem. But we have our equipment to clean. I jumped in and got mine done so I could sleep a little and write a letter. I am now sitting on my bunk writing to you. The weather here has got a lot warmer, but at night, it gets really chilly.

How is everyone? I am feeling just fine and getting along fine. We haven't started to pack yet. We were told we won't leave here till about the 21, but must be out before the 25. And we are to go to Tenn. So that won't be so far from home. But we will take everything. Then we don't know where we will go. This one thing, we won't be on maneuvers long, just one month, and then to go else where.

How is the church doing? Tell them I am thinking of them and for them to keep on doing good for God.

Myrtle, write to me. Even though we do move. I will get your letters and boxes. For they said we will get our mail. If I wasn't getting your letters, I don't know what I would do. They help me to know that no matter what happens someone is still there for me. At home things are still just like I remembered. I think of you all lots.

Can you get me some cookies or make me some. I really miss them. I was thinking about you the other night and how we can talk. Hoping you are allright. So if you can do it, please send me some.

Myrtle, has Lloyd left yet? I hope he doesn't get into a mix up over that. If he does go, I hope he gets along allright. How is everyone at home. Tell them to write. I have written over a week ago and no one has answered. Tell them I miss their letters. So tell them to write when they can.

Tell me the news in Fairchance. Tell me who the stork visited first. Ha! Ha! Jim, my buddy, has his wife down here with him. Boy, do I tease him. But we shore get along fine. I also got a letter from Bill Walls. He said he is getting along fine. I knew he would. Hoping he makes the grade. Well sister, I can't think of anything else. So please answer when you can and as soon as you can. I will be looking for one from you. So long Sister, till I see you, but don't know when it will be, but hoping soon, so long now and with love,

Your brother, Alfred

January 20, '44
Dear Sister Myrtle,

I received your letter the other day, but just couldn't answer it right away. For we really have been busy. We just got through about 2 hours ago washing down the dispensary. And what a job it was. But we got it done. But will have to work all day Saturday and Sunday for we are to leave Monday and still we have a lot of work to do. We had to pack our A Bag today. And oh how I hate to do it. For we have to put our good clothes in it. But I guess they will have to go.

Thanks a million for the box you sent me. The chicken really tasted good and, believe me, I ate almost all of it. After I ate most of it, I showed the bones to the other fellows, and you ought to have heard them. They could almost ate me for not giving them some sooner.

Yes, I know who that Wilson lady was. I shore hate to hear that she died. But I know she is better off there than some of us. For the days coming are going to be terrible, but I guess we will have it to do. So don't worry for me. I will get along fine. Don't worry about anything. And if you don't hear from me for several days, don't think I forgot you, because I haven't. The reason why will be because I won't have the time. But when I get a chance I will write to you. But write when you can, for I will like to hear from you and the rest. So don't let me down. My new address, I will give you at the end of this letter.

Boy, Ralph and Betty must shore like kids or something else. Ha! Ha! But I guess they know what they are doing, at least they ought to. I guess they aren't the only ones for the way you talk there are lots of other ones. Hoping some day to be able to have sons myself.

Am glad Lloyd went back. I hate to say it, but he is better there than he was at home. Hope he gets along fine. Tell me when he writes and send me his address if it is different than the last one.

How is the weather at home? It really has been real good here. It feels like spring. But just wait till Monday and watch it snow or rain. It always does when we move. For it will make a person feel worse to have to lay on the wet ground or snow.

I can't think of anything more to say. I have three more letters to answer. I got one from George Roupe, Eleanor Walls, and Leona Lewellen. So, I wish you good luck and may God bless you always.

Your brother, Alfred

Chapter VIII

Tennessee Maneuvers

Care of Postmaster, Nashville Tennessee
Somewhere in Tennessee
January 25, '44
Dear Sister Myrtle,

   Just a few lines to let you know I am well and hope you and your family are all well. We are here in Tenn. in which our maneuvers are to be going on. We got here Monday and was it a swell day to move. The weather down here has been fine. But today it has clouded up and it looks like rain. But only hope it doesn't for it if does, I shore will be muddy for there is plenty of it. But where we are set up is kind of dry. We have gotten fine meals since we been here. But when we start our maneuvers, maybe we won't get such good ones. Because we might get our kitchens captured and then we will be out of eats. I shore hope they never get captured, or me, or any one of our trucks.

   Myrtle, will you send me cookies, or even just bread, for we shore can eat bread. When ever you are out of food and besides I am getting tired of this bread. But is shore does taste good when a person gets hungry. Thanks for the cookies you sent me. They were in very good shape and were they good. I gave my bed buddy some and he said he wished his family could bake those kind for he really enjoyed them. If you can will you try and get me some film, size 6 X 16, and if you do, I will send you some pictures we take here, because you will like to see them. For all of us are growing a mustache and you ought to see mine. It is red, and it is growing. Some of the fellows has white and black, brown, red. I wish you could see us, and we tease each other about them.

Myrtle, how is Dad? Tell him I said "hello" and also the kiddies. Tell Harold and the rest you see about my new address, and everyone who wants to know. I have written several letters to the ones in my family. So if you will, you can put my new address in the church so the people will know my address.

How is everyone at the church and the Appleby's and the rest on the hill? How is the church doing now? I heard it was shore doing fine. I only hope it keeps on good.

Myrtle, don't forget to let Aunt Ella, Mildred, and Garnet know my address. I don't know when I will be able to write again. Don't forget to let everyone know my new address and tell them to write and I will answer when I can.

Send me a box when you can, but don't rob yourself or the kiddies. Send anything you want to. For I will eat anything you send. And if you can't it will be allright with me. For I know how things are to get.

I will pay you back someday for what you have done for me since I came in the army. I would get things myself here, but we can't get to town often, and besides things aren't as good as you send.

I will close for now and write when you can and tell everyone I said "hello." I will say so long dear sister till I hear from you.

Your brother, Alfred

Alfred and the other fellows were always doing things for fun. A bunch of them growing a mustache was obviously providing them with the excuse to joke around. Alfred never had one as a civilian. The guys used humor and teasing to its greatest advantage. It helped take the edge off of worrying about the future. War and death seemed a million miles away while 30 or 40 guys were playing touch football, racing to the chow line to see who would eat first, or putting frogs in one another's bunks right before lights out.

Another form of teasing and having fun with one another was in the nicknames some of the guys picked up. Paul Yee, the only one of Asian origin in the company, was called "Ting-a-ling." Alfred also had a couple of handles. Big Al, not a surprising tag, was hollered at him a lot. Because he was older than most of the guys, some of them started calling him "Pappy" early in their stint. Later on he picked up the name the "Big Stoop."

February 4, '44

Dear Sister Myrtle,

Just a few lines to let you know I am well and hope you are the same. I am writing you this letter while I am waiting orders to move again. We are in the wrong area and will have to move again.

I received your letter, but couldn't write because we were on a problem. I get your mail every day it comes in. So don't worry about me not getting your mail. You asked me if I got your box. Yes I did, and was it good. It really hit the spot.

I am shore glad we had today off. Because we been gone since last Monday. We haven't gotten very much sleep. But I have caught up on it now though. The other night, I just got laid down against a hay stack, and was all covered with 4 blankets, and was going to sleep. It was about 3 in the morning when we got there. Then a runner came over and told us we had to move again. Oh boy, how I hated to do that. But we had it to do. And then we walked about 9 miles with a full pack. Boy was I sleepy. Some of the fellows went to sleep walking. So you can imagine how sleepy we were.

I am putting the bonds I talked about in your name so you can cash them. For if I put them in my name, you would have send them to me. But I won't be able to do that till after next month when we come off of the maneuvers.

We shore are having fine weather. It is nice and warm in the day, but it really gets cold at night. But if you get to your blankets, you could keep nice and warm.

Well, how is everyone at your house. Tell Dick and Billie I said "hello" and tell Bill I said the same. Yes

Myrtle, I know how Bill likes to hunt, and he will do it no matter what you say, and I don't blame him. For he works hard, so he deserves a little pleasure, don't you think he does.

I am shore glad that they are getting along fine out home. I know they could have things different. I thank you a million for what you are doing for them out home. And don't worry when I get out of here, I will pay you back for what you have done for me and them. I can't hardly do it while I am here, but will when I get out of here.

Myrtle, don't worry about me, for I am getting along fine now. We went the other day to Lebenion, to take a shower and I really needed it. For we went a week without a bath. I don't know when we will this weekend, but hope it will be some place near us, for I dearly need one.

I don't know when I will be able to write again, but don't you stop writing, because I would like to know what is going on at home. I will write when I get a chance. Tell Dad I said hello and hope he is in good health. I borrowed this paper to write to you because my paper is in my A bag. And they haven't brought them to us as yet. I am closing now dear sister, with much love to you.

Alfred

The 328th Infantry Regiment had been reactivated on February 12, 1943, at Fort Jackson, just a few weeks before Alfred started his basic training. The enlisted men's scuttlebutt (the latest news attributed to rumor and the loose lips of a buddy of a headquarters clerk) was that there were too many soft, rich kids in the 26th Division, and that a little money in the right places had insured that this fighting force would never see action, except perhaps as part of the occupation effort.

Essentially, these men were ready for war. They had endured the rigors of basic training and had gone on to their specialized fields. Now, after almost a year of intense training and field maneuvers, they were more than prepared for combat. So their question was, why were they still hanging around stateside?

The most vocal of those asking the whereabouts of the 26th belonged to a journalist and radio announcer by the name of Walter Winchell. Through the medium of radio, he held captive the ear of a nation. Promptly at 9:00 p.m. every Sunday night, Mr. Winchell opened his broadcast with the same cordial greeting, "Good evening, Mr. and Mrs. America." Mr. Winchell was no novice at the microphone. He literally played it like a virtuoso plucking the strings of an old violin.

One Sabbath evening he went on the air at 9:00 and plied the airwaves with the dire plight of a man visiting in Florida who had suddenly hemorrhaged and officials were attempting to procure a rare blood type which Mr. Winchell named. He only used the bulletin twice, stating that only donors in Florida should respond. A few blocks from the hospital, a man heard the broadcast and knowing his blood type rushed to the hospital and in a matter of minutes they were transfusing the patient.[1] But the plea had been put out on the airwaves and America responded with phone calls and nearly 300 cars pulling into the Florida hospital. Even the airlines got into the spirit by holding up flights if anyone having the blood type needed to board.

Mr. Winchell was also a staunch supporter of President Franklin D. Roosevelt. At the time, some of the press and congress were taking political shots at the president by attacking his son's war record. Winchell personally knew of the sacrifices made by the President's family and asked "FDR" if he could make their war records public. The president's reply was "forget it." He even made a plea to his wife, Eleanor at Hyde Park, to see if the president might change his mind. Her reply was to do as the president asked. Winchell, however, was undaunted. That Sunday night he went on radio and in his own inimitable way, with a few words flung across the airwaves, he stood up for the president and very neatly shot down a vocal Congressional foe. Then he wished all a good night.[2]

I've always heard the quote "never underestimate the power

[1 & 2] **Winchell Exclusive *"Things That Happened to Me—and Me to Them"* by Walter Winchell; Prentice-Hall, Inc., Englewood Cliffs, NJ © Ernest Cuneo** of the press," or I might add, the power of a Walter Winchell discourse, articulately spoken through a microphone at 9:00 on a Sunday night, to an American audience who listened and believed every word and took them as gospel.

If one World War II veteran of the 26th Division told me about the Sunday night broadcasts of Winchell's, I know of another ten who also expressed an opinion or two. The men can't say for sure one way or the other, but they sort of feel Walter didn't do them any favor those nights when he just happened to mention the 26th Division.

During the spring of 1944, without fail, at the end of every program, he put the question to America, asking, "Well folks, I wonder where the 26th Division is tonight?" He of course asked the question rhetorically because he very well knew where the famed division was ensconced.

Everyone has their own methods of waging a battle, including Walter Winchell, so thanks to him, his listeners were kept apprised of the fact that the famed division was safely tucked away stateside. If it had been any other unit, other than the "Yankee Division," it could have possibly languished here in the states forever without catching any flack. But it wasn't.

The original 328th Infantry Regiment was formed in August of 1917. The 26th Division consisted mainly of men from the New England States. The Y D patch was formed and earned them the nickname "Yankee Division." During World War I, the unit, by virtue of the men who served in it, became equated with heroism and courage above and beyond the call of duty. The legendary Sergeant York of the 328th Infantry had left the 26th Division with a certain brand of notoriety. If they weren't blazing a trail in blood and glory, they just weren't doing their thing. And Winchell wouldn't let Mr. and Mrs. America forget it.

February 10, 1944
Dear Myrtle,

Just a few lines to let you know I am well and glad you are the same. I have been receiving your letters and those cookies. I really liked those cookies and I got them when I was really hungry and I ate almost all of them. I gave some of them to the fellows for they look for them as much as I do.

Shore glad everyone is well at home and also am glad they are doing good at church. Only wish I could see the church and all at home. But it will be at least two or three months yet. Because we only had two weeks of maneuvers and have 6 more to go. After that we will get at least 15 days furlough. That is what I hear.

Myrtle, we shore had a bad night this week. We were out in the field, and it started to rain. It rained all night and you ought to see how muddy it got. We had to set up a tent in the rain and that mud. But me and my buddy did pretty good at it. You ought to have seen us after it too. We were soaked to the skin and with water and mud. I wish you could have seen us. We looked like pigs. We looked at each other and laughed. For we were too miserable for it to be funny. Sometimes I don't get washed for three or four days and you ought to see me. We also have been sleeping on the ground most of the time, and boy, it's no pleasure either. You have to move around to find a comfortable spot. Sometimes I think a soldier would be better off dead than take this kind of a life.

I am sorry to hear about James Cunningham or anyone else of having to come to the army. Boy, I pray this war would soon come to an end. How really sick I am of this way of life. I would rather be home than in here. You don't know what will happen and you don't have a say in what will be. But I guess I will have it to do like the rest of the fellows.

Did you get the money order I sent to you and also the one I sent to Curtis. Hope you have gotten them. I am getting those bonds changed. See what you can get done with those you have already got. But if you have to send them to me for anything, wait till we get to our next camp, for it is hard to get anything done out here in the field. But see if you can get them changed at home and get your name on them so you can get them cashed. If

111

anything happens at home let me know if you can.

Put the same address on your next letters, but just don't get time to answer all of them. But tell all I still think of them and hope they all are allright. But tell them to write. And as soon as I get a chance I will answer. We shore have a terrible first Sergeant. He won't let us write or do anything. But just keep busy. But if he doesn't let up a little, someone is going to do something and I don't think he will like it either.

Tell Ellen I got her letter. I hope to answer when I get a chance to. I'm not supposed to be writing this one. But I am sneaking a little time to write to you. But hope to be able to write another one or two today.

The weather now is dark and dreary and it is just starting to rain and will it make it miserable for a couple days. I wish this maneuver will soon get over, so we can get back to our barracks, so we can get cleaned up for once. We get to go to town to wash up, but that doesn't keep up for a week. Right now I look like a pig. But hope to be able to go to town to take a shower.

We are getting good eats. That is when we can get them. We were captured by the blue forces and we didn't get anything to eat from breakfast till the next day at dinner time and boy was I hungry.

Jean wanted to know if she would send a box if I would get it. Tell her I will and to send it if she will, for I will enjoy it a lot, for we don't get things like those you or her send. Myrtle, send me some jelly and some homemade bread with butter on it, and send me some canned meat that is if you can get it. It doesn't make any difference what you send, just so you send me something good to eat. I will send you some money at the end of every month to pay for the postage, for I know it takes a lot to send a box. Would you see if you can get some olives for me, I mean stuffed ones. For it would really taste good out here in the field. We don't get to town to buy anything like that. I have been thinking of the olives Dad gets at home.

Tell Dad I said hello and also George Roupe. Tell them if I get a chance I will write to both of them. I really think a lot of those folks. For they really have been really good friends to me. I got a letter from Thelma, but just haven't had time to answer. Myrtle, how is Grandmother, Aunt Ella, Garnet, Mildred, and the rest. Tell them to write and let me know how they are.

Myrtle, I am glad Bill is well and still working in the mines. Tell him to take care of himself. Hoping he doesn't have to come to this hell hole of the army. It isn't a place for a married man. I sometimes wish I had gotten married before I came to the army. But just don't know who I want to marry yet. But even married I would have to come.

The towns around are small and there isn't much doing in them. And there is so many soldiers. You don't get a chance to do anything like you can at home. Please don't forget the box. For I will be looking for it. Just send anything you want to. I am shore glad they started on the church. I like to see it as soon as they get it done. Tell all at church I am thinking about them all and wish I could be helping them. But just can't, but hope to some of these days.

I got a letter now and was I glad to get it. I will see and get those things you asked me about. So you can be looking for a change in those bonds as soon as they get a chance to make it the way I want them. I now am closing, so I will say so long and may God bless you and all of my folks and with love,

Your brother, Alfred

It's when we can't have something that we want it. Alfred has been thinking about olives, stuffed olives, just like his Dad got at home. The mind can dwell on one particular thing incessantly until it becomes the most important thing in life, till it becomes an obsession. A whole jar of olives stuffed with a bit of red pimento, green, round, firm, a little bit tangy....

Then there's this terrible First Sergeant who he also happens to mention in his next letter. Alfred wasn't the only one who appreciated the sergeant. Another medic had a few tales to tell also, but in his words, "I wouldn't have used any kind language like Alfred did to describe that guy." It seems the sergeant was known to dirty nice shiny boots while on inspections and as one of the guys said, "He was a real pain in the butt." But they were stuck with him for quite awhile here in the states and for a period of time in France. The army saw fit though to transfer him back to the states before the war was over and his company didn't waste too much time mourning the loss.

February 15, '44
Dear Myrtle,

Just a few lines to let you know I am well and hope you are the same. I got your letter and one from Dad and several valentines. I still have them. I couldn't keep the envelopes, because we aren't allowed to have anything on us that will give our division. That is because we are the blues enemy. But we are allowed to keep the paper that has the writing on. These maneuvers won't last very much longer. We are to be over them the 21 of next month. So it won't be long, for boy does the time go.

We shore had a tough night Sunday and Monday. Sunday it snowed and we didn't have any tent up. I was sleeping and I had my face covered up. But some of the fellows sleeping with me pulled it off. The snow hit my face. I looked around before I covered up again and the ground was covered with snow and it turned into rain on Monday. Then we were on a truck for 17 hours and never got off. We were just sitting in it. I got so cold, I thought my toes were going to come off. But today, Tuesday, the sun is shining and it is quite warm. But just now the sun has gone down and it is starting to get colder. We will have about another night and day to go after today and then we will get a rest for 2 days. We shore did have to work all day Sunday. I don't like to but we just have to as the Army shore tells us what to do. But they don't respect the Lord's day much. I just got a box of candy and cookies from Eleanor Walls and boy do they taste good. I also got a box of razor blades from Melvin.

We haven't had any dinner from the kitchen. But we have a big box full of stuff the fellows try to keep, and we are eating that and those can rations that we were given. Boy, they shore do come in handy.

Well, how is everyone on the hill and how is the church doing? By now they ought to be done with the work they were doing.

I also got a box from Aunt Ella. It had waffles, bread, butter, gum, cinnamon rolls, and boy, did they taste good. I sure did appreciate it. If you see her before I write to her, tell her I said thanks.

We had an accident the other day. But all of the fellows that were in it weren't hurt much. Only shook up a bit. It was in a line company, not us. So don't worry about me. I am just fine and in good health, only wish I could be home now.

Myrtle, I will have to close because we might start moving soon. So I will close. I shouldn't be writing for if the First Sergeant would see me he would raise heck. For he really is a no good leader for soldiers. I will say so long and goodbye until I see you again or hear from you and may God bless you and your family.

Alfred

February 27, '44

Dear Sister Myrtle,

Just a few lines to let you know I am well and hope you are the same. I haven't had much time to write during the week, but have a little time today which is Sunday. How is everyone at home and on the hill? I shore would like to see everyone. But don't know when it will be. But hope soon. It won't be long now till we will be over these foolish maneuvers. I think we only have two more and they can't come too fast for me. Because I shore don't like the idea of riding in a truck in black-out and to go over some of these roads down here. Every night we travel without light. My heart is always in my mouth as we have seen so many trucks that was turned over and on fire. And with ours almost turning over, I just don't like it. But I will have it to take. I am going to try to get out of this week. I am going to ask to guard the base which we have to do.

I received your box and was very glad to get it. It really came in handy. For when I got it, we hadn't ate for three days, so you can imagine how I felt when I got to sit down with that box in my lap. And let me tell you, I didn't give very much of it away. But we get good meals when we are resting up. So at least we get ourselves filled up for a few days.

We shore have been getting a lot of rain. It has rained every day this week. And did we get soaked. Our blankets, and everything got soaken wet. And mud! It is terrible! Some places we can't get through with trucks. So you can imagine how it is to walk. We have to keep boots on all the time. We now are in mud about 6 inches deep. I have our tent stretched over a rock so we can sleep. Before we go to bed, we have our helmet filled with water, so we can wash our boots before we go to bed. So we won't get our blankets all muddy. The reason for that is when we get up, we won't get our shoes all muddy. I bet you the pigs around here have a better place to sleep than we do. But today the sun has shone bright and warmer than it has for two weeks. But still in two minutes we can have hard rain. How is the weather at home?

How is the church doing? How is the attendance? Tell me about the church and how it is doing.

Myrtle, have you received my last bond yet and tell me how it is. Is it in your name or is it still like it was. If it is the next one won't be that way so don't worry about it.

How are the kids out home and you getting along? I bet Dick and Billie are different now since I saw them last. Tell them I said to be good. How are they doing in school? I bet Dick is doing good.

Tell me how everyone is and getting along. Tell everyone I said hello and tell Jean to write and the rest too.

I can't think of much more to write about because there isn't much to write about out here in the woods. And it is dinner time now. So I will close, hoping to see you soon and to hear from you and everyone else. I am closing now dear Sister and may God Bless you and Bill always. Tell me all you can the next time.

So long sister, your brother, Alfred

It sounds like the rolling hills of Tennessee were not throwing out the welcome carpet of peaceful landscapes that their reputation conjures up for us in the 90's. It did not feel like home to Malvin L. Shar, either. He had been in the army's Specialized Training Program and was attending college. In his words, "From comfortable college dormitories, within about two days, we found ourselves dropped off into the hills of Tennessee and parcelled out to the different battalions of the 328th Regiment."

These men needed a crash course in the art of warfare, so the plan was for an already trained soldier to take one of them under his wing. This necessitated sharing a tent with him and otherwise showing him the ropes or to put it bluntly, how to stay alive in combat. Malvin had the pleasure of toting the other half of Alfred Wilson's tent.

In the time they spent together, conversations were about the future and speculation on what fate lay ahead of them overseas. Malvin wrote of my uncle, "Alfred had a philosophical/pragmatic outlook towards the future, but what I recall best and what impressed me most about his personality (in addition to his compassionate nature) was his wish, in the event that he was badly wounded and faced the loss of a limb. His desire was not to survive a crippling disability which he perceived would make him a burden to others and which would in turn interfere with his obligations to others. I don't remember the exact words, just the implication."

Alfred probably figured he wouldn't be much use to his dad and the kiddies if he needed more help than they did. It is my supposition that he carried a whole lot of pride inside him.

But I will be the first to admit that there is something in our spirited natures that compel us to be responsible for ourselves, to be masters of our own destinies. Any other state could be construed as not acceptable. But perhaps we underestimate the capabilities of those around us or fail to grasp that it is all an illusion of frailty for the expediency of a worthy opportunity.

March 2, '44

Dear Myrtle,

Just a few lines to let you know I am well and hope you are the same. I received your letter the other night and was glad to hear from you. I am glad to know that all of you are well and hoping you can always be that way. I am just fine but only a bit cold now. The sun is shining but it isn't very warm. Hoping it will be warmer later on in the day. The wind is blowing and I can't write very good because my fingers are getting cold. But while I have the chance I thought I would get caught up on some of my letters that I received the other night.

How are the fellows doing and what happened to them that took their exam? Tell me who all passed and when do they have to go. I only hope that Harold and Bill don't have to go. I only hope this war will soon stop so that all of us men can come home. It eats away at me because all of this misery because of one person.

How are things going at Fairchance and at the church? They all tell me that the church is very nice. Have they got it all paid for yet or how are they going about it? Please tell me all about it.

We will soon be out of the maneuvers. We have a couple more problems yet. We will be through about the twenty-seventh of this month. But don't know just where we will go after these maneuvers. We hear a lot of tales, but don't know where for sure. The general is in Washington finding out where we are going.

We are to get 15 days after these maneuvers, but they will be in mass furlough. So you know what that means. I only hope it isn't true. But they really said we will go this time. I'm no better than the rest, but I rather be on this side of the Atlantic.

I heard, or Ellen told me in her letter and sent me a clipping of Martha's wedding. She said she was going to get married after school. Did you see them? What did Aunt Ella say. I bet she didn't like it. Aunt Ella shore made a mistake by doing what she did for her. I bet you Martha don't do what she said she would do, and you know what that was.

Have you heard from Lloyd yet or has anyone heard from him? Let me know if anyone hears from him. Also let me know if he sends any money home. I shore am glad Dad got that money. He wrote and told me about it.

Tell the boys I said to be good. Tell Dick to do good in school. I bet he is as tough now as he was before. I shore like to see a kid that way. Because you know he will be able to take his part in everything he goes to do. Sometimes that's just the way it has to be.

I got your box and it was really good. You don't know how it makes me feel to get a box like that. For sometimes I could almost cry that everyone is so good to me. Especially when you are hungry at the same time you receive one. I will be glad to get one at any time. But one thing, Myrtle, when you send chicken, will you fry it. The one Dad sent was a little moldy. But don't worry, I ate it and am still alive.

We shore had another terrible week. It rained the first three days but I am glad it hasn't rained while we are resting. But the week isn't over yet. I wonder at what a fellow has to go through and still laugh and look forward to the next day. I think of coming home.

Closing with loads of love and may God bless you all forever, your brother, Alfred

Everyone can be wrong sometimes, and Myrtle could have collected on that bet of Alfred's. Martha Shaneyfelt, a cousin, had always wanted to be a nurse, but her family couldn't afford to send her to school for the training. So Aunt Ella pitched in and helped pay for the tuition and Martha agreed that she wouldn't get married till after she was done with school. That was the deal until she fell in love.

They got married in the middle of a war and nurses training, but Martha hung in there. A few years later she went on to finish her training and wear the white of a nurse's uniform.

March 11, '44

Dear Myrtle,

Just a few lines to let you know I am well and hope you are the same. I know you are wondering why I haven't written. Today is the first time I got to write this week. Because I am out with a Company and all my writing paper in my A-bag and about 60 miles away. But I borrowed this paper from some of the fellows in this Co. Pretty fancy letterhead with the outline of the state and all.

I received your box the other day, and also Aunt Zella. Did they come in handy. I was so hungry I could ate grass. All we were getting was C-Rations and they don't amount to anything. That was because they couldn't get the other food to us account of the blue forces would capture them, I mean the kitchens. But we are getting some fine eats today. Till Monday then the same thing will happen. But not as bad as when we were reds. We will be blues this week. But we won't have much more of this foolish work. For we will have only one more week after this. Then we are supposed to go to Fort Jackson, S.C. That's where we were before. But we don't know for shore yet.

Myrtle, how has Bill made out in his examination. I hope he doesn't have to go like Harold. I really hated to hear of him leaving. But I guess I can't do anything about it. I really hate to see his kiddies be without a Dad. I only hope he doesn't have to go. I hope that something happens in this war so he doesn't have to go. Maybe Hitler will kill himself and it will be over.

I got several letters today, one from Elna, Thelma, Mr. Roupe and was I glad to hear from them. You ought to read the letters I get from Thelma. She shore can make a person feel good and also when you and the rest write from home. So keep on writing.

Hoping soon to be able to talk to you instead of writing. We are to get a 15 day furlough, but don't know when they will start.

The weather down here had been terrible. I am safe to say it has rained 5 days out of every week. We have been out here for 8 weeks. Boy, will I be glad to get back in to Garrison again. At least we will be there for 3 months and then we are to go overseas. And maybe we will go sooner than that, because they are going to send 50 percent at a time on furlough. So it won't take more than a month to do that. I want to see you all again and then they can do what they want to. They are going to anyway.

I shore am glad to hear that the church is doing fine. Hoping it will always do good.

Hope to see you in a couple of months, so write when you can. Tell everyone I said "hello" and tell them to write when they can.

Closing with love to you sister and your family and mine.

Your brother, Alfred

Thelma is the daughter of Mr. and Mrs. Roupe and Elna Walls is the sister of Bill Walls, Alfred's buddy from Fairchance.

March 18, '42

Dear Myrtle,

Just a few lines to let you know I am well and hope you are the same. You asked me if I got your cookies. Yes, I did and was they good. You ought to have seen me eat them. When I got them we were out on a problem and we didn't get anything to eat for several days. And did they come in handy. I ate them like someone starved to death. And I nearly was. They sure came in handy. Thanks a million for them. I will repay you for what you have done for me and Dad and the rest.

We sure have had a terrible week just passed last week. It rained one night so hard you couldn't see very far. And it was at night so we had a miserable time in sleeping. You just can't find a comfortable spot. But the first two days were just fine. The sun was shining and it was really warm. And the general made us carry a full pack and overcoat for about 4 miles and it made us really hot. But the rainy night shore spoiled a good night sleep though. I hate the rain the worst at night. We also crossed a river in boats. And with all of our equipment. So you can see we shore have gone through with lots. I say again, I wish I was home. But this week will end us of maneuvers and I am glad. At least we will soon get to sleep in a bed. I won't know how to sleep in a bed. But shore will soon get used to it.

I am now at the church writing this letter. The church name is on the front and you ought to see how many beds they have here for us to sleep on. I mean cots. I will sleep here also with other fellows. It is really nice, you ought to see it. While I am in here I got a hair cut and a good meal. It is the first time I have been in town and it had to rain as usual. But I am in where it is dry. I really like that.

It is getting late now and the fellows are starting to come in fast now. It looks like some of them have had a good time. So I guess I will have to close for now. Hoping it won't be too long before I will be seeing you. How and what has happened to Harold. Tell them to let me know where he is, will you please.

Closing now with love to you all, Alfred.

After dinner one night in New York, Robert Marshall recalled how they used to call Alfred the "Big Stoop." While the 328th was in training stateside on maneuvers, everything they did was practice for the real thing. One of their practice drills was putting up a huge tent that was supposedly to house an aid station. As Bob told it, "We had this big tent folded up for transport and a couple of the guys had struggled with it but just couldn't pick it up. Big Al came along, sized up the problem and said, 'I guess you fellows need some help.'" He then proceeded to wrap his long arms around the tent and with one fluid motion, threw the tent into the truck by himself. This was one feat that everyone remembered and he never was allowed to live down.

Some of the men claim that is was after this incident that Alfred started being called the "Big Stoop" because he resembled a big and kind comic strip character of the same name.

Americans have always been enamored with the concept of the comic strip. Back in the forties a popular comic was one called "Terry and the Pirates." Terry was this swashbuckling handsome pilot whom the women fell all over themselves trying to get to, and of course, he had his entourage of buddies or pirates. Finding an old newspaper, I looked up the funny section and found Terry, a buddy, and a gorgeous brunette stranded on an island after their airplane had been shot down and they parachuted to safety. If you have to be in dire circumstances, it is rather nice to wind up with a lady on your arm and on a tropical island. So what if one of your crew member made it a threesome. Nobody said life was perfect, even for comic strip characters. As it was, the soldier, sailor, or pilot could identify with Terry and his men. They always made it, and one could always hope that anything was possible.

One of Terry's men was a big fellow called "Big Stoop." Robert and some of the other guys remember starting to call Alfred the name because he was so big and gentle.

Ironically, it appears that stateside he was assigned to an Intelligence and Reconnaissance unit. He went on their night patrols as a medic and as they skulked along, Alfred always walked in a stooped position to avoid attracting attention to himself. Calling him "Big Stoop" was never a slur against his character or mental capabilities but merely his size and slouching walk.

Since there are two stories regarding his nickname, no one will ever know for sure who can take the credit. It doesn't really matter who gave him the name or why, just that the name stuck and Alfred never took offense because of it.

March 24, '44
Dear Myrtle,

Just a few lines to let you know I am well and hope you are the same. I know you are wondering why I haven't written. But you know how hard it is to write out in the field. But will be able to write more often now. For we are over our maneuvers. We finished on the 23 and now are on our way to camp. But just don't know where we are going. But hope it isn't too far from home. We have gone 50 miles. But we are going to stay where we are for a few days and then go again. But just don't know. These trucks are sure bumpy to ride in, so I don't mind sitting still for awhile. Myrtle, how is everyone at home? I have been thinking of all of you. I hope to be able to come home soon. I was also thinking of Harold. I only wish I could have been home before he left. But I just couldn't. I only hope he does come back safely to his home and family. And if you see Winnie, tell her I said hello and hope to see her soon as I can. I don't know, we might be going to somewhere far. Hope we get to come closer home. So I can get home once more. Then I don't care where they send me. I shore have gotten tired of living this kind of a life, I want to go and see what will become of me. Either I come back home or that God will take me. Because the last three weeks I have been miserable. It has kept raining still the same and it also has been cold. The other night, I didn't think I had a right leg. For I was so cold that I shook and we didn't have anything to eat for 4 days only except can stuff and that doesn't go far. But hope we will have it much better from now on. Because we are going to a camp. It will be allright if we don't go somewhere else.

How is the church doing? Tell everyone I said hello and to keep on going to church. It shore has been a long time since I been to church. But when I get back to our new camp I am going to start going again.

I am glad to hear that Dick and Billie are getting along fine. I know they have growed since I last saw them. That is why I am growing to hate all this. Tell them I said to be good.

I heard last night that we would be in our new camp by Friday of next week. And will I be glad of that. I will let you know when and where we will be as soon as I can. I don't know if I will be able to write to you anymore until we get there. They might take our bag again and all my stuff will be in it. But will write when I can.

Tell Bill I said hello and hoping he is getting along fine in his work. Hoping to see him soon. I started this letter yesterday, but just couldn't get it finished. For I had to take several fellows to the aid station.

I will have to close because we are going to have an inspection soon and I still have some things to do. So long and hoping to see you soon. So long dear sister. Tell Dad I said "hello."

Regarding his brother Harold, he was drafted and went into the submarine service on March 24, leaving Esther and four-month-old Jesse at home with their mother.

March 26, '44
Dear Sister Myrtle,

Just a few lines to let you know what has happened since I wrote the last letter to you. We went to a big field and the colonel gave us a talk. This is what he said. But before I write what he said I am asking you not to tell anybody. I just mean for you to know. For I don't want anyone else to know till things happen. Because things can be changed in just a few hours. But as things are now this is the way. First we will leave here on the 30 and be in Fort Jackson, S.C. on the 31. Then after we get there and get our equipment cleaned and fixed up and everything else done that has to be done. Then we will get a 15 day furlough. When we leave the whole battalion will leave at a time. Then when we come back we are to get 2 months of training for there has been several hundred came in last week. Then after those 2 or 3 months we will be taking a boat ride. This one thing he said that we will go across. But please now, Myrtle, don't tell anyone yet.

Would you send me $25? When you send the money, will you sent it this way: Cpl. Alfred L. Wilson ASN 33429521 328th Infantry Co. C/O Post Master Tenn.

The reason for you to send it that way is because I now am with a company. But I don't know if I will be here all the time after we go to our new camp. I will be shore to get it here. But if you write a letter just put the same address as you have before. But please send the money as soon as you can. I will let you know if I stay in the Co or not after we get back to our new camp. But I have gotten all of my mail. Don't worry about anything being lost. I got your letter the other day and was glad to hear from you. I went to church today in memory of those who war killed during these maneuvers. There was over 100. I know at one time 20 were drowned at one time. What happened was the boat that they were crossing the river with turned over. And with the pack they had on, it held them down and they drowned. There was one lieutenant I helped pull out of the water. Several were killed by tanks and trucks overturning and by blasting and every other thing. And all of that just wasn't needed to be done but it is the way of things that all of them had to be there. It shore makes a person feel bad to hear things like that. But we just have to get used to it.

We are shore getting some beautiful days now. We have gotten several sun shining days and does it feel good. Only hope we have the rest like them.

It is getting around dinner time now. I will have to close. But hoping to be able to see you soon. Write when you can and let me know how things are at your home and mine.

Closing now dear sister.

Your brother, Alfred

Clifford Glazier called me one evening from Cincinnati, Ohio to reminisce about Alfred and some of his war experiences. After entering the 26th Division at the Tennessee Maneuvers, he was assigned to Company C until about the third week after the landing in France, then he was transferred to a sniper division.

Cliff told me an interesting story about Alfred that occurred on one of the famous 25-mile marches that the infantry was subjected to. On this trek, it was a typical hot and muggy South Carolina day. They started out full of energy and sound bodied. But the heat and distance soon made itself felt on muscles and nerves. Cliff remembers how Alfred, because of his enormous size and big feet, marched along with a sort of dragging gait. As the march wore on, many dropped out from heat exhaustion or just plain collapsed with fatigue. Unfortunately for the foot soldier, the part of the body they needed most for walking was the part that got covered by blisters. Out of the forty in Alfred's platoon, eight men made it back to throw themselves on their bunks in exhaustion. The rest of the unit were strewn out along the road and would be picked up by a truck and unceremoniously dropped off in front of their barracks.

Cliff Glazier made it back and hit his bunk, too tired to even move. His officer had told them that there was a medic down in the infirmary that would take care of their blisters and to go on down. As Cliff put it, "I was too tired to move. I waited till everyone else had went down, I was the last one in line. I didn't want to have to wait. I had blisters as big as quarters." Since he was the last in line, he and Alfred were the only ones in the infirmary. He happened to look down at Alfred's feet and noticed that both of them were nothing but blisters. He told Alfred that he could wait and to look after his own feet first as they were in worse shape than his. But Alfred insisted on taking care of him. He told Cliff, "We're trained to take care of the men first, and to think of ourselves last." Cliff remembers asking Wilson if he would do that in combat, to which Alfred replied, "I certainly would."

Cliff, now a businessman in Cincinnati, and at the time of Alfred's heroic act not with C Company anymore, heard about Cpl. Wilson's insistence on staying with his men and how the doctor in the aid station had told the litter-bearers to bring Alfred in by force if necessary. He remembered thinking right away that Alfred had done exactly what he said he would do.

Mr. Glazier survived the war, but as he put it, "I was more that lucky." He had been a sniper and with intelligence in a reconnaissance unit. He told how one morning, as the only man in his re-con unit with a rifle, he would unconcernedly lean it against a rock in front of a cave and walk by it a dozen times. That night he learned that another company had pulled 27 German prisoners out of the same cave a few hours later that afternoon. They had been there all day. He had been strafed by planes that first looked like theirs, but turned out to be the German Luftwaffe.

He had seen big, strapping men talk of bravery and then fold into a whimpering ball after suffering a nervous breakdown. He knew some who they suspicioned had shot themselves in the foot rather than face combat. Many soldiers appeared to possess a strong front, but when it came down to facing life and death situations, the false bravado of the outward man gave way easily.

The problem was that these were times when you needed to count on the courage of your buddy. His false front did you little good when you needed him to react quickly and decisively for himself and the safety of others. Cliff thought that Alfred had exemplified the trait of sticking to one's convictions admirably.

Chapter IX

Company C

Fort Jackson, S.C.

Right before leaving for Fort Jackson, each company was assigned three medics. Alfred became part of 1st Battalion, 1st Platoon, C Company along with T/5 Frank Novicki and Pfc Arthur Sturgis. From then on, the medic and his company would be inseparable. The rifle platoon of C Company and its medics would eat, sleep, hike, play ball, pray, fight, and take responsibility for one another until the hostilities ceased, and if God saw fit, only reassignment, injury, or death would part them.

April 2, '44
Dear Sister Myrtle,

Just a few lines to let you know I am well and hope you are the same. Myrtle, we are now at our new camp. We are at Fort Jackson and I am shore glad to be back to a main camp. Now we can have a lot of things we didn't have while we were out in the field. At least we can sit down at a table and eat in a goodly manner. And we won't get any dirt in our food and we also can have all the water we can drink. Boy, it really is fine to be able to be like humans again.

How is everyone at home? Hoping they are all well and enjoying the good old sunshine and life. How is Dick and Billie and William? Is Bill still working the mine at Kyle? I hope he is doing good in his work and hope he doesn't have to leave it for anything like this place.

Have you heard anything of where Harold is? I am wondering and hoping someone would tell me where he is. I haven't heard from anyone. I hope they write me soon and tell me what has happened and what is going to happen. For I would really like to know. So don't forget to tell them and tell them I now will be able to answer more often that before.

How is Dad? Is he sick or not. I wrote him but he hasn't answered. I know he answers, but don't know why he hasn't lately. I would really like to hear from him. If you see him tell him I am well and getting along fine.

I will be coming home soon. I thought maybe I will get home for Easter. But I don't know if I will or not. But if not, I think I will leave here no later than the 10ᵗʰ of this month. But don't tell anyone until I get home for Easter. I hope that is true. I want to surprise them at home and Elna. I just want to get home in time to be in Church on Easter.

Don't forget to send me that money so I will have it to come home on. Hoping you have sent it already. So I can have it before I come home.

Myrtle, I want to go to church. So I will close. Hoping to see you real soon. And when I do come home I can talk to you better and tell you everything. If I don't get home for Easter, I will or think I will leave about the tenth. So till I see you I will say so long and God bless you always.

Alfred

On Easter morning, Rev. Jones greeted Alfred as he entered the church. Everyone was glad to see him, there was a lot of hugging and hand shaking. Rev. Jones clasped Alfred in his arms and it was a while till he let go. They thought a lot of each other.

Alfred was home for Easter and he surprised everyone like he wanted to. He went up to Myrtle's house for one of her good meals. The Easter Bunny had been there and left a basket for each of the boys, and big-hearted as well as big-eared, it left one for Alfred too.

April 23, '44
Dear Myrtle,

Just a few lines to let you know I got back safely and in plenty of time. Before we went home or to camp, we went to a show and also got steaks and then went to camp. I took my time putting out my clothes and then took a shower and then got some real good sleep. We didn't have anything to do on Saturday so we took our time of getting cleaned up. But went to town in the afternoon and took in a show and got another steak. We, I mean Bill and I. Then we came to camp again and went to sleep. But today I am in Charge of Quarters and will be there or here until 12:00 tonight. I shore don't like it for you have to be in the orderly room all the time and have to get the men out for everything that someone wants. But I rather have it today instead of during the week. For then a person has a lot to do. I just came back from supper. We had only cold cuts, but they let us eat all we wanted.

How is everyone? How is Dick? Hoping he will soon get over the measles. I hope he gets along good. So tell him to be good. As soon as I get paid I will send them something from down here. Have you taken those pictures in yet? Hope you have and when you get them back give Dad and you the powdered or tinted. Then give Grandmother one please. Then after that give Winnie the negative so she can get one made for herself. Also get one painted and give Janice one and I will pay you for it. Would you do it for me please.

You can be expecting some of your money about the first of next week. When it comes you will know what it is for. We are to leave next Sunday for a week on the firing range. But we will get our mail. We will be wearing our summer clothing on the first of the month. I really will like it. For this winter stuff shore makes a person hot. And there isn't much you can throw off for you get hollered at. Have you seen Dad and the rest and how are they? Tell them I said hello, and hoping to hear from them. I wrote to Harold Saturday, hoping to hear from him soon. How is Winnie doing? Have you seen her since I left. Boy, how I hated to leave, she really cried when I left. Hoping that this war will soon come to an end.

How is everyone on the hill? Has Cordelia had her baby? When she does, let me know will you, also it's name.

We had a better time coming down than we did going home. But would rather be home. I seem as if I can't get started out as yet. But will have to in the morning. For tomorrow will be first day of the week. Hoping we won't have it too hard. I know it won't for the fellows said they didn't have much to do. I can't think of much more. Oh yes, I will see about the bonds and Dad's allotment as soon as I get up to the personnel office. And also tell the kiddies to use those food stamps up as soon as they can. Closing now with loads of love to you and all of the rest.

So long, your brother, Alfred.

Cordelia had her baby girl named Faye. Later she had another girl, they visited Myrtle and Bill over the mountain several times.

May 4, '44

Dear Myrtle,

Just a few lines to let you know I am well and hope you are the same. I am wondering how you and the rest are for I haven't gotten a letter since I wrote to you. Hoping to hear from you soon for I would like to know how everyone is at home.

We are out here as an aid man. But they are only shooting 22 rifles out of a 37 millimeter gun. And there isn't much to do. I write and sleep almost all the time. So you can imagine how hard I am working. Ha! Ha! But we are to start doing lots of field work when all of the fellows come back from furlough. But till then we are really having it easy. I don't care if we have it all the time. So don't worry about me doing hard work for at least two weeks. But as soon as those fellows come back we will start that walking over again.

Have any other ones been called from home? Has Tom Appleby went to the army yet? He told me the night he took me to town he thought he would go soon. Has Bill heard when he has to go or did he get deferred or what.

How are Dick and Billie? Tell them I said hello and to be good till I see them. I don't know when it will be, but hope it won't be too long. We might never have to go across because we haven't heard any more about it. But hoping to see them as soon as I can. I also don't know when I well be able to get them a trinket. I might get the money if I get to go to town Sat. But we are to leave here Sat. But some of the outfit are going to stay out here two days. Only hoping I don't have to stay with them. For it is a terrible place. We can't go no where out here. At least we can when in camp. Hoping I don't have to stay. Myrtle, how did my pictures come out? I bet they are terrible looking things. But hope one is good enough for you and Dad. Then you know where the other ones are to go. I might get some taken with my summer issue on. For we are to wear them this month starting Sat. But I think it will be toward the last of the month before I will be able to for I haven't much money. I only drawed $18.00. The reason why is because I took a full bond out. But I am looking for a bigger pay next month. How is the church doing? Has it been going on like it did before. Only hope it is. For I really like to see it doing good. Tell all I said "hello" and hoping to see them some day for good. Tell everyone to keep on going to church and to be good.

I can't think of much more to say. For there isn't much to say about this hot, sandy place. So I will close hoping to hear from you soon. May God bless you and all the rest forever.

So long, your brother, Alfred.

Tom Appleby never had to go to the army. He was later deferred because he already had three children. Uncle Sam didn't want to deprive three kids of their daddy.

May 11, '44

Dear Myrtle,

I received your letter today and was very, very glad to hear from you. I knew there was something wrong at your place. But just couldn't figure out what it was. I am very glad to hear that you are getting along fine now. But please Myrtle, don't forget to let me know when something goes wrong at your place or at home. Because I would rather hear about it than be like I was this time. For to be so far away and thinking that something is wrong is a terrible feeling.

Myrtle, don't think hard of me for writing the last letter the way I did. But I really felt that there was something wrong or that you forgot about me. But I was looking every day for a letter from either you or some one from home. So don't pay any attention to the last one I wrote.

Please take the next bond for yourself and then we will always be square. And maybe after a few months I won't be even able to send a bond home, for we are going to take a test soon and if we don't pass it we will all be broken. (Our present rank will be stripped from us.) I am going to take a test I don't know much about. The major said it isn't fair for us to take that kind of a test. But he said he didn't have any thing to do with it. But will see what he can do about it. He said not to worry, but I am trying my best to do what I can to hold my rating. But if I can't pass it, I will just miss out on the money I get now. But don't tell anybody till it happens.

We don't know how long we will be here now. For we really are getting some overseas stuff before we go. There is a lot of things we are doing now that looks like we won't be here long. And everything we do now is put down on a chart and we have to sign our name on everything before it goes on it too. So you see we are getting ready for something. And are they getting stricter and stricter every day on things. Only wish it isn't true but if it is we will have to do as they say. I only hope it is over before we go. I really hate to hear of Ralph and of the rest having to go. But just as I say there isn't anything we can do. Ralph is shore having trouble too. I only hope all will be able to take it. And look for the rest to be happier and better days of time to come.

Yes Myrtle, I have even heard down here that people know he is going with her. Someone has seen the two of them together. I only hope he doesn't get her and him into trouble. But if he keeps on he will. He ought to do better than that. It was bad enough for me to go with her. I have sure learned.

How is the church doing now? I got a letter from Winnie and she said it was going down instead of going up. Have they heard anymore about the seats or not. Let me know when they get them. I bet I know it will shore make a big difference in the church. Hoping people helps pay for them and treat them better than the chairs.

Myrtle, did you see Melvin graduate? I bet he really looked nice when he was all dressed up. Only hope he gets a good job like the man said he would. Tell him to do as good as he can. Also have you heard from Lloyd lately? Is he still out where he was or has he changed his place of work or not. Let me know where he is and what he has written to Dad or you or Curtis.

Tell Curtis I said "hello" and hope he doesn't have any more trouble like he has. Hoping his chickens are doing good. Also tell Ellen and the rest the same. Hoping to be with them forever soon.

I can't think of much more. So I will close now. But hoping you will get well again and watch a little more closer the next time when you go to do anything like that.

Oh yes! Myrtle, you know next Sunday is Mother's Day. But you know where ours is. But we can think of her. I am going to church Sunday. For they are going to have a program for the ones with and without mothers. So when we go don't forget to think about her. Let's hope some day we all will see her on high. I really have thought about her often. Sometimes I really dream of

seeing her. I shore had a funny feeling. I did or don't
know what made me dream that way. But I know it is
meaning something. I shore have missed her. If only I
could see her like she was when she was with us. But I
do know she is up there watching all of us. I am going to
see her some day soon. I also talked Bill and Jim Wilson
to go with me at church Sunday. I know their mothers
will be glad to hear that.

I will have to close now for it is about 10:00 and the
bugler is blowing lights out. For tonight it sounds sad to
hear it. So till I hear from you I am wishing you and all
of my family God's richest blessing and hoping to see you
as soon as I can again. So long dear sister for now.

Your brother, Alfred.

Melvin was the first Wilson boy to graduate from high school.
Everyone was real proud of him and his Dad bought him a watch
to celebrate the event. Alfred's younger brother, Lloyd, was still
working, but it wouldn't be long until he too would leave home to
go into the Navy.

May 18, '44
Dear Myrtle,

I received your letter yesterday and was very glad
to hear from you. But I was going to write to you the
same day. But we were having a big inspection Friday,
Sat. and Sunday. So we had to mark all of our clothing
and what a job. We also had to scrub our hut and
everything in it too, even the windows. We had to turn
in everything we don't need now. Boy, it shore is a noisy
place here now. But we have almost all of our work done.

Myrtle, don't tell anybody what I am going to tell
you. We aren't doing this just for nothing what we are
doing. I really think we won't be here very long because
since I came back they have been doing some funny
things. I would like to tell you but I am afraid for I don't
know when they might look in our letters. But what has
been going on and the way the officers tell us we might

only be here a short time. I only hope we aren't going. But now we don't know from day to day where we might be or go. So don't be surprised and don't worry about me. I will have to go just the same. So if ever you don't hear from me for awhile you will have a good idea of what has taken place. Please Myrtle, don't tell anyone. I don't know if it is really true or not but we are wondering ourselves what is going to happen. Only hope this will soon get over with.

Myrtle, I am glad you are better and that it wasn't too serious. But you better watch of doing things like that. Also am glad to hear that Dick and Billie are getting along fine. Also that William is well and that he doesn't have to go. I really hate to hear of Ralph leaving. But other ones had to go. Boy, they shore are having their troubles. But I hope Betty will get along fine and hope she doesn't worry about him too much. How are the rest on the hill.

Myrtle, it shore is hot down here now. It is over 100 degrees now. You only have to just walk around or even sit around and the sweat runs like a creek. You ought to have seen the fellows and me after a march. They are soaken to the skin all over. And we went on a 25 mile march and they dropped out like flies. We aid men were pretty busy. And we will be having one every week too. So you can see they aren't doing it for just to pass the time away.

The red cross called up and wanted a fellow volunteer to give a pint of blood. So four of us fellows went. And they took me for it. I gave it and I didn't even feel it. They asked me if I have ever gave blood before. I said no. After they took it they said I was really the best one yet. For I had big veins and a lot of blood. Boy was there some beautiful nurses and did they talk to me. They asked me all kinds of questions. You can imagine what they asked. Where I was from. How old, how heavy, how tall, and every other thing else. I really enjoyed it. I will get my name put in the paper also. We all got a $1.50 but we didn't want to even take that, but they really made us.

About my pictures. If anyone else who wants a picture, let them have the negative and let them get one themselves. I couldn't afford to get them all one. So do that for me please.

Hope the church is doing fine. I bet they had a real Mother's Day program Sunday. We did down here. But I would rather been at home. But I just couldn't. I also wish they would let Dad have a rose pinned on him by Melvin. I also wish he has done fine at the service. I wish I could have been there.

I can't think of much more to say and besides I have to do some more work. So till I hear from you, I will say so long and may God bless you always. I will be gone till 12:00 now. They are hollering for me, so I will have to go.

So long, your brother, Alfred.

May 24, '44
Dear Sister Myrtle,

I received your letter today and was very glad to hear from you. I am very glad that you are well now, also all of the kiddies and Bill. As for myself, Myrtle, I am well and getting along fine in my work. But the weather is making it sticky for it has been from 98-105 degrees. So you can see it really is getting hotter and hotter every day. Hoping it isn't that hot at home. I only wish I could be home now. For I know it is swell there now. But I guess I will have to wait.

Yes Myrtle, I only wish I could see the yard. I know it took a lot of work to do it. But it really is worth it. Hoping some day I will have a home as beautiful as yours. At least I will try to have one as nice as yours.

How are the kiddies doing and getting along at home? Hope just fine. Myrtle, I always think of them all the time. When I close my eyes at night, I can see them. I sometimes just have to cry on account of thinking of how they have to live. But I know they are getting along fine. But I know they are missing a lot in life. Curtis, Melvin, Bernice, and Ellen are the most I think of. Boy if only I get the bonds I will shorely do all I can for them all. But I thank you, Myrtle, a million times of what you have done for me and them. I'll never be able to repay you for what you have done for us.

Myrtle, I got a fine letter from Mr. and Mrs. Roupe and a real one from Thelma. She is writing very good and steady to me. But I don't think I will get her to be my girlfriend. For she is going with a fellow where she is. But if she doesn't, I only wish I can have her for my wife if after the war and if she ever comes home single. I will shorely try real hard for I really think a lot of her. But you ought to have read the letter Mrs. Roupe wrote. She shore did make me feel fine.

Hope she is right too about this war going to be over soon. But please never let anyone know what I say for they might tell things different.

Myrtle hoping the church keeps going up like it is now. The last person I wrote to told me it was doing fine. Hoping it always does fine. For we really need the churches but the people in them better get good and live a better life.

I am going to church every time I can and doing as best I can, so don't worry about me please. I hope Dad hasn't lost any time. If he does he better get the old car fixed up so he won't miss anymore time. Also hoping Harold gets home. Wish I could see him.

I will close now, so until I see you or hear from you I will say may God bless you and your family forever.

Your brother, Alfred.

May 27, '44
Dear Myrtle,

I received your letter yesterday and was very glad to hear from you. I am really glad to hear that all of you are well and getting along fine. As for myself, I am swell. Only for the heat it really is hot. It has still been over 100 since the first of the month. So you can imagine how it is down here. I really felt it the other day. For I went on a nine mile hike. When I came back from the hike of 2 hours, I was soaken with sweat. But I got the rest of the morning off. And I really rested up. But had to go out in the afternoon. If it wasn't for the heat, I would be really fine. But I guess I will have it to take.

I am glad you took Dad down to see Grandmother and Aunt Ella. I know they have been looking for him to come down. Also glad to hear Winnie went also. For she told me she wanted to as soon as she could. Also glad to hear about Harold getting to come home. I know she was really glad to see him. I wish I could see him too. I hope he is getting along fine in his work. I know he is. Hoping he gets a good rating out of it.

Myrtle, I can imagine how Melvin felt about the watch. I know he is proud of it. Only wished I could have given him something too. But you know how it is with me. Hoping some day to. Myrtle, do as I said about the bonds. I am trying to get those bonds changed. I saw the fellow again and he is trying to get it changed. But if not, you send me two as I can sign, and send them back to you. So do as you think best. Hoping you can get my pictures for I know you want one.

Myrtle, I shore would like to see you again. So as to hear of what is going on the hill. Also to see your home. I can imagine how it is. Just the place to be comfortable. Hoping you always have a fine home and I know you will. Myrtle, don't let yourself get down account of working too hard. But hoping you will get it all done so as to let you have a lot of enjoyment.

As for the chicken, you said you would send. If you would put it in a jar and seal it, it would be allright. But don't send it just by wrapping it up, for it will spoil. As for being here to receive it, I will, for we will be here now for a couple of months as I hear. So don't be afraid to send it, please. As for the cookies, I didn't get them today with the letter, but hoping to get them tomorrow, that will be Sunday. I am writing this letter today, Saturday. I haven't anything to do now for we have the rest of the day off. It is now about 7:00. I am just waiting for it to cool off. So I can take a shave. I was going to take one sooner, but I would just be as hot a before. I will wait, so when I do, I will be able to keep cool.

Myrtle, I am still going to church and hoping you are too. Hoping our church is still going up instead of down.

May God bless you forever.

So long dear sister, your brother, Alfred.

At Alfred's mention of cookies, Myrtle faithfully sent him cookies almost once a week. When asked where she got the sugar she said, "I saved all my sugar for cookies." She had cookie-making down to a science.

Among Alfred's favorite cookies that traveled well were: chocolate chip, pineapple, and a brown sugar cookie that was made with molasses. Myrtle also made a plain sugar cookie to which she would add a generous portion of raisins.

June 7, '44
Dear Sister Myrtle,

I received your letter and was very very glad to hear from you. I have been looking for a letter from you all the time. Boy, was I glad to get this one from you. You don't know how it makes me feel to receive letters from you. So please don't make me wait too long for a letter. But I know how it is when you are cleaning your home, but if you only write a few lines I will shore be glad. I know you will. I will write you the same way. But you know we just can't sit down and write when we want to.

I am glad that all of you are well and getting along fine. Hoping that you will be that way all the time. As for myself, I am getting along fine. I am getting all I can eat and lots of sleep. We have had it really easy this week so far. But oh, Friday and Sat. will be a hard day for we will have a 25 mile hike with everything just like in the real war. I think I don't want to be in the real war, but if I do I will just have to go.

Boy, has it been hot down here. It has been 105-110 almost two weeks straight without a let up. Only hoping I will get home soon to see you and the rest. But I will have to wait.

I shore hated to hear about Ralph C. But I couldn't do anything about his trouble like I can't do anything about mine. Only hoping we all will get back safely. I wish I could have seen Harold. I shore really miss him and everyone else. I hope Lloyd would get a job instead of going to the Navy. For there he will find out it isn't as he thinks it is. He ought to think twice before he does that. But if he insists, I would leave him go.

I can't tell you much now. I don't know how long we will be here now since what has happened in France and at different places. I am only hoping we don't have to go elsewhere. For I really hate to think of it, but all of us who are here at this camp are glad of what has happened. We sat around and listened to all the news we could get. Hoping they will soon kill all those Germans off. So we can come home and live a real life. And maybe we won't have to go over until it is all over there. I hope I will get home instead of going there.

Shore am glad that William and the rest had a good time in the mountains. If I ever get out of here I won't set a foot in the woods. For now I can't think of any kind of killing even of animals. But maybe I will change my mind.

I will always thank you and everyone who sent me a box. For I always will like them no matter what you send. So tell Augusta I said thanks for what she will send.

Write and tell me all the news you know of home and on the hill. Hoping you always keep God in your life and mind. I am doing the same. So long now dear sister until I see you or hear from you.

Your brother, Alfred

June 16, '44

Dear Myrtle,

Just a few lines while I am sitting here with nothing to do. Boy is today hot! We marched just a few miles and I was soaking wet. It was at least 115 today. Boy I wish we were out of here to a place cooler. But when we move this time which we are in the very near future, it will be at a hotter place than here. For there will be shells flying. Boy the way things are going it won't be too long either. For we are doing things now that we haven't did before. Boy the way I hear it we will only be here about a month and a half. They just won't tell us the real time. So you can be expecting to hear about it almost anytime. But please don't tell Dad what I have said. We had a big day yesterday. We had a big parade and 630 men received a medal. It really does look good too. We won't be able to get it for it is only for the rifle company. But what they had to go through with isn't worth it. For they really had a hard job to do before they got it. Then after the parade we had all we could eat. Then after supper they had a big street dance and was the place crowded. There were 25 men to every girl. I felt sorry for some of the girls for the guys wouldn't leave them alone. You ought to have seen it. But I didn't stay long. I went to the show and then went to my hut and went to sleep.

I got a picture of Harold from Winnie. Boy, he shore does look fine. I only wish I could be there instead of here. For I think it is better than in here. For we have walked at least twice a week to a distance of 25 to 30 miles each time and it really makes a person go to the dogs. It is on account of the heat. For the men really fall out that never did before and I really felt it myself this time. But we won't have them anymore.

I will have a chance to come home. But I will only get about 24 hours home. But Myrtle, I really think it is worth it. For we don't know when I will get to come home and I really think we won't get any more now. But I don't have the money. But if you will send me $20 I will

143

get to come home. But please send it real soon so I will get it before next Friday. I will give it back to you and if Grandmother is still bad sick go into the Red Cross and tell them and they will come out and investigate and I might get more than three days. But don't tell them I mentioned it. Just say that she wants to see me. That is if she isn't any better. And if you think it isn't right, don't do it. Myrtle, just forget about what I just said. I don't think that it isn't right. But if you think it will be all right, do it. But see what the Red Cross might say. Do what you think is best. But anyway I will do the best I can on three days. I will try and get all the time I can. So please send me the money if you can as soon as you get this letter. Don't tell anyone of this. I want to surprise them. But don't forget to send me the money, will you. If I don't get home this coming week, I will the next. Saying so long, hoping to see you as soon as I can.

P.S. I have a lot to tell you when I do come home. So long now.

Your brother, Alfred

Alfred made it home yet another time. Following his usual pattern, he surprised his Dad and the kiddies, went up on the hill to visit Myrtle, and then went the rounds, visiting all the aunts and uncles and grandparents. Jesse had taken him down to visit Aunt Ella and Grandma Wilson, who had given him the Bible that he carried with him and who hadn't been feeling well.

On this pass, Alfred used his precious gas coupon and, borrowing the car, headed over the mountain to Windber to visit Alice Mock. Almost a two hour trip, it was a long way to go just to visit a friend.

June 30, '44
Dear Myrtle,

I am writing you this letter to let you know I got back safely and in time. I haven't had time to write till tonight for I have been real busy. Hoping I will be able to write to you the next time sooner. But now we are going out in the field to stay at night. We will be there for 2 days and a night. We will go out this week twice like that. The next one will be a little longer. But won't be till later on. But after that we will be doing something different you know what I mean. So when you see a different address on the letters I send you don't get excited but please don't let Dad worry about it. See when he gets it that he doesn't worry about it. Try and change the subject when he does talk about it. Please don't tell him till you get the new address. I will tell you first. So you can be there when he finds out. I could tell you more but I am not to say anything about it or the time of the movement. So as I say don't worry or shed any tears for it won't be as bad as it might seem to you. Please don't let even Bill know, will you. I am trusting you to do so. I only want you and you only to know. "I can trust you, can't I?" I always have when I say things to you, please keep it to yourself.

What has happened since I left? How did Janice and Mrs. Wilson take the terrible shock. I really feel sorry toward them. I am glad I wasn't home for the funeral on Thursday. I just can imagine how those folks felt. But there is no use to, for they can't bring him back. But they can go to him. Have you seen Janice since? How does she feel since he is gone? Please tell me what you know about it. I do know Janice is heart broken.

You don't know how much better I felt since I got home and came back. Since I came back I sleep better and I don't worry like I did before I got to go home. I feel like a new person. It seemed as if something was taken off my mind. Boy those few hours shore did help me. It was worth a million dollars to be home just those few hours. Hoping soon I and the rest will get to come home to stay forever. But we will be seeing some hard times before we do get to come home. I shore do feel a lot better since I seen Dad and the rest of the kiddies.

Have you sent Alice that big picture of me? If not please send it as soon as you get this letter. Will you. Her address follows. Be sure you send that picture will you. Also the rest when you get them. I say again, don't forget to send Alice that picture I told you to. Please. How is everything at church? Hoping real good. Has Jones came back yet? Tell him I said "hello."

The next couple of nights I am working at the dispensary, that is where we treat all the fellows. I will be in charge all night till in the morning.

Tell Dad and all I said hello and what I told you about getting back safe and in time. Hoping to write soon to them. Closing now for I have my bed to make before 10:00 and is 9:30 now. It is real fine here now. It rained and it cooled off for a good sleep tonight. It has been that way all week.

Saying so long now sister, and with love to you,
your brother, Alfred.

I would like to jump in here between letters and say that we once again hear Alice being mentioned. On Alfred's leave he had sort of surprised everyone by taking the car and disappearing for a whole day. Alfred told Myrtle, "I just went and done me a little visiting to one of Harold and Winnie's friends," who happened to be Alice Mock.

Even though they had known each other for three years, suddenly friendship was not what they were feeling for each other. Almost overnight, the tiny fire of romance had been fanned and had started to burn quite brightly.

He wrote Myrtle a lot, but from this point on he wrote Alice every day. He had chased the girls and they had chased him, but suddenly, the game of catch was almost over.

Another subject that concerned Alfred was the terrible shock that Janice and Mrs. Wilson had sustained. Janice Grimm Wilson, now a 70-year-old widow living in Annapolis, Maryland, remembers Alfred as a tall skinny guy. When she was fifteen and had to walk home from school, she would poke along until Alfred and his father came by on their way home from work. They would always stop, pick her up, and give her a ride home. Still full of spunk and merriment, Janice smiled and said, "You know, I always thought

I'd marry Alfred. He was sort of special and you don't forget men like that. But I guess I couldn't stay away from a Wilson because I wound up going through three of them."

Although Janice maintained a friendship with Alfred, she had given up on him romantically. So while she was home from D.C. to help out in a family crisis, she met O.J. Wilson and they fell in love. But he too went into the army and wound up in the Pacific theater of battle. They had wanted to get married before he went overseas, but family members persuaded them to wait till he came home.

Despite the uncertainty, Jamice recalled, "O.J. sent me money to buy my wedding dress." Separated by war and an ocean, their wedding plans continued, but their luck did not.

Sometime after he left for combat, the family and Janice received word that O.J. had been wounded and was in a hospital in California. He had lost a limb but was recuperating, and as soon as he was ambulatory, he would be put on a train for Pennsylvania.

With hope to spur them on, the bride-to-be and the family went ahead with their wedding preparations and looked forward to seeing O.J. They didn't care if he came off the train hobbling with a limb missing, or swathed in bandages. Janice soberly recalled, "He was so quiet and considerate. Just to have him would have been enough."

But prior to O.J.'s arrival, the family received another telegram from the army. They gave the time of arrival of his train, but the family would not rush to the station to greet him. Only his father was there when the train pulled in and a couple of soldiers gently took a coffin from one of the cars and placed it on the platform. PFc O.J. Wilson had come home, but there would be no wedding. Janice would wear his engagement ring on her left ring finger along with the wedding ring of a younger brother for the next fifty years or so. He was another Wilson not to be forgotten.

July 12, '44

Dear Sister Myrtle,

I received your letter the other day, but I just couldn't answer it. For we left Sunday and had to stay for four days out in the field. And when we came back today, we had to scrub and clean our equipment and get ready for a big inspection on Monday. We will be doing it all the rest of the week. We won't even have Sunday off. So you can see we are really busy. So, I hope you don't think I have forgotten you and the rest at home. I don't know if I will get to write to you or Dad anymore or not. But if I get a chance, I will. For Myrtle, we are going and going soon. But we don't just know when it will be. But if you don't get a letter from me in a few days or a week, you will know I have been on the move to somewhere we don't know. So don't get excited or worry about me. But as soon as we get to where we are going, I will write you.

Hope everyone is well and getting along fine. Tell Dad I am always thinking of him. And also tell him not to worry about me. For I will always be allright and will come home safe and sound. Tell the kiddies I said hello and hope to see them soon. But I don't know how soon it will and where we might be before I do get home. How is everyone on the hill? How is everyone at home? Also how is the church doing now? Tell Pastor Jones to keep up the good work for people will need it. How is Janice by now? Let me know how she is doing.

Will you send me three pair of undershorts. I will get them for we will be here till at least the end of the month. My size is 38 or 40. If you can get 38, get them and if not get the other.

Tell Bill I hope he will always do good, also the rest of the men.

Myrtle, this is all I can tell you about. For a person don't know when they might inspect our letters. I will say so long with loads of love. Always thinking of you and home. Hoping this war will soon come to an end. Closing now for the lights are to go out in about 5 minutes. Write when you can and as soon as you can.

Your brother, Alfred.

Friday evening 8:00, July 18, '44
Dear Myrtle,

I have just got through writing a letter today to Dad. Now I am writing to you. Hoping by this time you all are well and doing fine in everything you do. As for myself, I am fine and getting along fine in my work. But I shore am doing a lot of sweating doing it. For it really has gotten hot the last few days. Only hoping it doesn't get any hotter.

How is everyone on the hill? Who does C. baby look like? How are the Cunningham boys doing? Also how is Dick and Billie doing. Tell them to be good boys. How is Bernice doing at camp. Also how is the church doing. How is Grandmother? Tell all I said hello and hoping to see them all as soon as I can.

We will be here till the end of the month. But from then I don't know where we will be. So till I am here, I will write to you as much as I can. We are always working now. We didn't get done the other night till 10:30. We were getting ready for the big inspection we had today. So you see we are always doing something. We will have a hard day tomorrow for we really have to go through some real tests. But after that we will be doing some packing and getting things ready to move when that day comes.

I am hoping to come home again soon. But it won't be this week. But maybe next weekend. But whenever it is I will let you know the day. I have told Dad also about it. So you and he will know when I will get home. But I am saying if I don't get home don't be disappointed. For things can happen here over night. Also don't worry about me. I will get along allright. Hoping to see you soon for the rest of my life. Hoping this war will soon come to an end.

Myrtle, it is hard to write now. For I am really afraid to tell things I shouldn't tell. For a person don't know when they might look into our mail. And I wouldn't want them to say I gave important information out. I know you understand. Please don't ask me what things they are for I won't be able to tell you anything about it.

Dear Sister, only hoping I will be able to see you as soon as I can. But till I can I will say so long and may God bless you and the family. Tell Dad to write when he can.

Closing now with love to you dear sister,

your brother, Alfred.

Alfred saw his family after he wrote Myrtle the middle of July. But he knew when he walked into the kitchen at home that this would be his last time home before he was sent overseas.

In letters, Alfred and Alice arranged for her to be staying with Winifred in Fairchance on that last leave, but Alfred saw more of her than Winnie did. It was one of the few times she remembered spending any real time with Alfred. From the moment Alfred had met Alice, she had grown from a seventeen-year-old teenager to a woman of twenty. And from what we can gather from letters and Alice, it didn't take him long to sweep her off her feet. Alice said, "He was a charmer, but he was all man."

Every minute that they could be together was spent sipping Cokes at the Dairy Bar and walking Church Street hand in hand. They'd also visited Grandma Wilson and the aunts and had dinner at Myrtle's one Sunday afternoon. Alfred and Alice had naturally showed up at church together. With a man ready to be shipped out, two days with someone you think might be the one you've been waiting for, was like sitting a starving man down to a meat and potato meal with the promise of dessert.

It was Saturday night on a starlit summer's eve, they were two lovers caught up in the torrent of emotion and courtship, so it's not surprising that Alice said "yes," when Alfred asked her to be engaged to him. That Alfred wasn't a romantic is dispelled as we read of him taking her high school ring off and putting it back on her ring finger with a spoken promise. Alfred had been caught. The game was all over except for throwing the rice.

With hands clasped and faces close together, they whispered into the darkness their promises, hope, dreams, and plans hastily made and just as furtively to be carried out. War would put quiet desperate faces on men and women who had things to do and no time in which to do them. Uncle Sam had little compassion for those in love. Duty, unfortunately, had first call over any future that might come after the war.

Alice had already gone home when the family gathered for a really big picnic and family reunion at Aunt Ella's. Everyone was there except those away in the service. Augusta said, "We had a ball." They had all the tables set up outside when it started to rain and storm, so they gathered everything up and moved the whole thing into the basement. She said, "Nobody minded, didn't think a thing about it. Of course we were all young."

There were lots of good eats, and Alfred, who showed up dressed in his light khakis, did away with his share. Augusta remembered, "Chicken, oh, lots of chicken, Myrtle had made all this fried chicken, and Ora Fetcho Doyle had made chicken and homemade noodles in a roaster. I never saw so many chicken and noodles in my life. I can remember those two things always stood out in my mind because everyone went for the noodles and chicken. Oh, we had everything, green beans, cake and pie, lots of pie." Alfred would say after the third plate and third piece of pie, "I don't think I could eat another bite." He had ate "a little more."

Everyone remembers the laughter and the good time they had that day. There was a lot of hugging, but Augusta remembers there was sadness, too. "Everybody hurt when they knew he was going to leave. Everybody hated to see him go. As this one or that one left, it was sad. They'd say goodbye and wish him the best of luck, which he didn't get. After everyone had left, Alfred stuck around and helped Mom and Dad clean up. And I think he had to leave real early the next morning."

Alfred had hung around, as if staying could prolong the last few precious hours of his leave. It was hard to let go of the love and fellowship of family.

Amid all the reunions and family and Alice, Alfred was certainly having his best time home. Everything was working out great and he was enjoying himself immensely.

But in the midst of the good times, there was this intuitive feeling that he fought to put out of his mind, but with a volition all its own, it invaded his thoughts from time to time. He kept thinking that this might be his last time home, even voicing his fear when he visited Bill Wall's wife before reporting back to base.

Ann and Bill had set up housekeeping on May Street and she had been alone with baby Will, then five months old, on a typical July day. Alfred walked up on the porch, knocked on the door, and came on into the living room.

Ann said, "Bill hadn't come home this time, and I was holding Will and we were standing in the living room." Alfred said to her, "I stopped to tell you goodbye and I'm going back to the base. I wanted to know if there was anything you wanted me to say to Bill when I get back?" Ann's reply was to tell Bill that they loved him and missed him, and she continued on, "Alfred asked me if I minded if he held the baby?" Ann said of course not and held him out to Alfred. He took the baby in his big hands and cradled him in his arms against his chest, and held him there, all the while holding onto one of Will's small hands.

The next thing Ann heard was Alfred saying, "Well, I know that Bill is coming back, but I won't be coming back." As he talked, she remembered him choking up and both of them got to crying together. Laying her hands on his arms she'd responded, "Don't say those things. Don't feel that way. We'll be praying that you all get back." Alfred had said, "I have to say it because that's what's going to happen."

Ann said, "He was serious, never batted an eye. He wasn't joking this time. He was standing there holding Will, it was like he was thinking of how it would be to hold kids of his own."

Alfred had stayed for a good while and they had talked about family, friends, and church. When he went out the door to leave, they were joking and laughing. But Ann had said, "It was like he knew what was going to happen."

August 1, '44

Dear Myrtle,

Just a few lines to let you know I am well and that I got back safely and in time. I was here in camp at 11:30 Monday night. I took a shower and then went to bed. I really felt good too. For we went to sleep when we got on the train and I didn't know much until we woke up when we got to D.C. Boy was the train hot after we left

Washington D.C. But we opened up our window and it soon cooled off.

You really don't know how I enjoyed that short time home. I really felt better than when we were home on furlough. One reason was because I see Alice and also the rest of my family. But only wish this war was over. So we all can come back and live as we did before we came in here. Because I will soon have some one to live for besides Dad and the kiddies. Only hoping some day soon we all will come home.

I hope this war will soon come to an end. Oh yes? We might be here until Sept. But it only is a rumor. Only hoping it was true because the way things are going on the other side we might not have to go. Hoping they soon knock Germany out.

Myrtle, I got your cookies today. The mailman didn't eat them and boy were they good. Just now the fellows are eating some and say, "boy, those cookies are good." And I really love them too.

Myrtle, hope you aren't holding anything against me for what happened Sunday. I will take the blame for some of it. Hoping you know it won't happen again. Forgive me if what I done to make you feel unhappy.

I washed out my clothing tonight before starting this letter. So I can have all my clothing clean before we move out. Besides I made a dollar. I washed a fellows clothing when I washed mine.

I will close and may God bless you always,

your brother, Alfred.

Sunday morning 8:30, August 6, '44
Dear Myrtle,

While I am waiting for the time to go to church I will start writing you this letter. Hoping all are well and enjoying life.

As for myself, I am fine. We shore have had some hot weather lately, but today it is just fine. We had a rain and it cooled off.

We are to have a fine dinner today. For we are going to have chicken and everything that goes with it. And then on Monday we are to have ham. The reason why I know is that I was on K.P. yesterday. And was it hot. But we were through it early. Usually it is 8:00 before we would get out of the kitchen.

How is the church doing? Is it just the same or has it growed. Hoping it will grow for if ever we need it, it is now because of what has taken place. Only wish it would be over. For I really want to come home. So to be near you and the one I love. Because, Myrtle, I am going to tell you something that I know will surprise you. Myrtle, I hope you won't get angry with me for it. So Myrtle, I will tell you and after I do, tell Dad when you tell him, please tell me what you think and of what Dad said and please tell me all he said. Also I want you to tell me if I have done wrong or not. So here is what I have done.

Myrtle, you know when I was home the last time and that Alice was there. Well, Saturday night as we were all alone, we were talking and I asked her about us getting engaged. And shore enough she said yes.

For I told her I loved her before she came down and I said I wanted to talk to her about something and that was it. She knew I was going to ask her for I told her in my letter. But before we would agree I wanted to talk to her and she also wanted to do the same to me. So we got together and planned out what we wanted. So after we got through talking, I took her school ring off and put it back on saying this is a symbol of being engaged until I give you the real one. So now I am saving to get her the true ring. Hoping it will only be but a very short time until I will be able to get it and send it to her. I am going to get both rings. But I will send the wedding ring to you. I am asking if you will keep it for me until I come home for good. And then her and I will be married as soon as we can. You and Dad will be there I hope. Myrtle, don't think Alice asked me first, because I was the one who asked the question. I hope you don't think hard of her for saying yes because I wanted her to say that. If you say anything, blame it all on me for I was the one who started it. Myrtle may I ask what you think of her? Also tell me what Dad thinks of her. But for myself I really love her. For she is really a fine lady and I really love her. For me she is the only one now. For when you do that sort of thing as I did, you really mean it. Myrtle, I really have faith in her. For she told me she really means what she told me and that she wants me to do the same. In which I am going to do. For I now have stopped writing to some. The ones I write to is the ones who are one of our own. But I now will write to her and tell her what I have told Bernice and Ellen, but they didn't believe me. But what I have told you is true. I was going to tell everyone Sunday while we were eating, but Alice got a little bashful and told me to tell you later. So here I am telling you now. So I ask you again what do you think. So please tell me. I know you are going to tell me I said I wouldn't do such a thing in times like this. And of what I have all ready seen. But, dear sister, there is a time when you have to take a chance. So here I am taking that chance. There is always a time when a person has to decide things. So here I am deciding. I think I deserve to have a happy time like others have. I really think I deserve to have a future and to have a wife like other young fellows. You and the rest of my family has done as they thought and you have had a happy married life I hope. So I decided to have a happy life too. I hope you don't hold this against me. For I love Alice and I mean to have her as my wife. I don't want to be smart, but don't you think I deserve to have a dear wife and to have a happy married life. You and the other young people have been able to do it. I think I can support a wife too. I really hate to leave Dad. But I have and I will always think of him and do as much as I can for him. With you, I think we both can keep on helping him and he will continue getting his allotment and to get my insurance if anything happens to me. In which I hope nothing will happen to me. I will always think of you because you really helped me and also Dad and the kiddies. I thank you a million and I will never, never forget you. We always will be close together, won't we. I know you won't like it of what I have done. But truly sister, I feel as if I should have a chance to have a wife and a family like other young fellows and ladies. So I ask please don't think hard of me. I know other people will say things and will be surprised too. I know Grandmother and my Aunts will say he shore has changed his mind of what he has told us. But I know they won't mind or care. For they will say he's the one doing it. If you want to you can tell them. They will know who the lady is for Alice was with me when I went down to see them. Tell me what they say too. I ask again please write and tell me what all has been said. I know they will say a lot of what I have done. But I can't help it now. For it is done. Now I am on my way to be a married man, and to have a dear wife like others have.

Before we go across, I will make a allotment out to you. And when you receive it, I want you to take out what I owe you and then keep the rest for me. But if any one of my dear family gets sick, take what you have and use it for them. I want you to tell me what I owe you. I mean all. So I know what I really owe. I have forgotten it. The reason why I want to know is I can put it in my book so I won't forget.

The reason why I said that you will get a class C allotment is because we won't be here long. For we are doing the last thing now and that is loading the freight case. So you know what that means. But don't know when the time for us to go. For the General said there is only one who knows when and where we are going.

I also don't want you to worry about me for I will come back safe and sound. All I ask is that you pray for me and I will do the same for you.

Would you keep whatever I send you? Would you?

So dear sister, I will close and may God bless you

and keep you till he calls you home. Saying so long now until I hear from you or see you. Write as soon as you can please.

Your brother, Alfred.

P.S. Please tell me what you think of Alice. I will tell you she is 20 years old. Also please don't think hard of her. For she isn't the cause of this. But because I love her is why I feel this way to her. As you might think she is the cause, but I told her I want to see her at my home. I am glad I waited until I got the real thing. But I am going to tell Janice. So I thought I would tell you and Dad and my relations first.

Saturday afternoon, August 12, '44
Dear Myrtle,

I am writing this letter now because I can for we have the afternoon off. But I will have to go to work at 5:30 for it is my night to work in the dispensary. But will have all day off tomorrow. I am hoping this letter finds all of you well and enjoying life. Tell all I said hello, and hoping to see them as soon as I can. But the way things are now and what has already happened, it might be awhile before I will get to see any of you. But please don't worry about me. For I will be allright. I can't tell you when or where or what has happened. I wouldn't if I could. For too many lives are involved in what is to take place in the future. I know you can understand the reason why I can't say anything about what is to take place. But please don't tell Dad until he hears from me. For I don't want him to worry about me until he has to. Wishing he won't if anything happens in the future. I know he will, but I hope he doesn't, for I will be allright and will come back when this is all over and to live as I have lived before I came into the service.

Myrtle, will you do something for me. I can't do it myself, also because I think it is wiser to do it near home than down here. For what I want they will soak me for

157

it here. And besides, you can do it better than me. Will you go to town and see what a set of rings cost. I'd like to get a fairly good set costing about $120 to $150. But if you can get a set for $100, get it. But don't pay more than $150. Get the engagement ring first and if you have to put some money down on the wedding ring, just put down enough to hold it till I send you some more money. I think maybe you could get an engagement ring for $50, which I am sending you with this letter. But as soon as you get the engagement ring, will you send it to Alice. I will write to her and tell her why it will be later getting to her. I have told her she could be looking for it soon.

I know I am asking for a big thing and I know you will say that is a lot of money for a thing like that now. But Alice deserves it. To me she is the finest lady in the world and I want to get the best I can for her. I know you are saying I shouldn't be doing this, but I had to decide sooner or later, so since I feel this way to the lady, I think it is the time to decide this sort of thing. Hoping you won't hold this against me, that I am doing wrong. I was the one who thought of doing this and she accepted when I asked her.

Why I asked you to see if you could hold the other ring is because I would like to have them matched. But if you can't get both, just get the engagement ring and leave the wedding ring go. When I come back I will try and get it matched.

I will pay you for what you are doing for me. I know we are going across, so before we go I am going to get a class E allotment sent to you. That will be money that I won't need over there. It will at least be $20 a month. So when you get it, take out what you need on the wedding rings. I will send you some money every month until we go. But I don't think we will be here long.

I hope you have done what I told you to do about the money I owe you. Don't let Dad pay you any out of his money for I know he would try to help me.

Remember if you get the wedding ring to hold it for

me until I get back home. For I am coming home to live as before and maybe better.

I am trusting and depending on you more than anyone else. I know I can really trust you with anything. Hope you won't say I am just a bunch of trouble. Hoping I haven't asked too much of you. I know I am asking a lot for I know how you feel.

Closing now and may God bless you always.

Your brother, Alfred

P.S.

I know I shouldn't ask you to do this for it means a lot to do as I ask. But to me it is the best I think. I know you will do the best for me. Write as soon as you can and when you send her the engagement ring. Insure it, you better. Please pick the ring that you thing will be the nicest. If you can, get a yellow gold, if not, get the other.

Along with the August 12th letter my mother received a packet of pictures from Alfred. A few were of family members, but the bulk of them seemed to be of girls. He evidently was making good on his recent commitment to Alice and was getting rid of the pictures he had in his possession of old girlfriends. He believed in carrying things through all the way.

Postcard No. 1

Hoping you are well and enjoying life. Hoping to be able to see you soon as I can. I forgot to tell you one thing in the letter I sent you. About what I wanted you to do, so I am telling you on this postcard. The ring size is 7 1/2. Hope you understand. Also if you can get a $75 one, get it. Hoping it is a good one. I know it will for you know how to choose things like that. Tell me if you get one for that much or if you can get both for that much. Saying so long now. Write as soon as you can to me.   Alfred

P.S. Get something like yours with little diamonds in it please.

Chapter X

Post Master New York, N.Y.

Postcard No. 2
August 18, '44   USO

Sis, have you gotten what I asked you to. If you don't know Alice's ring size, it is 7 1/2. Don't worry about me for I am well and getting along fine. Did Rev. Jones read a letter in the church yet. If so, tell me what was in the letter. Sis, I really mean what I have done and hoping everyone will do as I have.

I am closing and hoping to hear from you as soon as I can. May God bless all of you and good luck. Alfred

Somewhere on the East Coast August 19, '44
Dear Myrtle,

I received your letter today and was glad to hear from you. Glad to know all were well and enjoying life. As for myself, I am fine. Getting along fine with my work. Hope everyone keeps on working. For now is the time a person can save a little, so I hope the work keeps on going till this is all over. Also after this war is over so when we come back we can get a job.

We have moved. Where we are at is really fine. It is cool and nice. We also had some rain. But it really is better here than where we came from. Only wishing we could be home instead of here. But I guess we will have to go like the rest and do our part in this war. Hoping Milton will get to come home. But anything can happen now. How bad is R.C. Wilson? I bet he is shore in terrible shape. Tell me what happens when they tell him about O.J.

I am glad you and Dad like Alice. But as for myself,

I love her. I know you never seen or heard about her, and maybe to you and Dad it does seem as if she is young. I know she is young, but she is 20 years old. I really think she will make me a fine wife. I tell you Sis, she really is a jokey person and she loves to enjoy the pleasures around her. All of her folks seem to be jolly and lively just like her. Hoping some day you will meet them.

I really enjoyed what you said in your letter. Hoping someday to have all you said come true. And that really is what she and I have already said. I know we decided quickly, but I really couldn't go and leave her because she really appealed to me. So that is the reason I done as I have. But don't worry that we won't know each other well enough, for we have talked about not being married till after the war. That's the reason why I asked you to get both rings and to hold the one for me.

I ask you, please, as soon as you can, send her the ring. For I really want her to get it as soon as she can. Don't worry about the money. Don't worry about me. For I will get along fine no matter where we go. Only hope we soon get this all over with so we can all come home.

We are getting fine meals here. I have all I want to eat. It really tastes good too. But would rather be with Alice or at home. But don't worry, it won't be long, I hope, before we will be able to get home. It can't last forever. I know or hope to come back for I am trusting in God to let me come home and to enjoy life as I had when I was home. For Myrtle, I really have changed my ways. Hasn't Jones gotten a letter yet and hasn't he read it in the church. But if he does you will understand what I mean. I really mean what I said too.

Tell all I said "hello" and hoping to see them in the future at home. Also tell Janice I will write to her as soon as I get a chance. But tell her to write. Tell her that Alice and I aren't married, but just engaged.

If you want to, you can put our engagement in the paper. But before you do, please write to Alice asking her. You know how to put it in. The date that we were engaged on was July 30, Because that is when I took off her school ring and said as I put it back on that from this day on we were engaged. She was to keep the ring on until she got the real one. When you do, please send me the clipping of it no matter where I am.

What I write in this letter will be read. But the officers said it wouldn't be told to anyone and I believe them for we have got some fine officers. It is their job and it has to be done as you will see on the outside of the envelope.

Closing now with loads of luck to everyone at home and may God bless all of us and the other fellows who are like me here in the service and you and all the kiddies.

Your brother, Alfred

Chapter XI

Somewhere In France

This is a picture taken by black light camera. The fellows are me, Jenkins, the one in the little picture I sent you, and Will. A fellow who came in with us. Show who you want.

Between the letters with a New York postage and the censored ones that came out of France, the officers must have kept the men too busy to write home. The 26th Division was on the move again, but this time, their mode of travel was not within the confines of a bouncing truck. This time, they rode the swelling white capped waves of the Atlantic Ocean on one of the forty-seven ships in a troop convoy heading for Cherbourg, France, and the United Kingdom. As they pulled out of New York Harbor, the decks were crowded with guys taking their last glimpse of the land of the free and home of the brave. Keeping her vigil in the harbor, the Statue of Liberty stood in the morning mist and everyone waved a last goodbye to the lady.

Alfred made the crossing in the liberty troop ship SANTA MARIA. Built as a freighter in 1942, she had been converted to a troop ship in '44 and this was her second crossing with her holds filled with a human cargo numbering 1,417. The 1ˢᵗ Battalion of the 328ᵗʰ spent 10 days between the shores of home and the uncertain shores of the French coastline.

While at sea, the guys mostly remembered the aircraft carrier with planes sitting on deck that rode the water ahead of them. They also couldn't forget the long chow lines (if you could eat), how long the trip seemed, and how seasick a lot of the men were. They had encountered a couple of storms coming over and Alfred definitely hadn't fit the sailor mold. Bill Walls said Alfred was hanging over the rail or had his head in a bucket most of the time.

Frank Novichi was a sergeant when they went across and he had talked several times to Alfred during the trip. He had asked him if he had a girlfriend and tried to encourage him about getting engaged. Frank had told him to save his money and get a proper ring and go ahead and do it, and not to worry about what might happen over there.

Again, Alfred had expressed his fear, "I have this feeling that I'm going to get killed, I won't be coming back." Novichi had replied, "Get that out of your mind."

Over the phone he spoke of Alfred, "You couldn't miss him, he was big and gentle with a heart as big as the man. He never had a bad word to say about anyone and he'd help anyone who asked him. We loved that man."

While at sea, the men couldn't write, couldn't do anything. Robert Walls said, "There were a lot of fights. Everybody and everything got on their nerves." They were worried. Nobody knew what war was really like. The French already knew, though.

Bob Walls shared an emotional story that foreshadowed what the men of the 26ᵗʰ had ahead of them.

Months after being in combat, some of them were bivouacked along a road leading into a small French town. As they lounged around, a very pretty young girl came down the road pulling a two-wheeled cart. Bob was fluent in French so he spoke a greeting to her, asking how she was and where she was going. She informed him that she was going to church and as she started to move on, Bob remembers her looking back over her shoulder at him asking if he wanted to go with her. It didn't take him long to think it over. He told her to wait a minute and he ran to find his captain to ask if he could go to church. He received permission to do so if he got his butt back there right afterwards. He agreed, of course, and off he went to escort a pretty young girl to a church that he estimated would hold about twenty or twenty five worshipers. They came back the same way, he bid her goodbye and she went on her way.

Sometime later after he had been wounded, he had some extra time and went back to try and find the town and the girl. What he found though, was pretty much of a shock. The quiet country village was gone. Even the church. All that was left were a few burned out walls and foundations and holes in the ground. Bob said that he stood there and felt like he was in a dream. He didn't know if maybe this was a dream or if he'd been dreaming of the girl and the church or what. He said it was the strangest feeling standing there in the middle of nothing. He flagged down farmers and anyone he could find and inquired of them as to where all the people had gone. The only response he could get from anyone was, "C'est La Guerre," meaning, "It Is the War."

But for now, as the flotilla of boats neared their destination during the night, Alfred and some men of the rifle platoon stood on deck. They heard one sailor say while looking at the faraway search lights moving across the sky and hearing the faint noise of what sounded like rifle fire, "They're sure catching hell in London tonight," he said.

At the end of ten days of "walking on water," with full packs and rifles, the 26th Division climbed hand over hand down the ropes of a cargo net that kept moving at the wrong time, and tried to jump into a bobbing landing craft. Then, just like the landing force which had proceeded them on June 6, 1944, three months before, the navy sailors drove them into Normandy and landed them on Utah Beach. But thankfully, the calendar had been turned, and all that greeted them was a few spiraling streams of smoke and an upside down helmet embedded in the sand, and at places, a rifle stuck barrel first into the sand to show where a GI's body was buried.

Burial detail hadn't gotten around to digging them all up yet for identification. It sure gave the boys an eerie feeling.

Most of the guys didn't mind at all when the army held them at Normandy for about a month waiting for supplies to catch up with them. But the respite didn't last long, and the grand scale of things started changing. The 26th was on the march to join up with Patton's third army. Supplies and men rolled along the one way highway named aptly, the "Red Ball Express," which ran from Normandy to Paris to wherever Patton was.

Somewhere in France September 12, '44
Dear Sister Myrtle,

Just a few lines to let you know I am well and hope you are the same. I know you were wondering why I haven't written. The reason was because we were on a ship and didn't have much to write about. Even now we can't write about the trip or where we are and what we have seen. I mean by the way we come. But will try and let you know as much as I can. So don't think I won't write and let you know where I am if we can. For I will when I can. But we had a good trip and have seen a lot. Yesterday we went several miles to take a shower. It was really worth it and we also saw a lot.

But don't worry about me for I will come home to be able to talk to you and the rest and will tell you things that we can't write about. Please write as often as you can. I will say now that maybe I won't be able to answer all of them. Don't think that I have forgotten you if you don't receive a letter from me for several days because I can't write when I want to.

I hate to hear about Bill. I only hope he doesn't have to go. Wishing this war would stop before he has to come in. If he does, hope he doesn't have to come over here, but stays in the states. I hope he is well and enjoying life, also tell everyone and the kiddies that I said "hello."

Was glad to hear what you said in your letter about sending Alice the engagement ring. I only hope she has gotten it by now. I know Alice will like it. For she said no matter what she gets will be allright. All she wants is to get it. She said she was going to write to you when she gets it. Let me know what she said please. I am only hoping to be with her as soon as I can. For then I will be very happy and she will be too. She does write some good letters and I believe her for the way she writes seems to me as she really means what she and I have done. One of these days I will show you that she means it. Only wish it could be tomorrow, but hard to tell when I will get to do that. Myrtle, I am sure you did allright by the ring. Since you are getting it, get the one you want. I know you got her a nice one. So don't think she won't like it. Tell me what it looks like and see if you can get me a picture like it or something.

Put a nice announcement in the paper but first see what school she graduated from and also her fathers name. When you get it send me a clipping please.

Will you send me a bottle of ink. But wrap it so it won't break. I got a good pen. Alice sent it to me for my birthday. It won't be only 6 more days until I will be 25. I said before I wish I could be home for this one, but I am many miles away from home. Hard to tell where I will be for the next one too. Hoping I will be home for it. Tell Dad I am always thinking of him. I only wish I could be with him on his birthday. But I wish I could be with him all the time.

Myrtle, I always go to church and I am trying to be as good as I can from now on till my life is taken. I pray every night and read my Bible that Grandmother gave me. I know God will spare my life and other fellows lives that are with me here. Hoping he will make other fellows change their ways and live for him. I always think of you and everyone who is in our family. Hoping you are doing the same.

I saw Bill Walls today. He is fine and getting along good. He and I shore been lucky. We been together ever since we came in the army. Also came over here together. I shore liked that. Tell Elna or whoever you see, he is fine.

I can't think of much more to say. I hope you will send me what I asked for in this letter. Send me some air mail stamps too. Closing now with all my love to you and may God bless all of us.

Your brother, Alfred

Even as Alfred wrote about Alice getting her ring and the hopes he harbors in his heart for them both, he was blissfully unaware that a young woman's dream has already come true in the middle of a hay field.

Thursday, September 7th, was Alice's day off. She writes that on this morning she had been out in the hay field watching the cows. At about 11:00, her sister Leora, picked her way across the field with a package in her hand. "I was very excited and tore it open out in the field, and much to my surprise, there it was. A beautiful ring. I wish Alfred could see it. I know he would love it," she wrote to my mother. Alice's exuberant response to receiving the ring must have been a balm to my mother's worried conscience that Alice wouldn't like the ring she had chosen. But Alfred had not put his faith in my mother's impeccable taste without good reason.

Alice went on to say that she couldn't have picked a better one herself. The box and ring had arrived in good shape and the best part was that when she slipped it on her finger, it fit perfectly.

Alfred also mentioned in his letter that he hoped the other fellows change their ways.

Robert A. Walls spoke to me from his country home in Maryland, "Al was a complete gentleman. He was always trying to keep the other fellows straight." He laughed and continued, "I mean, he was trying to keep us from those bad French women."

Sometimes the men would kiddingly call him "Preacher Al" because he'd tell them they shouldn't do this or they shouldn't do that. "When the guys were coming home on the train, Al would say to those drinking, 'If you don't straighten up I'm going to write home and tell your mother,'" Bob chuckled. Alfred kept his uniforms clean and spit and polished his shoes. He'd be after the other guys to maintain themselves just right.

One time Bob recalls, "They were shelling us and down this road comes this jeep with four stretchers on it, dodging back and forth when all of a sudden it got hit, and that jeep just rolled, the driver was killed, so we jumped into it, Al was with us that day, and we had to rebandage those guys up. It was something."

Somewhere in France Sunday Afternoon
September 17, '44

Dear Myrtle,

Just a few lines to let you know I am well and hope you are the same. We shore had a fine dinner and I had what I wanted to eat. Only hope we always can get it. But if not we all will have to do as we best can. Hoping you and the rest of my family are well and having what they need.

The weather is fine here. Only hoping it doesn't get too cold if we are over here this winter. I got a letter from Alice telling me she got her ring. She said it was a beautiful one. And if we were to have gotten it we couldn't have gotten a nicer one. She does really like it, but she is hoping soon to have me put the other one on and I am hoping the same thing. Please tell me if Bill has to come in or not. Hoping the war will be over before he has to go.

I thank you for what you have done for me and hope some day to repay you back for what you did for me. Hoping it won't be long either.

I will close for now, but tell everyone I said "hello." Also don't forget to send me the bottle of ink. Closing with all my love and hoping to see or hear from you real soon. May God bless you and the rest.

Your brother, Alfred

P.S. If you can, send me a fruit cake.

Friday evening September 29, '44

Dear Myrtle,

I am fine and getting along good in my work and with the company I am with. They shore treat us fine. Also we get plenty to eat. The other day we had turkey, mashed potatoes, carrots, bread, butter, coffee, and fruit. It shore was a good dinner. But I wished I could have been with you. For I really enjoy that sort of thing and the way you fix things. But I just can't be there for that, but now have to take what I can get and like it. Hoping to be home in the near future and to enjoy things like I did when I was home. Myrtle, thanks a million for what you have done about the ring. Hoping some day to do something for you. I will like it. Just so Alice was pleased is all I wanted and she is. You ought to read the letter she wrote me about it and you. She thinks a lot of you for the way you chose it and the way you wrote to her. It will always be that way. You shore will be at the wedding when I get back home. I know you will like that. Hoping that day will be soon.

How is Dad, Grandmother and the rest? Hoping all are well. Shore hated to hear of those sick around there. Hoping they get better and all the others who are sick. So tell all I said to think of God and he will heal them.

Tell Dad and all the family to write to me. I will write when I am able. I shore miss you and all the rest. Hoping this war gets over so we all can get home and live a good life as we were doing before we came in here.

How is Dad taking this, me being over here. And what does he say? If he seems to take it hard, please try and make him forget about me and tell him not to worry for I will come back to him some day in the future. Please do that for me.

When you write to me, send your mail by air mail because it will come faster. Myrtle, don't forget what I asked for and please write, it's been a long time since I heard from you.

Can't think of much more so before I close I hope and pray to be able to see you and the rest as soon as I can. Keep praying for me and the rest. I will do the same for you and the rest. May God bless you and all the rest forever. Saying so long for now. Answer soon.

Your brother, Alfred

P.S. When did you know I was here in France. Let me know the dates.

Somewhere in France
Wednesday Afternoon October 11, '44
Dear Sister,

Just got some paper from a fellow here, so while it is light, I will write to you. I received a letter several days ago. Boy was I glad to hear from you. I was wondering if you knew I was over here. Didn't hear or get any letters for awhile. But one day I got 5. They were from you, Dad, and Alice. The last I got from you was 29th of Sept. But even at that I was glad. It told me about the ring. Was glad to hear you done that for me. Alice has told me about receiving it and she was pleased with it very much. Will send me a picture of it as soon as she can. Thanks for doing it for me. Will pay you back for everything you have done for me now or till I come home.

I got two letters from Dad and one from Jean. Please tell all I will answer when I can write and when I can get paper and stamps. I think of all of you at home and always will. I have been glad of what you and Bill have done for us at home. I like all and think of the rest just the same, but you are my best one.

Hoping I will get home real soon after this war is over. For I really miss home and my loved ones. I am praying and hoping God will stop this war soon, so all will get home to be with their families.

Myrtle, have they cut very much out of my letter I send you. Tell me if they do. Dad sent me our announcement and was I pleased to hear about it. Now, hoping to be able to put the other one on. Boy will it be a happy day. You will be the one who will be able to see that happen. Hoping that it won't be too long.

Will you tell me how much I have in bonds. I would like to know. I can't count on what I send home in the class E allotment for that is to pay you back what I owe you. I got it straight now. You will be getting $10.00 in the class E allotment. But I am going to get $10 more added on. But will have to see the clerk before I will know. Dad and Curt will get theirs, but I owe you more.

How is everyone around there? Send me some air mail stamped envelopes and some paper. Are you sending me a fruit cake? I will miss that. Send me some candy bars too.

Myrtle, what are people saying about what was in the paper? Dad said they were surprised about it. Tell me what they say, also if you or Dad see George Roupe, tell them I said hello and hope to hear from them.

I saw Bill Walls. He shore is a good pal. He and I are really glad to be able to see each other every day. I showed him the piece that was in the paper. You ought to have seen the expression on his face. Also the other fellows. They all congratulated me. They said they wanted to dance at the wedding. I said there wasn't any drink or dancing. Then you ought to hear them.

I always go to church when I can out here in the field. I also read my Bible every day and pray every night. For you and all the rest and I ask God to take care of us all. I know you and Dad are doing the same. For now we need that more than ever since we are here in France. I know God will take care of us. I really have changed my way of living and will do all I can for God now and when I get home, because before I left camp, I couldn't sleep for two nights. So I went to our chaplain and told him everything. Then when I went back, I felt much better. Did Jones ever read a letter from a chaplain, if so did Jones read it to the church. Tell me if he did or not, please.

Closing now with all my love to you and home.

Your brother, Alfred

Alfred never received the answer to his question.

Reverend Jones did get a letter from a Chaplain Gordon. But he never read it in church, preferring to believe that nothing would be gained by a public reading of the letter from Fort Jackson. He wrote to my Mother, "I thought it best not to read it because I know that the church thought as I thought, that Alfred was alright and I still think that it will be alright with him."

The Chaplain's letter had merely stated that, "Alfred came to me deeply moved by his inward repentance over some sins which he said he had committed in the past. He desired forgiveness and absolution from Almighty God and any who might have been affected. After prayer, he asked that I write to you, indicating his sincere desire to enjoy again the full fellowship of the congregation in as much as he had deigned to refuse the communion on an occasion when he was home on furlough. I told him that I would write, explaining his state of mind and heart."

This incident has taken place the first week in August of '44. Alfred had now found peace with God and with himself. He was sleeping nights now!

John Dobos Jr. from North Versailles, PA., expressed the opinion that thoughts of God were preeminent with many of the men. One soldier commented, "I don't believe that there are any atheists in a foxhole."

Bill Walls told of being in a foxhole during a mortar attack and having a clump of dirt fly and hit him on the leg. "My first thought was," he said, "I'm hit, I'm hit! I said every prayer that I was ever taught as a child in church. Then I looked at my leg and saw that I was okay and it was just a big chunk of dirt that had hit me. Was I ever thankful!"

Father Bransfield, a Catholic priest, often found himself conducting services from a jeep out in the open spaces wherever a group of men happened to be gathered. The jeep served as an altar with the surrounding countryside their cathedral. Even though there were no elaborate trappings like in Europe's finest cathedrals, there was no mass more holy to God or men, than that held with helmet in hand, and kneeling in the dirt behind the good Father.

Alfred's last letter to sister Myrtle.

October 19, '44
Thursday morning Somewhere in France
Dear Sister Myrtle,

I hope this finds you well and enjoying life. As for myself, I am well and getting along fine. Getting lots of sleep and eats of what I have been getting, even though they are C rations. That is meat and beans, vegetable stew and hash and in between hot meals. I like them pretty good.

About the mail. I have gotten your letters right along, and have been writing. I know one thing. Sometimes it takes a long time for you to get them. I have gotten 3 at a time. So you see how it is. But, Sis, I write to you when I can. Our mail now has caught up with us. There for a while I wasn't getting any. But now I am. Thanks for the clipping. Everybody around here is congratulating me. Boy do they say funny things. Shore have a lot of fun. You know how fellows talk about getting married or engaged. Alice shore will be glad I know about the announcement.

What dated letter told you we were in France? Before we came here, I wrote almost every day to you. Bill told me you knew it on the 19ᵗʰ of Sept.

Hoping Curtis gets better with this medicine so he can enjoy life better. I don't know where Lloyd or Harold are. Boy, am I going to tell them. I'll write if I know their address and they should do the same.

Myrtle, hope Bill never has to leave home. Because where I am now, shore is muddy and wet. But can sleep in a dry bed at night.

I haven't as yet received any boxes. I don't think we will get them till Christmas. Hope we would for I need ink. This is the reason I am writing this letter in pencil. Hope you don't mind it.

When you send me your next box, send some stuffed olives, candy bars, pineapple juice and pineapple, and a fruit cake and sweet pickles, please. They are the things I think about most.

You asked me if I saw any French people. Yes I have. But I take the people in the good old USA. I can't talk to them because I can't speak French. But I know some things. We can't buy anything in the small French town. I visited Paris, but that is all I can say. Please don't ask me what town I am near for I can't tell you. But when I can, I will tell you what towns I visited. I know you understand the reason why we can't.

Tell all I said hello, hoping to see them all when I get home. Has Dad gotten a cable gram yet?

Sister, can't think of much more to say. So I will close and may God bless you and my dear family forever.

I know that it is true what you say at the end of your letters. For some has already come true for me since I been here. I pray every night since I left Jackson. Closing now and will write when I can and you do the same.

Your brother, Alfred

P.S. I just got a letter from Dad, dated Sept. 28.

After their landing on the 7ᵗʰ of September, peace was to be an elusive phantom to the 328ᵗʰ Infantry who fought against the faceless Nazi war machine.

The Battle of the Bulge began in earnest the first of November and continued on relentlessly for Patton's army. After a successful beginning, planes, tanks and men were now being stymied by rain and snow with no end in sight. The mounting frustration for Patton as American youth were being slaughtered, evidently inspired him to ask his chaplain to inquire of God just whose side was He on anyway. The now famous prayer, delivered by Patton just before Christmas, suggested that God had in some way changed horses in midstream. Of course, he promised a Christmas present of the entire German Army to God's Prince of Peace in exchange for four perfectly clear days of weather.

One of the first orders issued in France was to turn in gas masks. The men sort of figured someone had goofed. But it just so happened that the Germans didn't have gas masks either, so despite the hostilities, both sides agreed not to employ gas warfare.

About this time the Germans started to pull an old trick. The Heinies would capture a soldier and take his uniform, coat and helmet. With the captured uniform, a German soldier could walk around disguised as an American.

By the time a G.I. found out that the fellow standing guard next to him couldn't speak English, it was probably too late to save himself.

So some smart officer went back to Paris and got the gas masks hauled up to the front lines and ordered that every soldier carry one or else. Then when someone without a gas mask came around, he was easily identified as a German. Problem solved.

During combat, nothing could be taken for granted. Not your life, not your friends and not a national holiday like Christmas.

When they first fought their way into German territory, headquarters commandeered the same homes that the Germans had just left. In one particular house, two company clerks decided to explore the attic, not really expecting their predecessors to have left anything behind that was useful. Much to their surprise though, they found all kinds of handmade Christmas ornaments and an old train set. The two clerks decided to pack up all the stuff in a couple of boxes, and conspired between them to pull off a surprise for the men later on.

By this time the Bulge came along, and headquarters got moved a dozen times. But the dynamic duo always managed to move the boxes along with everything else.

Right around Christmas, Battalion Headquarters got trapped at a large and isolated insane asylum.

The two intrepid company clerks had a room with two bunks and a few other odds and ends on the second floor. In line with their plans, they had managed to appropriate cotton balls, soda straws and anything else that they could use for their big surprise.

There was one little hitch though. They hadn't yet found a tree. But, providence provided.

Growing outside the window of their room happened to be a twenty foot pine. So, a few nights before the holiday, climbing out the window and into the tree, one of the clerks cut about six feet right off the top. Then he dragged it back through the window into their room.

Santa's two angelic helpers then set about hanging ornaments and snowballs, and turning green branches into a resplendent snowy vision of beautiful Christmas trees past. The piece-de-resistance of course, being the miniature train encircling the base of their masterpiece. The ingenious pair had even managed to make a few presents for the other company clerks. What would Christmas be without presents!

On Christmas Eve, they nonchalantly invited all the other clerks to their room for a little get together. At the appointed time, the door swung open, and what to the wondering eyes of the clerks should appear, but a magnificent Christmas tree bursting upon their sight, shining with the light of beauty and hope. In the midst of a war filled with fear, hopelessness and uncertainty, it was quite unexpected.

They couldn't believe what they were seeing. The two perpetrators of saintly deeds told them, "Don't ask us no questions, just enjoy it."

For one GI, the clerk's Christmas tree was a blessing he'd remember the rest of his life. Because of heavy fighting, he had become separated from his platoon and had been wandering for three days in enemy territory, barely escaping a couple of times with his life. In the late evening hours on Christmas eve he had stumbled onto the wall surrounding the asylum and a guard on duty. When the guard called out for him to give the password (there was a new one each day), he didn't know it, so the guard hauled the guy back to his captain for interrogation. In the end they got his story and found he was a legitimate American GI who had gotten lost. The poor guy hadn't eaten for days so they sent him to the kitchen for some chow after which he promptly fell asleep. By chance or not, it happened that the two clerks with the tree put him up in their room for the night.

The next morning, with light streaming in the window, the GI woke up and the first thing he saw was the sparkling Christmas tree. He would later tell the clerks, "I had given up on living. There wasn't anything or anyone left to live for. Then I saw that Christmas tree standing there and just like that, I knew I wanted to live. It gave me a good feeling looking at that tree and thinking about Christmas. I wanted to make it back home."

Later on Christmas day (there are no secrets in an army), the Captain found out about their show of Christmas spirit and told them they couldn't hide it in their room, but to take it to the mess hall for everyone to enjoy.

Thousands of miles from the circle of family and home, the Christmas spirit still warmed the heart and gave hope to the hopeless.

In a war, some problems are easily solved, you cut the top out of a tree. But then there was Bob Walls, a medic friend of Alfred's whose problem didn't have an easy solution. Bob had fallen victim to that great malady of the German field of battle, trench foot. One of the medics thought that more soldiers suffered from this than were wounded by the enemy.

The German soldier, unlike their counterparts on the Eastern front who suffered from the very severe Russian cold conducted to the foot by the steel nails in the boot, fared much better than the American foot soldier. The other major factor in their favor was that they were hunkered down in secure defensive positions. The American G.I. was on the offensive and thus exposed to the elements of nature.

When an officer approached Bob and asked how he was doing, he'd reply, "Just fine sir, or doing good Sir," while in reality, his feet were swollen and in very bad shape. But early on in the campaign, the quickest and best remedy for trench foot was amputation. Bob was a medic, so he knew what the score was regarding his predicament. Bob said, "I was going to bring my feet home with me no matter what," thus the lies about how he was doing. Thankfully, he held out just long enough until some new treatments started being used in England.

Alfred's writings to his sister and the experiences of his friends in war, have set the stage for one more scene. But we cannot stand over Myrtle's shoulder and read about it in one of Alfred's letters. There are no more.

The old faded candy box has yielded to the hunger to know the heart and soul of my uncle, though it is not empty. In the bottom lie three letters and a card commemorating Alfred's twenty-fifth birthday. They are dated from September 30 thru October and November. They were written by my mother, and sent with every hope that they would reach France, and somewhere along the way with the help of the US Army, they would be laid into the hands of her brother. But the fortunes of war turn the most precious of hopes into the darkest depths of pain. They are an unopened, silent reminder that somewhere in France, they didn't make it to their destination, and if they did, there was no brother, with eager hands, waiting to tear open the envelopes and devour the words which he desperately looked forward to. He would not read the birthday card that would have made him smile and conjure up images of other days with cake and ice cream and family all around.

Chapter XII

Bezange La Petite '90 and '44

Since Alfred wrote no more letters from France, I found that I yearned to touch my past and go there myself. To breathe French air and walk on its soil, would be almost like walking in Alfred's steps and seeing with his eyes. Only by following Alfred and reliving those tumultuous days, could I hope to understand what he had done. Traveling across continents and an ocean, God and Alfred would be my companions.

It is 1990, and it is my first overseas flight to Europe. Feining nonchalance, I stared out of my window into the black abyss of space, and contemplated the obstacles ahead. I can't speak German or French for one thing. I have no friends here. I vacillate between extreme excitement one minute and acute apprehension the next.

Alfred and I have a date with destiny.

Arriving in Frankfurt, I picked up my Opel Cadette and after a couple of hours driving, jet lag forces me to spend my first night in a country inn outside of Kaiserslautern, Germany. Snuggled up under a feather tick and watching German television, my mind struggled with reality. "If I venture nothing in life that requires me to look beyond myself," I wrote in my journal, "I will never know what I am truly capable of accomplishing." Dreams and plans have given way to a menu I couldn't have deciphered if my life depended on it, and wooden shoes sitting outside their owner's doors.

The next morning, the seventh of November, I look at the maps Bob Marshall has supplied and that prove to be a godsend.

It is a beautiful sunshiny day as I entered France from Germany. Clear, but chilly. Sunlight streams down through the semi-bare branches of the trees, but when I got out of the car, it is cold. The air penetrates. It is one of Alfred's worst fears. It feels like winter.

Close to the town where Alfred and his men were in '44, that afternoon I check into a hotel at Chateau Salinas.

I stow my gear in the room, then set out to explore the rural, narrow, and it seems, almost forgotten roads of France with the goal of finding Bezange La Petite.

Leaving Lezey, France behind, I wound along for a time and then topping a small knoll, I see a nondescript sign bearing: BEZANGE LA PETITE. We were finally there.

Making my way down the only main street, I gaze curiously at the buildings, most of which are house and barn combinations.

Manure lines the road.

Asking directions to the local cemetiere (French spelling), I am directed to the outskirts of town. After parking the car, I walk up to the cemetiere and open the gate. Walking among the flowers and slabs of marble, I can almost see and hear the Germans in Bezange la Petite, just a few hundred feet away, and litter-bearers carrying Alfred through this very place while a sniper takes shots at them.

Beside the cemetiere is a dirt road. I pass a farm on the right. Across from it a little further up the hillside, sheep graze in a pasture. If I can get into the field, I will practically be standing in Alfred's size thirteen and a half shoes. It is an experience I have longed for with my whole heart. But not yet.

I head out following the line of red arrows Robert Marshall

had drawn on my map. On another narrow, quiet back road, I enter the hamlet of Richicourt where the First Battalion Aid station was located. Red roofs shine in the soft waning glow of the late afternoon sun.

The rolling hills of eastern France surround it like the undulating water of an ocean around an island.

A farmer drives his tractor along the road and parks it in a garage off of Richicourt's main street. There are more tractors than cars here. The buildings lining the streets are light brown stucco with red tiled roofs. A man with only one leg hobbles up the street.

I have looked forward to seeing this place, but now there is also a feeling of dread clutching at my chest whenever my gaze wanders down the street toward the building whose picture I carry.

A beautiful old church is sitting along the main thoroughfare and I parked in front of it.

There is a Frenchman doing masonry work on the walls of a balcony, so I am not alone as I pass through the massive wooden door and sit in a pew. The magnificent architecture of dark woodwork and ancient carvings imbue me with peace, an almost ethereal quality which makes me weep.

I hesitate to move on, because I know the house down the street awaits me.

At last my heavy feet take me where I do not wish to go.

It is yet another house and barn combination.

No longer an aid station, it is a private home with autumn flowers blooming in window boxes. Somehow though, neither the flowers nor the sun can enlighten my darkened heart.

A rooster crows and a motor hums. It is quiet. The sun is

leaving me alone with these hills. The day is spent.

Shortly I will leave. I must journey back with my Uncle Alfred to relive another night exactly forty six years ago.

It was the night of the 7th of November, 1944.

Reichicourt

The light of the sun has passed over the horizon and given way to the black vagueness of night. It is the time when life seems to slow into mystery with the comings and goings of man.

Darkness has overtaken Alfred and the men of the 26th Division, 328th Infantry. For them, the cold realization of war has not totally penetrated their minds. So far, the aid men have tended blisters, trench foot, fatigue, and boredom. The full impact of what is to be has not yet touched them.

Frank Novichi and a few other guys stretch out in an old forgotten barn and still others curl up in an aid station. While in Moncourt Woods, platoons of men try to sleep in foxholes they have dug that day. They are cold. This French air penetrates to the very bones. One medic crouches in his hole with his men of C Company.

What thoughts flash through the brain at such a time? Everyone is scared, for sure. It seemed everyone prayed. These last hours of darkness may be a blessing. They are a calm before the coming storm of day.

Perhaps they think of tomorrow. It will be heavy combat. The Heinies are entrenched at Bezange La Petite.

These fighters are to take the offensive against the town. For this they have trained for the past year and a half.

Alfred feels in his pockets for a picture of his little sister, Ellen, that he carries with him. Someone beside him digs out a cigarette, fumbles in the cold for a match, and after a few attempts, a small

183

light flares in the darkness. It glows long enough in the fox hole for Alfred to get a glimpse of her face and dark hair.

Then, darkness engulfs the men trying to find some comfort in this dark hole in the ground.

Around the perimeter of Bezange La Petite, this scene repeats itself countless times. The coming of dawn will be remembered as long as memory lasts.

The glimpse of the brown haired girl in the picture leaves a kind of glow for Alfred. It brings back the warm feelings of home, Dad and the kiddies, Myrtle, Bill and the boys. He lets his mind linger on Alice's face. There had been lots of girls. But he knew she was the one for him. Myrtle had got the ring for her like he'd asked. She was crazy about it. She'd said that they couldn't have picked a better one themselves. He would have liked to have given it to her himself. Liked to have seen it on her finger, all sparkley and pretty. A man lived for his hopes and dreams. Someday!

The still night hours glide by as some of the men doze off, waken, rearrange themselves, pull a blanket a little tighter, think, then try not to think, and go back to sleep.

The clock at Battalion Headquarters haunts those who know that life or death may await its next reverie.

Then: The 8th of November has begun. Only God knows what this day will bring to the lives of these men. Hold onto this moment. It's cold, feet are numb, there's a loneliness for loved ones that eats away at you insides. But so far, you're alive.

Alfred dozes, then wakes. It feels so cold. Back home in Fairchance, it sure didn't seem this cold. Why, sometimes in November it's still right nice. Dad and Bill are probably in the middle of small game season and bringing home lots of squirrel and rabbits. Alfred thinks of Myrtle fixing up a skillet of fried rabbit, can even smell the meat frying and hear it sizzling in the pan. A mound of fluffy white potatoes and gravy. Sure would be fine to sit down to some home cookin'.

His eyes close, and sleep brings an end to the parade of memories. His body relaxes in rest.

In a cramped position, a muscle goes into a spasm, he is pulled awake by the pain. He rubs his leg until it is gone. His mind is alert again. His eyes scan the surroundings. Can dawn be far away?

It is not yet time.

He leans back in the foxhole, tries to rest his head. The helmet is uncomfortable and he takes it off. Pulling his olive green toboggan down further over his ears, he waits. He thinks again.

Alfred always thinks of home. If he gets back from here, he and Alice can go to farming over in Meyersdale with Bill and Myrtle. Not that there wasn't good farming in Fairchance or a job in the mines with Dad waiting for him, but with Alice from Windber and all, maybe they'd just move somewhere in between. They could visit with each other's families without too much trouble and be on their own. Sounds real fine.

That is, if he gets home. He keeps getting this feeling. He had told some of them, "I won't be coming back." He had told Ann Walls his fears when he visited her home on his last leave. He had found himself breaking down. They had both cried.

Don't know why or were it comes from, just have this feeling. Everything to come back to, a family and fiancee.

Well, seems a good time to pray.

He prays for all of the family, and the other fellows too.

It is now that part of the night when an unearthly stillness languishes like a spectra over the land. Those who lie awake, thinking, praying, are lulled to sleep once more. Little by little while they try to sleep, the dawn of November 8th changes the darkness into the gloom and cold dreary dampness of the early morning. Outside an old barn, there is no gentle early breeze rippling the air, nor does the mourning dove beat its wings against the dawning sky. Everything waits. War sleeps but little, too.

The men and medic of Company C awaken then doze, while the sounds of their own artillery shells being lobbed into Bezange break the silence.

With the start of a new day, some of them watch as tracers trail through the still dark, but gray sky. They are still observers of war, but that will change. Behind each wall and bunker ahead of them is a piece of a deadly puzzle called the German war machine.

While the men of the 26th slept in '44, I also waited for the morning of November 8th. Crawling out from under my warm blankets, I felt an eagerness that I could not explain in words. This day I would share with Alfred.

An early sun had given way to a few clouds, so I donned a warm sweater and coat. Earlier in the morning my French phrase book had come in handy as I finagled an old blanket off of my cleaning woman to sit on in the field. I knew better than to ask my landlady. She would not have complied with my request. It was time to head back for Bezange La Petite to recapture another day and time.

Leaving Chateau Salinas, I wound my way through several small hamlets down Bezange's main street to the outskirts of town and parked the car. Following the red arrows on my army map, I proceeded up the dirt road toward fields and a farmhouse. Even with the chill in the air, I was about to find warmth in the heart and smile of an elderly French lady.

The day before I had noticed sheep grazing in the field that I had determined was approximately where the men of C company had stood. As a stranger, I hesitated at crossing a fence and going eye to eye with the wooly creatures without getting permission to do so. Across from the field was the barn and house combination with the red roof shining under a partly sunny sky.

Armed with my French phrase book and some note cards explaining in French why I was standing on his doorstep, I knocked on the door of the house in hopes of rousing the farmer who owned the land. After several knocks with no answer, I was about to give up and walk away, when the door opened and a very old woman stood staring at me. I said "Bonjour" and showed her my card saying that my uncle had been killed here during World War II. To my surprise she motioned for me to come in. She ushered me into an entry way, up some steps and through a door that opened into a kitchen.

The room was as unpretentious and plain as the shawled and kerchiefed woman who sat me down in a chair and tried to understand my broken French. She and I carried on a strange conversation. We would look at my book and with bits and pieces of phrases we talked. She found the phrase "very much" and "thankful." I'll never forget the tears which sprang up in her eyes as she told me she was very much thankful for Americans. She had been living in Bezange La Petite during the war.

Containing little beyond an old black coal stove and a wooden table with two chairs, I spent about an hour basking in the warmth of her quaint French kitchen and watching the browned and crinkled face, that to me was a paragon of French womanhood. It was the study of a face that living had etched perfectly.

I even got to watch her as she haggled vehemently with a grocery vendor over some cheese and bread, his little van cram-med with meats, cheeses, breads, and even yogurt. It was just like a small grocery store roaming from village to village. Standing there watching and listening to the harangue of these two, I felt as if time had been standing still in this rural hamlet of France. The 20th century loomed far away and seemed to have little to do with this woman and her plain existence.

War Survivor, Bezange La Petite

All too soon I found myself taking leave of my new friend. I had accomplished my mission and obtained permission to roam the pasture. I knew the chances were great that I would never encounter this lady again. I didn't even know her name, but I had been deeply affected by our meeting. Life had thrown us together for a few brief and precious moments, but the mark she left on me would last all my days to come. We were moved to tears as we hugged one another. She kissed me and I in turn pressed my lips to her leathery cheek and we bid each other goodbye.

I crossed the dirt road and ducked through the strands of barbed wire and entered the pasture.

With trepidation, I walked through the field until I found a spot that most likely was where the men of C company had stood that morning before all hell broke loose.

Located on a gentle slope of a hillside and with a few old fruit trees dotting the pasture, this now bucolic place was where it had all happened. Below me was the cemetery the litter-bearers had carried Alfred through as a sniper fired on them.

A gentle breeze touched my cheek. I spread the blanket out on the grass and after sitting down, I let my eyes wander over the peaceful French countryside.

Right, the cemetery Alfred was carried through. Below, the battlefield site.

I have no explanation for what happened next. It was kind of like deja vu. I had never been here before.

But Alfred had.

As I sat there, a kind of metamorphosis occurred inside me. The clock of time wound backward before my eyes to November 8, 1944. The roll and thunder of artillery fire sounded in my ears, and I could see a fine cloud of smoke hanging over the valley. This was a battlefield. For the next five hours my world stopped while Alfred and the men of C Company faced their fates.

"And yea, though I walk through the valley in the shadow of death, I will fear no evil." Psalms 23.

I wrote:

The 8th of November is a cool, dreary, overcast day, with rain intermittently. It has rained for three solid days. Everything has turned to a brown, sticky mud.

We are on the move. The 26th Division is fresh and the push is on to drive the Germans back. General Patton's Third Army is about to move the Lorrain offensive from command headquarters to the field. The 1st Battalion is ordered into a holding position.

The Americans send their artillery shells screaming into Bezange La Petite, early this morning. The Heinies return likewise and the explosions vibrate the earth and rattle the soul. The stench of acrid smoke and fire fill the air. As quickly as the shelling had started, it ceases for a space of time.

Then, the sharp crack of rifle fire resounds on the ridge where A Company is entrenched. Already the wounded are crying out for a medic, and as a new shell finds its target, screams of terror and pain ring across the hillsides.

The aid station in Richicourt is seeing a lot of activity already. It so happened that a Negro tank division had earlier come storming through the center of town firing away with everything they had. Fortunately, someone made them aware of the fact that they were in the wrong place and the tanks got turned around and headed down the road for Bezange. Thankfully, we were at the end of town, and no real damage was done. But they sure caused a lot of guys to sweat.

On this particular morning, Able Company, occupying the eastern hill overlooking Bezange, had taken the brunt of the first shelling. Under fire, they lost some of their medics. The call came down for medics willing to help them out and Alfred volunteered. He had just broken the cardinal rule of soldiering, never volunteer for anything! But war was raging around them and he felt obliged to aid his comrades.

During the morning hours C Company was moved into a position on the western perimeter of Bezange between Able and Baker company. They were located on the edge of a small wooded area with a graveyard further down on the slope.

Then: the safety of the foxhole is left behind. Now, your heart beats a little faster each time you move or even stand still for too long. The morning gives way to afternoon. Still the battle for Bezange La Petite rages in earnest and casualties are pouring in.

The aid men and medics have now had, as Bill Walls said, "Our baptism by fire." They possess memories that will stay with them till the day they die.

Cpl. Alfred Wilson finishes up his job with Abel, and is relieved of his duty with them. He stops briefly at the aid station to replenish his aid pack, but is in a hurry to get back to his own men. A medic just naturally worries about his men. A part of him is afraid that they might need him and he won't be there.

NO TIME TO WASTE. HURRY! JUMP THE GULLY, DODGE THROUGH THE TREES. The sound of rifle fire, artillery and mortar shells exploding in the distance drives him to get back to his men as soon as possible. Peering through the mists of war, Alfred sees a group of men standing around, and instantly recognized Captain Kixmiller, Lt. Swan and the others of C Company. He breathes a sigh of relief. They're okay! He made it!

It is well into afternoon now. They can hear sniper fire in the direction of Lezey, and at times, uncomfortably close to their own position.

Nonchalantly they appear to stand around, but that would only be to the casual observer. As they stand, every nerve is taunt and ready for what they do not know. Some are talking. The inevitable cigarette is lighted and held between fingers that are willed not to shake. They try to relax, talk, and keep each other calm.

Now it is coming! They hear the sound of a German artillery shell from Bezange La Petite as it screeches through the French sky for some thirty seconds, but they have no warning where it will impact. The G.I.s have a saying that each shell says, "To Whom It May Concern." But this one was very specific. It bore the names of "C Company and its medic."

With unscrupulous intent, the shell propels itself near the platoon of riflemen and Cpl. Alfred Wilson. The shell bursts, sending instant missile-like metal projectiles hurtling through the air in every direction. Nothing remains unscathed. Even as a young sapling is torn apart, the shards rip and tear into the soft flesh of the soldier's bodies as many of them try and throw themselves to the ground.

If any scene in life can be described as hell, this would be one of them. As the noise and smoke begin to clear, the carnage can be seen and heard. Men who could find voice in the midst of their pain cry out, "Medic! Medic!"

Captain Kixmiller realizes he has not been injured by the blast. He picks himself up and looks around him. Lt. Swan, who he had just been talking to moments before, lies a few feet away, dead. He had just gotten married. Everyone seems to have been hit. His eyes pick out the red cross insignia of his medic, Wilson, lying on the ground, and he immediately yells at him to see to the wounded.

But no such order needs to be given to this man. These are the men he has come to look upon almost as family. They have laughed, cried, eaten, slept, and faced death together. They have bonded with one another through circumstances that now make them closer than if they had been brothers.

He remains immobile for only a few seconds, then reaches automatically for his pack of supplies. His trained eye and the cries for a medic tell him many are wounded, some seriously. Alfred looks down at blood oozing from his thigh and with the pain in his arm, knows that he also has been hit. But he is a man of great strength and stamina. His men are depending on him. There is no one else. He wills his mind not to succumb to the thralls of pain as he crawls over to the nearest man and starts to patch him up.

Alfred is the only medical personal on hand. But already the word is flashing to the aid station where Lt. Robert Marshall is in charge of the evacuation unit. He gathers the men under him together and with an evac plan already in place he sends them to Company C's position which has just come under fire. George Trabucco and Robert Jenkins, a litter-bearer and a driver, are among those who head out.

Alfred crawls to the next man—knows he is wounded. But there is nothing he can do for this one. He was a good kid. He frees him of the helmet that holds his head unnaturally, smooths his hair back in place, and crawls on. He cannot feel the pain. He has a job to do. He can save them. He can't let them down. He whispers a prayer to God. In one of his letters, he told Myrtle that prayer was almost second nature to him.

He hears that call again, "Medic, Medic!" Recognition of the voice is instant. He gains new impetus as he makes his way to the man's side. The wound is bad. As he pours the sulphur on and gives him a shot of morphine, he tells him that he'll make it, to hold on, anything to give the fellow hope. He stops the bleeding.

The litter-bearers are here now. Alfred tells Trabucco and Jenkins to take this fellow out first. Alfred keeps on going. The pain in his left leg is excruciating. He stops to put a tourniquet above the thigh where the bone is almost protruding through the skin. His hands are covered in blood. It's not a very good tie, but it will have to do. Have to get to the next guy. I'll be okay.

Captain Kixmiller glances at Wilson crawling among the men. He notices for the first time that Wilson is hit, one leg practically torn off, while he has bad holes in the other leg and an arm. He is covered with blood. Kixmiller thinks, "He's a medic. He knows what he's doing."

Trabucco asks Alfred to take his sulphur tablets, but Alfred refuses. "Don't have time!" he says. One of the litter-bearers suggests that maybe Alfred better get back to the aid station himself. He notices that Alfred's leg looks pretty bad.

Alfred scoffs it off casually. "It's only a scratch. Some of these other boys are worse off. Take this one next. He needs plasma. Stopped the bleeding as best I could." The litter-bearer obediently listens to the Medic.

Alfred continues to crawl to another man. Time moves by quickly now. He needs more time. Must help everyone. His Dad's words ring in his ears, "Don't try to save everyone by yourself." Another man is loaded onto a litter. One more taken care of. Again Alfred refuses to let Trabucco take him out.

Second Lieutenant Arthur Morales is passing through and sees this great big guy who is a medic kneeling beside a badly wounded soldier. He thinks it is that Wilson fellow but is not sure. He notices that his right leg is laid open and bleeding. He asks if he needs help and the medic responded, "I'll be alright. Get out of here Lieutenant. This ain't no place to be." With the sound of screaming shells in his ear, the lieutenant moves on.

It is hard crawling around now. Alfred finds that

perhaps he hasn't the strength he thought. He offers up another silent prayer. Afternoon is waning. Not all the men have been evacuated. The job's not done yet. But with the passing of the afternoon, the cold air turns perceptively more frigid. There is now no sense of warmth coursing through Alfred's body.

Alfred can no longer crawl about. He props himself up against a tree and motions for Trabucco to pull a man over. Alfred's great stamina has started to ebb away. A weakness steals through his veins. It is a chore to even move his hand. He tells Trabucco what to do for the wounded soldier, who is soon taken out. When George returns, Alfred looks at him and inquires, "Did you take care of him?" George reassures Alfred that he has, then once again attempts to persuade Alfred to leave.

Alfred looks about him. His eyes fall upon those still suffering and in pain. "Not yet fellows. Get them out first." His voice is still strong and commanding. "He's the Medic," they say.

The work continues on, but more laboriously for Alfred. Trabucco and the other men follow Alfred's verbal instructions, give aid, and move the men out. At last one of the aid men approached Alfred and must lean close to his lips to hear the whispered instructions. Trabucco knows they must get Alfred out soon. They tell others at the aid station that their medic is badly wounded, but will not come in. A Lieutenant vows to take Alfred in himself. Darkness will soon be upon them. Shadows start to steal along the trees and through the cemetery.

Alfred's ability to function is now minimal. He cannot keep his mind clear. He tries to will himself to think, but finds he cannot.

The men are almost all gone now. One more. Trabucco hastily returns to Alfred's side as he lies slumped against a tree. He speaks Alfred's name, but Alfred cannot reply. The whispers have ceased. His eyes have closed.

The Lieutenant arrives and gives the orders to get Wilson out of there. Everyone is gone. Alfred is the last man off the hill.

Hours have slipped away since the initial burst of the shell. Alfred is a big man and they finally manage to get him on a litter, and tuck a blanket around him. He is not easy to carry. But Lt. Marshall and his evac men toil the best they can. The mud is so deep, it's impossible to make any time. They feel an urgency as they wade down the hill. They decide to go through the graveyard to save time. But as they do, a sniper still lurks and a shot rings out. Alfred is dropped as they plunge to the ground for cover. After a minute or two, they try again. Hands return to grasp the litter and proceed toward the evac position. It is a hard and arduous trip. An hour is spent just getting down the hill to the jeep with Alfred. Other hands take over and he is loaded onto the conveyance and strapped on. It is now totally dark. The jeep makes its way over the rough dirt road the army has made to the aid station in Rechicourt. It is Alfred's last ride. He did his duty. He has tried to save everyone.

The evac jeep finally pulls up in front of an old dilapidated two story house in Rechicourt, that is serving as their aid station. More hands heave to the task of getting a man of Alfred's size into the house. He has lost a lot of blood and is in shock. But he is still alive. For how much longer they cannot tell. Desperately, they try to give him plasma, but his veins have collapsed. Too much time has elapsed since his injury. He is too far gone. It is only a matter of time. But the surgeon, Captain Dedick, tries all that he can for this wounded medic. He knows Alfred well and has heard how he refused treatment for himself and waited till all of his buddies were brought in. Alfred still hangs onto life. There is little reason to see to his many wounds, but they labor feverishly on. There is still hope.

His left leg at thigh level is in terrible shape, a piece

of bone can be seen. The other leg has also taken some shell fragments as well as one arm. Still he breathes. His body is young and strong. Perhaps he will beat the odds and make it. There is a frenzy in the aid station to do all that is within the scope of their learning, despite the odds.

Sometime later that night, as darkness swirls around the little hamlet, the gentle giant succumbs to the loss of blood and shock. With the glare of the aid station lights in their eyes, the doctor and aid men watch the slow rhythmic rise and fall of his chest until all movement ceases. The Battalion surgeon, Lt. Andrew P. Dedick, pronounces Cpl. Alfred L. Wilson dead. Among those listed on the casualty log for the 1st Battalion Aid Station are at least ten men who were treated by a wounded medic. Also listed was:

"Wilson, Alfred T/5 C 328th Inf. KIA"

With the writing of the abbreviation for Killed In Action, I look around and notice how the shadows have lengthened on this hill and how cold my fingers have become. And the poor sheep! They probably thought I was going to take up permanent residence in there little corner of the world. Still I linger, sitting here in this grassy spot. The truth is, I am reluctant to leave for Rechicourt and break the magical spell that has weaved itself into my being. I had fulfilled my dream of walking in Alfred's footsteps 'almost literally,' as reality had far surpassed anything that even I could have envisioned. As I lived and breathed, I had reached out and touched my uncle.

Finally, I made my way down off the hill, through the cemetery, and climbed into my car. Starting the motor up and releasing the brake, I put my Opel in gear and drove the paved road into Rechicourt a few miles away. As darkness stole its way into the evening, I stood across the road from the house where Alfred had died. I cried once again. For him, for me, for the things that were, and for things that death had cheated us of. How I wished with all my heart that he had lived.

On the eve of the eighth, Alfred's best friend, Bill Walls, working out of the aid station at Richicourt, didn't know his friend was wounded until he got word that they were bringing him in. By the time he got to the aid station that night, Alfred was gone. After he was told, in a state of shock himself, he remembered walking over to where he laid, lifting up the blanket, and seeing that it was Alfred. It would be several years after coming home from the war, before he would allow himself to remember Alfred and talk about him. And even then, it would be with a certain amount of perplexity. Without a doubt, Bill thought that if Alfred would have allowed himself to be brought in sooner, he could have been saved. Bill had seen enough to ascertain that Alfred's wounds might not have proved mortal if he had been treated in time. In my interviews with other medics, they echoed the same opinion, and knowing that, it didn't made it any easier to take. It just hurt all the more.

At first, when anyone died, if he was your buddy, you took it hard, the guys in your company who knew you, took it hard. When Alfred died, the whole 26th Division took it hard. Everyone knew who the "Big Stoop" or "Pappy" was. He was a gentle giant. The Medics took it hard. There just wasn't anyone like Big Al. He had symbolized for them all something bigger than life. He had attained what they all wanted. Respect, friendship, a reputation for being the kind of guy you wanted to know, and he did it by being himself. He had been compassionate, considerate, a fine loving fellow, and he didn't even try. As Captain Ed Kuligowski had said, "We loved that boy."

Back in his hometown of Fairchance his family would find the pain piercing their hearts like a thousand arrows. On November 22nd, the telegram had arrived at the house on a cold, oppressively dark morning, and one of the girls had answered the door. Melvin quickly carried the news to other sisters. Alfred had delivered a cryptic note to Myrtle in one of his letters. It had stated that if something happened, and she knew what, she was to go home right away, and she did. They were all there when Grandpap Wilson came home from work later in the afternoon. When he walked in and saw all the children gathered, no one had to hand him the telegram. Throwing his arms into the air, and with the anguished cry of a devoted father, he screamed out, "Oh no, no, not Alfred!"

The telegram read: "The Secretary of War desires me to express his deep regret that your son T/5 Class Alfred L. Wilson was killed in action on 9th of Nov. in France. Letter follows."

WESTERN UNION

A. N. WILLIAMS
PRESIDENT

CLASS OF SERVICE	SYMBOLS
This is a full-rate Telegram or Cablegram unless its deferred character is indicated by a suitable symbol above or preceding the address.	DL=Day Letter
	NL=Night Letter
	LC=Deferred Cable
	NLT=Cable Night Letter
	Ship Radiogram

The filing time shown in the date line on telegrams and day letters is STANDARD TIME at point of origin. Time of receipt is STANDARD TIME at point of destination

Dunaway's Pharmacy   Washington, D.C.
18 Church St.   Nov. 22, 1944
Fairchance, Pa.

Mrs. Jessie Wilson
Box 405
Fairchance, Pa.

The Secretary Of War desires me to express his deep regret that your

son T-5 Class Alfred L. Wilson was killed in action on 9th. of Nov. in France.

Letter follows.

                                   Dunlap- Adj. Gen.

Myrtle called Alice Mock in Windber and informed her of Alfred's death. She had just gotten two letters from Alfred. There were no words of comfort.

The next day word had spread through the community. A favorite son was gone and the whole town mourned his loss. At the mine where he had worked, the men who had timbered alongside him entered the shaft this day with tears coursing down their cheeks. After hearing that he was dead, George Walls would lean his head against the walls of the automated cage, and cry the whole way down through the shaft till it hit bottom.

A few days after the eighth, on another cold and dreary November day, a group of infantry men, with bowed heads, gathered in front of a flag-draped coffin beside a mound of earth at

Limey, France. A Protestant chaplain would commit to the ground one of their beloved comrades. In the midst of their silence, they could still hear the scream of artillery fire echoing back from the front lines.

When the service was over they stoically climbed aboard their jeeps and headed in the direction of the mayhem that awaited them. The hell of war would write each one his own page of history along with the ten men Alfred had saved. Alfred had written his own story with the blood of his sacrifice. His war was over.

He was where he wished himself someday to be....

"He was home, with his mother, on high."

Sometime later, the family would hold a memorial service at the Fairchance Church of the Brethren, with his friend and pastor, Rev. Ewing Jones, officiating. It would be four years before his body would be brought back home for burial. But Alfred had already carved himself a place in history.

Chapter XIII

The Congressional Medal of Honor

Plaque at Arlington National Cemetery
Washington, D.C.

"Alone and far removed from earthly care
The noble ruins of men lie buried here
You were strong men, good men.
Endowed with youth and much the will to live
I hear no protest from the mute lips of the dead,
They rest, there is no more to give."

Poem by Audie Murphy
Recipient of Medal of Honor

THE CONGRESSIONAL MEDAL OF HONOR

Congress has stipulated that:

"The President is authorized to present, in the name of Congress, the Medal of Honor only to each person who, while an officer of enlisted man of the army should hereafter in action involving actual conflict with an enemy distinguish himself conspicuously by gallantry and intrepidity at the risk of his life, above and beyond the call of duty."

He who possesses the Medal of Honor is the holder of the highest military award for bravery that can be awarded to any individual serving any of the armed forces in the United States of America. Bestowed upon this man is a great privilege—that of being named among those few heroes who have been honored by the award of the same Medal he wears and to be assured of their rightful place of distinction in history.

Awards for valor and noble deeds have been imparted to the brave since the time of the Greeks and Romans. Napoleon established the Legion D'Honneur for soldiers and citizens. Inspiring loyalty and bravery with the people, he once said that Europe could be conquered with lengths of ribbon.

In America, George Washington established the first military award for the common soldier. For "singularly meritorious action," the Badge of Military Merit, instituted on August 7, 1782, was awarded to only three men. In 1932, the badge was renamed and a new recognition surrounded those receiving the Purple Heart. A small box containing this medal reposes with the rest of Alfred's memorabilia.

The history of the Medal of Honor as we know it today started in earnest with the Civil War, but there were problems. The guidelines were vague and a medal could be earned by simply capturing a Confederate flag, and of course, the recipient was eligible for a 30 day furlough which was probably never turned down. In one case, the names of a whole regiment were submitted on the premise that they had volunteered to stay for the defense of Washington, when in fact, less than half had stayed while the rest went home, and an accurate list of those staying could not be procured. The men themselves applied for the medal some even thirty years after conflicts had been resolved. In certain cases, because of time, inaccurate and even no records, it could not be proved for certain whether a man justly deserved the medal or not.

During the Indian Wars in the west, much confusion existed even though the guidelines were beginning to tighten up. The surviving commanders of Indian raids recommended large numbers of men for Medals of Honor. These were rejected by a review board, because it was deemed that the men had not acted in any capacity other than what was normally expected of them.

One of the first men to earn the Army Medal of Honor, as it was called then, was a surgeon Col. Bernard J.D. Irwin, February 14, 1861. He had volunteered to take command of troops being sent to relieve the men of the Seventh Infantry Regiment who were surrounded by the Chiricahua in the Arizona Territory. They set off in the midst of a snow storm, but persevered and arrived the next night in a canyon leading to the stranded outfit. Upon arrival they freed the trapped regiment, attended to the wounded (which was why Irwin volunteered in the first place), and went on to accomplish the original mission of the Seventh Infantry. However, he was not awarded the medal until January 21, 1894.

The first medals awarded were handed to six soldiers in Washington by Secretary of War Stanton, on March 25, 1863. The six men were part of a twenty-man unit who had volunteered to carry out a sabotage mission against the Confederacy.

Boarding a train disguised as civilians, they later stole it as it sat empty for twenty minutes while passengers and trainmen ate their breakfast. With an engine and boxcars, James J. Andrews and his volunteers chugged through Tennessee tearing up tracks, pulling down telegraph poles and trying to cause as much destruction as possible to the south. Their plans aside, the Confederates started pursuit on another train, causing the Union men to drop cars, rails and anything they could get their hands on to slow down the enemy. Despite their valiant efforts, and 90 miles of flight, they were left at the end with twenty one men clinging to the sides of a locomotive that had run out of fuel and steam. Faced with little or no choice, Andrews and his men abandoned their set of wheels and fled into a wooded area on foot.

A few days later all of the conspirators had been captured, with Andrews and seven men being executed, and the remaining fourteen incarcerated in prison camps. Eight of these men escaped their guards, while six survived starvation and beatings in prison until they were paroled in 1863. These six men were called to Washington and after giving evidence about the raids, they were taken to the War Department Building and after an explanation about congressional authorization for the medals for bravery, Secretary of War Stanton gave each man his medal. Later on they were to have an audience with President Lincoln at the White House where he received them with great "warmth of feeling and....utmost sympathy for their sufferings."

Up until the late 1800's, various awards and certificates had surfaced. A rosette appeared in 1887 to be worn with a ribbon around the neck. And if a man wore out his ribbon he could apply for a new one. The Navy had established its own medal, but similar to the army's. Another important change was that claims now had to be submitted by a commanding officer and substantiated by witnesses. It was decreed that there had to be uncontestable evidence of the deed and it must be clearly distinguished by extraordinary merit.

In the early 1900's legislation passed, pushed by the Secretary of War, Elihu Root, clearly defined procedures for awarding the medal. A time limit of one year was established to consider an application. A special board was set up to examine applicants and make recommendations, and a new medal design was adopted.

The original basic star shape was maintained, and in the center was the head of the goddess, Minerva. A laurel wreath surrounded the points of the star and oak leaves were positioned in the star points. The words "United States of America" encircled the head. The emblem was then hung from a bar which is inscribed with the word "valor." On top of the bar was an eagle clutching the olive branch of peace with one talon and the arrows of war with the other. The eagle's head is turned to the arrows of war because it is valor in war time that earns the Medal of Honor. It is then suspended from a ribbon of light blue upon which 13 white stars appear.

In 1903 it was decided to make the presentation of the Medal a special and solemn occasion, and when possible, it was to be made by the President as Commander in Chief. Under the new orders, President Roosevelt presented the first medal to James R. Church on January 10, 1906 in a special White House ceremony.

A group called the Medal of Honor Legion pressed for legislation giving the Medal a military position enjoyed by similar medals in world governments. A Congress approved pension of ten dollars per month for life, was to be provided to Medal recipients.

Before World War I, the wording of a new bill excluded anyone receiving the award other than those men who in actual combat, distinguished themselves by conspicuous gallantry or intrepidity, and at the risk of life, above and beyond the call of duty. A review of all recipients was made public in February of 1917, and 910 men and one woman were removed from the roll. Some of those included Buffalo Bill Cody, civilian scouts, President Lincoln's funeral guard, and a woman surgeon, Mary Walker. In 1977, her descendants lobbied for her reinstatement as a recipient and today, she is the only woman to have been awarded the Medal of Honor.

Eventually a "pyramid of honor" was established by the government recognizing stages of bravery, thus protecting the legitimacy of the Medal of Honor at the top of the pyramid. As late as 1963, congress was still establishing airtight guidelines for the medal that were the same for all the branches of the service.

With the award come a few privileges. Each recipient receives $200 a month regardless of age. He is allowed free travel on military aircraft, may be buried at Arlington National Cemetery and his children may attend the military academies without a Congressional appointment. Their names are written down in honored places, and some of them get places named after them. They are the only ones allowed to wear the medal itself.

The present day medal has a pad of blue with stars on it, attaching the medal to a blue ribbon. It is the only United States medal worn around the neck.

To date, there have been 3,394 men and one woman who have received the Medal of Honor. Under loose guidelines, over a thousand medals were awarded during the Civil War and very few of them were won posthumously. One hundred and eighteen received the medal for valor during World War I. The unknown soldier of each of our wars has been presented the award.

But by the turn of the century and World War II, posthumous awards outnumbered living awards and the same has held true for the Korean and Vietnam conflicts. Earning the medal was one thing, but living to enjoy it became quite another.

T/5 Alfred L. Wilson fulfilled that criteria the afternoon of November 8ᵗʰ, by putting his own welfare in jeopardy for the lives of his men in Company C. It was a sacrifice that would not go unnoticed.

One of Alfred's litter-bearers, George Trabucco, took little comfort in the fact that the next day his company commander told him he was wanted in Battalion headquarters. When he asked why, they inquired if he hadn't been with Wilson the day before, and he said yes. Headquarters wanted to hear the whole story on Wilson from someone who had been there. He tried to get out of it saying he wasn't the only one there, but it was orders, so he went. He didn't want to take any credit by being the one to tell what had happened. At the time, a G.I. wasn't thinking of purple hearts, bronze stars or any Medal of Honor. God! You just thought about staying alive.

When I interviewed George Trabucco in Providence, Rhode Island the summer of '92, he still appeared nervous and reluctant to talk about Alfred. The emotion showed in his eyes, voice and a lit cigarette that was in constant evidence. Like a majority of G.I.s during the war, he had gotten into the habit of smoking. But like he said, "I was just a kid." He had been drafted a few weeks after turning eighteen. Anyway, he just wanted to forget.

There had been heavy casualties on that first day of major battle, and at least four men had been sent out that afternoon. Lieutenant Marshall was in charge of the evacuation team. George especially remembered Bob Marshall and how he always thought a lot of the Lieutenant, and it was his opinion that he was one of the best officers they had. That day he had pointed to litter-bearers and evac men, and said, "You, you, you, and you," and they had quickly gathered what they had needed.

The evac jeep took them to a pick-up position located in the rear of the front lines. George had thought of it as a sort of crap shoot. He was just lucky enough to be in the wrong place, at the wrong time.

So he reported to Division Headquarters that day and gave them the whole story about how a medic who wouldn't quit until all his men were out.

By January of 1945, Alfred's Captain, Ed Kuligowski, had started the ball rolling by putting him in for the Congressional Medal of Honor. "I never dreamed he'd actually get it," Ed told me in a telephone conversation. But they all thought so much of Alfred and what he'd done that day by not giving up on any of the men when he could have saved himself. Well, that was Alfred, and you just couldn't let a thing like that go by. He was just a big gawky guy they called the Big Stoop, but they would have gone to the ends of the earth for him. But he did it first, for them.

Ed said, "When it's something as big as the Medal of Honor, you go for it knowing you got a good chance, but when it actually happens, you still can't believe it."

They were all proud of him and glad to know that he had gotten the Medal. The whole damn regiment was proud. He'd be the only one to receive it in the 328th.

One June 14, 1945, Grandpap Wilson received the following announcement from the War Department:

```
Dear Mr. Wilson:
     I have the honor to inform you that
by direction of the President of the
United States, under the provisions of
the Act of Congress approved 9 July
1918, a Medal of Honor has been
posthumously awarded by the War De-
partment, in the name of Congress, to
your son, Technician Fifth Grade
Alfred L. Wilson, for conspicuous
gallantry in action above and beyond
the call of duty near Bezange La
Petite, France, on 8 November 1944.
     The Commanding General, Third Ser-
vice Command, Baltimore, Maryland,
had been directed to select an officer
to represent the President in present-
ing this decoration to you.
     May I again extend my deepest
sympathy in your bereavement.
```

On June 26, 1945, the presentation of this nation's highest military honor was posthumously awarded to Cpl. Alfred L. Wilson, and my Grandfather, Jesse Wilson accepted it at Allegheny County Airport in Pittsburgh. Brigadier General T.N. Catron, at a ceremony attended by Alfred's sisters, Bernice, Jean, Mary, Ellen, Myrtle, a brother Melvin, and other family members, extended the open box containing the medal to Jesse. Upon receiving the General's congratulations, Alfred's father accepted the medal in Alfred's memory and made a poignant statement that has forever lingered in the memory of the Wilson family. "I accept the honor, but the price was too high."

I think the whole family felt the same, I know my mother did.

The whole ceremony was one of those military doings with a military band and the formality that goes along with a presentation of this magnitude. There was also a certain dichotomy about the whole thing. At the same time they were presenting the medal to a man whose family would never see him again, the airport was teeming with friends, family and the press, ready to explode with exuberance, as a plane carrying 64 heroes of the war in Europe were coming home. As the saying goes, "but for the grace of God."

Part of the ceremony was the reading of the official citation — tears mingled with the emotions of pride and sadness as the family listened.

❖

Honoring A Hero...

...A Family Remembers

❖

Medal of Honor Citation:

He volunteered to assist as an aid man a company
other that his own, which was suffering casualties from
constant artillery fire. He administered to the wounded
and returned to his own company when a shell burst
injured a number of its men. While treating his comrades
he was seriously wounded, but refused to be evacuated
by litter-bearers sent to relieve him. In spite of great pain
and loss of blood, he continued to administer first aid
until he was too weak to stand. Crawling from one
patient to another, he continued his work until excessive
loss of blood prevented him from moving. He then
verbally directed unskilled enlisted men in continuing the
first aid for the wounded. Still refusing assistance himself, he remained to instruct others in dressing the
wounds of his comrades until he was unable to speak
above a whisper and finally lapsed into unconsciousness.
The effects of his injury later caused his death. By
steadfastly remaining at the scene without regard for his
own safety, Corporal Wilson, through distinguished
devotion to duty and personal sacrifice, helped to save
the lives of at least ten wounded men.

Later that evening, a dinner and reception was held at the
William Penn Hotel in Pittsburgh which my grandfather and mother
attended. Grandpap took Mom to the gala because she had been
closer to Alfred than the rest of them. I know she did talk of that
dinner a few times. It was quite elaborate with Maine Lobster
Thermidor as the main course and my mother never quite got over
the sight of a lobster with eyes that looked at her while she
attempted to figure out how to eat it. It was quite a day for the
Wilson family.

At approximately the same time as the Medal ceremony,
thousands of miles away across an ocean, another man from
Company C would take time out to remember a medic's heroic
deed. He would think about the price of dedication and why some
had made it through the war and some had not. The fighting had

The President of the United States takes pride in awarding the MEDAL of HONOR posthumously to

TECHNICIAN FIFTH GRADE ALFRED L. WILSON,
MEDICAL DETACHMENT, 328th INFANTRY
UNITED STATES ARMY

as set forth in the following

CITATION:

"Technician Fifth Grade Alfred L. Wilson, while serving with the Medical Detachment, 328th Infantry, near Bezange la Petite, France, on 8 November 1944, volunteered to assist as an aid man a company, other than his own, which was suffering casualties from constant artillery fire. He administered to the wounded and returned to his own company when a shell burst injured a number of its men. While treating his comrades he was seriously wounded, but refused to be evacuated by litter bearers sent to relieve him. In spite of great pain and loss of blood, he continued to administer first aid until he was too weak to stand. Crawling from one patient to another, he continued his work until excessive loss of blood prevented him from moving. He then verbally directed unskilled enlisted men in first aid for the wounded. Still refusing assistance himself, he remained to instruct others in dressing the wounds of his comrades until he was unable to speak above a whisper and finally lapsed into unconsciousness. The effects of his injury later caused his death. By steadfastly remaining at the scene without regard for his own safety, Corporal Wilson's distinguished devotion to duty, and personal sacrifice, were prime factors in saving the lives of at least ten wounded men."

Harry Truman

ceased, and in a French cemetiere, evening shadows were falling from hundreds of plain white crosses dotting what had once been a pasture field. The uniformed soldier made his way among them purposefully. In his hand he carried a fresh wreath. Stopping in front on one, and kneeling down at the grave of Cpl. Alfred. L. Wilson, Army Serial Number 33 429 521, he placed it against the white cross. It was the least he could do to show his respect for the man who had become a martyr for love of his friends.

It was a simple gesture of thanks to the medic who had saved his life.

The next day, on the front page of the Uniontown paper, a photo appeared with Alfred's father, shoulders thrown back, hat in hand, and head slightly bowed, shaking the General's hand and looking at the medal. Lined up behind him, head and shoulders erect, and with expressionless faces, were four of the sisters. There was pride, but it was too soon not to be tempered by the sense of what they had lost, a big brother, whose laughter and caring, had made him almost a second father to them. I can only imagine how hard it was to mourn Alfred's death in any of the usual ways. All they had was a piece of paper to prove he was gone. None of them would ever see his physical body and as yet there had been no funeral. No way of really saying goodbye. Most of the family existed in a strange kind of limbo. They knew he was dead, but somehow it just didn't seem to be real. My grandfather would suffer from dreams for many years in which he would see Alfred begging for him to come get him. He would always think that there was a chance that Alfred was still alive somewhere.

In the picture, my mother's face is almost lost in the background. Because of the close bond between my mother and her brother, she had found it exceedingly hard to come to terms with Alfred's death. He had always told her not to worry, for he would come home. The pain and grief would never totally leave for the rest of her life. She would never again roll out filled cookies without thinking how they had been Alfred's favorite or hearing his voice asking what she had baked today.

Emotionally, it was hard to mourn Alfred's death in any of the usual ways. His cousin August said, "Even after he got killed, and they said they buried him over there and all, you lived in a fantasy world. You'd think they could be wrong. They weren't and you knew it, but you kept thinking something could have happened. You wanted to see him come back so bad."

Jesse took the medal home and placed it in a china cupboard, and a picture of Alfred in uniform graced a side table in the parlor room for quite a few years. I personally have a very vague recollection of seeing it during the fifteen years that I visited there.

The family was proud of the medal and an article appeared in the paper some time after the award ceremony when sister Bernice took the medal to work with her to Moser's Confectionery. It seemed that most everyone in town dropped by to get a look at the coveted medal and walked away feeling quite privileged. The newspaper described the medal in great detail for the benefit of those who didn't have a chance to see it. Bernice had been quiet about bringing it to work to show her friends, but once a few knew, the word spread quickly. I don't blame them at all for taking advantage of the opportunity to see a Medal of Honor. Very few people have ever seen one.

Presently, my Uncle Melvin has the medal in his possession and up to February of 1990, I had never seen it. But I asked my uncle if he would show it to me and he did. I'll never forget him bringing it into their kitchen and handing me the opened box. Even though the blue ribbon is a bit faded, the sight of the medal itself still leaves a sense of awe inside one's spirit. You cannot explain it, you can only feel it.

I also was shown Alfred's Purple Heart. I remember going home that day and thinking how it seemed that Alfred had exchanged his life for those two little pieces of metal and crying out how unfair the trade had really been.

We Americans have this saying that "it ain't over till the fat lady sings." In this case, amid the telegrams, words of sympathy, and the awarding of a medal, nothing could be put to rest or really be over, not until a casket had been lowered and the mournful sound of taps played.

It would be another three years before my grandfather's request to have his son brought back home would be fulfilled, and even then, I'm not sure it was over.

Chapter XV

A Flag Draped Caisson

The year was 1948. My parents had fulfilled both their own and Alfred's dream of buying a farm, and had moved from Fairchance to Meyersdale in Somerset County. I was seven months old on the auspicious occasion of Alfred's funeral Sunday, August 15th, at 2:30 p.m.

Three years, eight months, and seven days after Bezange La Petite, the army had finally arranged to have Alfred brought home during a spell of summer's hot and muggy heat. He came in on the train with a military guard, and J.W. Goldsboro picked up the body at the station and transported it back to his funeral home. It was time for the family to say goodbye.

In the summer of 1991, I sat in Mr. Goldsboro's home and talked with J.W., as everybody calls him. The conversation centered around Alfred himself at first, then turned to J.W. and the long association he has enjoyed with most of my family as a distant cousin. He shared how the Wilson family really were "good Brethren" and I thought how that heritage has woven itself into the lives of quite a few of the children down the line.

J.W. brought out the photographs of Alfred's funeral and pieced together the picture of those painful days, from the time the casket arrived, until the echoing sound of "Taps" had been burned into the memory of those present.

J.W. had just entered into the undertaking business the year before and he was sort of the new kid on the block when it came to burying folks. Right off the bat he knew this was going to be one of the largest funerals he would ever have, and one of this magnitude was a little out of the ordinary in a small town. But none the less, he felt good about being able to help Jesse, and honored to be the one to bury Alfred. As funerals go, he determined that this one was to be different and special. So he set about working out the details for the burial of Fairchance's first Medal of Honor winner.

"It just didn't feel right to use a hearse," J.W. said. He called around, and at Greensburg he located a jeep-drawn caisson and had the army bring it down. It was Alfred's last ride on home soil, and it seemed a fitting mode of travel for a man who had given his life for his country. There'd been that other ride on a jeep in France.

The casket had arrived closed with orders that it wasn't to be opened. But he'd asked Jesse if he wanted him to open it up so he could see Alfred. My grandfather declined the offer.

The flag draped casket, with a picture of Alfred, the Medal of Honor, two crossed flags along with a military guard, laid in state at the J.W. Goldsboro Funeral Home for two days. An older cousin, Esther Winters, still remembers the soldiers standing at attention, eyes staring straight ahead, gun at side, not even moving a muscle in the hot August weather. The round hand-fans, with the J.W. Goldsboro Funeral Home imprint on them, were brought out and the mourners made good use of them. The guards found the heat hard to take too, and it was little wonder that during one of the soldiers stint on guard duty, he crumbled to the floor, fainted dead away from heat prostration.

J.W. had put a small light on the picture and award. It stayed that way even through the night.

On the morning of the fifteenth, the military pallbearers, some of whom had served with Alfred, loaded the casket on the caisson, and then climbed aboard, three sitting in the front, and the rest standing in the back. Mrs. Goldsboro stood at the door of the funeral home, weeping uncontrollably as she watched the military pallbearers load the casket onto the jeep. She said, "I don't know why I cried, except that it was just so sad watching it all, it was just so sad."

The entourage then rolled away from the funeral home and proceeded to the Presbyterian Church. It was decided to hold the funeral there because it was the only church in town that would hold the expected crowd.

Again, the pallbearers unloaded the casket and carried it down a walk lined with men in uniform, and into the sanctuary. Along with the military, the church was filled with family and friends. Alfred's fiancee, Alice, attended the service, sitting beside her old friend, Winifred. It was standing room only for the funeral service of Cpl. Alfred L. Wilson, conducted by his old pastor, Rev. J.E. Jones and assisted by Rev. Robert Kneff.

After the service inside the church, the honorary pallbearers carried Alfred to the caisson back through two columns of soldiers formed from every branch of the service, and loaded him on the conveyance which was to take him on his last ride through the town he had loved so well.

Looking at the pictures of the funeral, I was startled by the crowds of people lining the streets. My inclination was that they'd all come out to watch the parade. I mean, nothing like this had ever been seen in the little burg of Fairchance before, and as a baby boomer, it hadn't been my experience to see much fervor in attending funerals, military or otherwise. J.W. said, "The funeral was like a parade, and everybody turned out for it, but I don't think that was why they were there."

The war had been over for three years. Men and women were trying to put their lives together, put the past behind them, and settle back into the routine of a normal lifestyle. They'd had time to reflect back on things, heal their wounds, and put things in perspective.

They knew now just how bad the Holocaust had been, especially those men who had freed the concentration camp at Dachau and others like it. They really had saved part of the world.

It still hurt to remember all they had endured, but the sacrifice had brought about results. They'd shown the world that oppression never works in the end. There was a general feeling of national pride. Call it patriotism if you will. And then along came this funeral of a Medal of Honor winner who had finally made it home. They knew him and his story. If anyone or anything deserved their respect and admiration, it was this procession that wound its way down Church Street to Maple Grove Cemetery.

A lot of men pulled their uniform out of mothballs, and if they could still fit into it, got all dressed up again. The ones who had taken too many second helpings or the last piece of pie, and couldn't quite button all the buttons, put on their medals and uniform hat and stood with the crowd.

They had all come to see the entourage that assembled to accompany Alfred's body from the church to the cemetery.

As tradition would dictate, the military band went by first, playing a funeral dirge in a very slow cadence. Next, picking up and setting down their feet in time to the music, came the flag bearers. Behind them with wheels moving slowly, moved the jeep, pulling the red, white, and blue covered caisson with Alfred's body. When the caisson went by, men and women who had seen the face of war, gave in to their impassioned spirits. All along the route there was a flurry of salutes toward one of their own, while others simply took off their hats or held their hands over their hearts. The onlookers were for the most part, silent.

The family and military units followed on foot as the procession moved down the street, past the fire hall and center of town, to the cemetery. The whole county lined the streets to see the caisson go by. It was indeed impressive. Just hearing the band, you knew it was not an ordinary band. They played no lilting melody of joy or expression of march that one usually associates with a marching band. But rather a somber mournful dirge laden with the cadence of grief.

At the cemetery, Alfred was laid to rest beside his mother and baby brother, Wallace. There would be a short message of internment and after the removal and folding of the flag, it was presented to Alfred's father, Jesse. Then amid the quietness some distance off, an order to "fire" and the booming sound of cannonade reverberated all around. As everyone sat in their own private world of numbness and grief and with the still faint sound of cannons hanging in the air, a rifle squad raised their weapons to their shoulders, fired off a twenty-one gun salute, and a lone bugler raised his instrument to his lips. The sound of "Taps" resounded along the hillside and over Alfred's hometown.

He had been welcomed back into the bosom of the place he called home. The family had finally said goodbye.

But was it really over?

Most forward grave is Alfred's.

Chapter XVI

The Mortal - Immortalized

What has man done that we should give them honor and praise so long after human frailty has claimed their body and God has claimed their soul?

Since the beginning of Adam, man has diligently searched almost every corner of the globe in the sometimes elusive quest for immortality. For many it is an innate desire to leave something of himself behind to insure that they will not be forgotten. Others want to know that a work begun will be finished, and in the end, it and they will have made a contribution to history. The reasons for perpetuating the existence of man are infinite. Some are remembered simply because they have lived.

Men and women are immortalized through cities, buildings, parks, roads, foundations and trusts, and a myriad of other ingenious methods down to naming plants and animals after themselves.

While Alfred was alive, there was no voice raised in proclamation that he had any right to fame and adulation, and if he had lived, he would have shunned it if there were. But in death, he inadvertently achieved what so many mortal men aspire to, immortality.

Two and a half decades after his death, we can find his name remembered in various and sundry places. Some are incongruent with his basic aversion to killing and war. But at the same time, the dichotomy of the situation gives us a sense of admiration and respect for the kind of man, who against all odds, wound up a hero.

To the peacemaker, he was the epitome of all that word implies. As much as his nature and inclination permitted, he made himself a friend to most, and lived at peace with the rest. Bob Walls said of him, "He was a prince among men."

To the soldier or those that believe struggle is an inevitable part of life, he was the embodiment of that very ideal. Superbly trained, mentally and physically, he lived with and for his job and men. As a fellow soldier had described him, "He was dedicated." For that November day, there was no one anymore fit for the situation than Corporal Alfred L. Wilson.

For those who are not driven by any particular passion either way, but prefer to languish somewhere in between the two ideals, Alfred's story is still unique. He was just exactly where he was supposed to be. He was the kind of guy that would have handled any situation with aplomb and come out smelling like a rose. Or we could say, for the sake of history, he was destined by some master plan far beyond our human minds, to be standing on a field in France at just the right moment, to make the choice that he made. No matter who you are or what your philosophical leaning, there is some element of Alfred's character that everyone can identify with.

The role he had played in life and death, had now transcended him from the little town of Fairchance into the annals of historical prominence.

Medal of Honor Hall - Pentagon, Washington, D.C.

Alfred had made his mark on the world, and my family and I were led to the Pentagon in Washington, D.C. on a gorgeous September day in 1990 to see the proof of it. We were there for a tour of the facility and especially the Medal of Honor Hall where the name of Alfred and others are on display. The arrangements for the big day had been made through Pennsylvania Congressman John Murtha and I felt like a kid being allowed into a candy store for the first time.

Arriving early at the reception area, we gave our names and who we were to see. It was a few minutes before a liaison person, Tony Zaccagnino, appeared and we were off on our personally conducted tour.

My two sons, my husband and I were duly impressed with the aura at the hub of this military establishment. There's just something about a uniform. Tony was a superb guide, doing it with just the right touch of class and courtesy. It didn't take long to figure out that here was a fellow who was going places. He walked us along the corridors of power and let us peek into a few offices of the upper brass with names that we recognized immediately. They were becoming household words because we were just getting into the Gulf crisis and either the President or some military figure was constantly being flashed across the television screen with updates on Sadam's latest escapade. We felt like we were walking through living history. Tony reeled off all kinds of information about the huge five-sided complex as we negotiated the hallways, doors, and were swished in and out of elevators.

Impatience tugged at my heels, however, and I thought Tony was never going to show us the Medal of Honor Hall. But, he had done his homework. I was taken by surprise when we were walked up to a wall lined with small brass plates, and he pointed out the name of my uncle and discreetly disappeared. I cannot explain the flood of emotion that swept through me causing me to break down into tears. I was not prepared for the stark reality of seeing Alfred's name printed there in this place. It is a simple thing: a small brass plate about one inch by four inches with Alfred's rank, name, date of death, and place where he earned the medal.

My feelings ran rampant within me, enveloping me in grief. A question nagged at me.

Why couldn't he have lived? Why was his name on a plaque? Why wasn't he laughing, living, growing old?

Even with the uncertainty, a sense of pride welled up within my soul. He was my uncle, blood of my blood, and bone of my bone. Some of the same genes that coursed through his veins now are part

Medal of Honor Hall, Pentagon, Washington, D.C.

of my nature. His heroic action, part of the legacy he would leave for us to ponder and try to live up to.

We walked around the room looking at all the brass plates, knowing that each one represented an extraordinary life, each one no less special than the next.

In the center of the room were replicas of the Congressional Medals given out by the three branches of the military. I wanted to grab a man and woman close to me, who were also touring the facility, and point out Alfred's brass plate and tell them that he was my uncle. I was overwhelmed by feelings of absolute and unutterable pride. At that moment, I did not think it possible to be any prouder of Alfred. But, I was wrong, and I knew it the minute I stepped into Arlington National Cemetery.

Arlington National Cemetery

At the Pentagon, Tony had told us that there was a room on the second floor of the Amphitheater in front of the Tomb of the Unknown Soldier, where we would again find Alfred's name on a bronze plaque.

Just being at Arlington is enough to give a person goose bumps for a week. To walk among those tombstones and watch the guard, with bayonet fixed, walk his lonely and silent vigil in front of the Tomb of the Unknown Soldier is a riveting experience. I don't think anyone who has ever been there forgets the sound of heels clicking together as he makes his about face at the end of the rubber walkway or the call for silence that accompanies the ritualistic pomp of the changing of the guard. It makes me cry.

We watch the ritual and then walk up the steps between the colonnades into the room beyond. It is filled with military memorabilia. Even though the steps leading upstairs are cordoned off, we have been given permission to go to the second floor. The walls in one room are surrounded by the flags from every state in the union. It is beautiful and we raptly walk around the room looking at the display. Along one wall are giant replicas of the medals, each one distinct, and touching. The bronze nameplates are on another wall and I touch Alfred's reverently. Here again, I experience the same feelings of pride, awe, and sadness at seeing his name.

HALL OF HEROES
MEDAL OF HONOR GALLERY

Arlington, Virginia

After a while, I am alone in this great room. I stand and read Audie Murphy's poem. It says it all.

Outside, a funeral is being held for a general, and we are privy to view a horse-drawn caisson making its way through the cemetery. Standing silently, we watch the black horse move slowly by. Walking to the car through the cemetery, I stop and look back at the Tomb of the Unknown Soldier. I think to myself, "What a place in which to be immortalized." On these Virginia slopes rest Army privates, a prize fighter, and a President. Alfred couldn't be remembered in more fitting company.

Fort Riley, Kansas

Zipping along Interstate 70, the country is open and I never tire of the constantly unfolding landscape outside my window. Before I know it, the signpost for Fort Riley flashes by me and I turn off the highway and into the Fort's compound.

At Wilson Barracks, Sergeant Bruce Hawley introduces himself and gives me the grand tour starting with the entry area, where a brass plaque, Alfred's picture, and a description of the citation hang on a wall. No matter how many times I see Alfred's name, that same feeling of sadness prevails. The picture is a familiar pose with

Alfred's characteristic smile. The sergeant says that everyone at Wilson Barracks at one time or another reads the plaque bearing Alfred's name and his citation. I hope they do. It would be a shame for anyone to pass through those front doors, live in these quarters, and never know the man whose name this building bears.

As we walk along the corridors, I learn that this is a medical barracks. These men and women are nurses and technicians in the hospital that is close by. It was first named and dedicated at a ceremony held in 1959. My grandfather, a number of Alfred's sisters, and a brother attended.

I came here prepared for a cold, impersonal army facility. What I found at the heart of the place was a home. The austerity, shrouded by a cloud of individuals, who by pulling together, turn a barracks into a warm personal abode in which to sleep, talk and dream.

Army life can be transient at times. They are here, make the best of it, then move on.

Sitting in the recreation room, I listen to the chatter of a couple of soldiers while they watch television. It is a very relaxed atmosphere. Life in all its orderliness marches along. If Alfred were here he would have joked and laughed right along with them. He would have thought this a pretty neat place to bunk. He could even enjoy a red pop if he wanted.

Wilson Range - Fort Benning, Georgia

Wanting to do something and doing it are sometimes two different things. My desire has always been to visit all the places where Alfred's name appears. Unfortunately, that has not been accomplished as of the writing of this manuscript, but hope still springs eternal.

At Fort Benning, Georgia, a firing range was named in honor of Alfred. It is simply called "Wilson Range."

I mentioned the place to Tony Zaccagnino when we were at the Pentagon and he remembered seeing Wilson Range on one of his trips to Fort Benning. At least I know it is still there. Alfred put some time in on a firing range during his basic training. He had scored pretty good with the rifle, but had never used it in war.

Fort Belvoir, Virginia

Many of the buildings the Army chose to name after Alfred have something to do with a hospital. It's understandable.

On June 29, 1968, Wilson Hall was dedicated at Fort Belvoir, Virginia, in honor of Alfred L. Wilson. My mother, Myrtle Cunningham and her brother Melvin and his wife Lil and daughter Susan made the trip south to lend some credence to the day. By this time, my grandfather had suffered a disabling stroke that confined him to a wheelchair and he did not attend.

As the program read, "...building 815 will henceforth be known as Wilson Hall. It will provide billeting for Nursing Service, and Supply and Administrative personnel assigned to Dewitt Army Hospital. In addition it will maintain general purpose office space and company Supply." Wilson Hall also provides an air-conditioned Day Room and recreational facilities...all the comforts of home.

Abel Hall - Medical Department Medal of Honor
Fort Sam Houston, San Antonio, Texas

I had fallen in love with Texas. The drive through the state had left me enthralled by a magnificent expanse of the rolling grassland they call cattle country. It was the only state where I saw a cowboy sitting his horse along a fence row. I had trouble watching him and the road at the same time. Thankfully, I managed it and made my way south through Dallas, Austin, and finally to San Antonio. I had negotiated the roadways safely and since it wasn't too late, I had no trouble checking into a hotel.

Ronald Still, Regimental Historian for the US Army Medical Department, took me to the Combat Medical Museum at Fort Sam Houston and introduced me to its director. The two gentlemen then escorted me through a very inspiring collection of military medical history. Starting in the Revolutionary War era and through Vietnam, from a dirty and bloody Civil War operating room to a Mash unit in Korea, the story of saving lives on the field of battle unfolded.

An ambulance from World War I was on display and I could have stood all day examining it. I tried to fix in my mind the details of a World War II medic uniform behind a glass case. Through the use of words, pictures and memorabilia, I saw the reality of how men and women have devoted their lives to the preservation of life in the midst of death and terror. For some, like Florence Nightingale, it was an idealistic calling. For others, well, they would rather have been elsewhere given the choice.

In Abel Hall, just inside the main foyer of the building is a small medical memorial. Lining a wall to the left are the pictures and citations of all the Medical Department Medal of Honor recipients. A velvet and brass rope in front of them keeps visitors at a respectful distance.

The third picture from the right was a pose of Alfred with his citation. I read it for the hundredth time and memorized the wall. Touching the glass enclosed picture and plaque was as close as I could get to Alfred. Somehow, it was enough. I had seen and been comforted by his immortality.

Ron had been super in taking me around and showing me everything, and I appreciated his own personal thoughts about his work with and for the Medical History Department. I can see that he is a man dedicated to his work and to the army. Our brave will not be forgotten as long as men like Ron persevere.

At the facility in San Antonio, there are plans to name another building after Alfred, but as of this date, the details have not been finalized. It will be one more place bearing the mane of an ordinary man who had the courage to do an extraordinary deed.

Alfred L. Wilson Memorial Award
Boston, Massachusetts

In 1958, the Yankee Division Veterans Association donated a Paul Revere Trophy Bowl to the 26th Division in Boston in memory of its own Alfred Wilson.

It was determined that an award in Alfred's name would be given to the most outstanding soldier of the 26th Division for that year. The bowl itself remains a permanent possession of the 26th Division and each recipient has his name inscribed on it.

The first soldier to be recognized in 1959 was Specialist 4th Class Charles W. Campbell. My Uncle Lloyd Wilson flew to

Boston to present the award to it's first recipient at the YD's Annual Military Ball. The whole affair was a great success and the 328's treasurer, Robert Clapp, still remembers that great evening.

The tradition of the award has been upheld through the years by the announcement of the recipient, and a Military Ball held in December when it is presented. My heartiest congratulations to all who have earned the Alfred L. Wilson Memorial Award. Due to the deactivation of the 26th Division in August of 1993, there will be no men honored in the future.

Alfred L. Wilson will be, as long as our nation maintains a military, a significant part of the history of the 328th Infantry Regiment or the Yankee Division. With a total of three medals to its credit, Alfred was the only man to be awarded this medal in the regiment during World War II.

Wilson Barracks, Landstuhl, Germany

Of all the places where Alfred is remembered, the most moving for me was in Europe, at Landstuhl, Germany, where I saw Alfred remembered on the face of a stone.

With the adventure in France behind me, I forged ahead into a new country. On a Friday I made it into Heidelburg and Camp Campbell. I use the terminology "made it," loosely. If you can call driving on a highway approaching the city, six lanes each way, and the going speed of traffic about 140 kilometers or more, making it. I was a nervous wreck! I hung grimly onto the steering wheel with such ferocity that my palms sweated. Just to keep up with traffic, I had to maintain a speed of about 120 kilometers, or 80 miles an hour. I thought that was flying. But the constantly passing streaks, some of whom made my little Opel Cadette feel like a sailboat being rocked back and forth by a tidal wave, made me realize just what going fast really meant. But I made it!

After arriving at the base, Captain Jepson came down to meet me. I didn't know if I should kiss and hug him or fall into his arms weeping hysterically in relief. Thank goodness I did neither and maintained a proper sense of decorum. I sure was happy to be able to breathe normally again and see and hear another American.

While stateside, the Pentagon had informed me that there

were three places named after my uncle in Germany, but I had no idea where they were. Captain Jepson did a great job finding out that two of the installations had been turned over to the Germans some years ago and no longer bore the name of my uncle. However, Wilson Barracks at Landstuhl, known during the war as The Kiechberg Kaserne (English translation Hilter Schule or School), was still named after Alfred, and was rededicated as late as 1984. The captain made arrangements for me to go there and see it.

I drove into Landstuhl on a foggy, dreary day. But after a stint driving the autobahn, I was glad to be anyplace in any weather. The ambiance in Landstuhl felt really neat. It was definitely a German town with small shops, bicyclers, and German signs. But the Pizza Hut at one of the lights helped me feel right at home.

I made a last turn according to Captain Jepson's map, headed up a hill and through a set of gates into one of America's most important hospitals in Europe. The Landstuhl Army Regional Medical Center.

Marie Shaw, a German nationale, escorted me around and we stopped first at the signpost with Wilson Barracks printed on it. Winding further up a gentle hill we parked our cars at what looked like quite a number of buildings spread out on top of the hill. Marie walked and talked us over to a huge stone that designated the name of this compound.

Landstuhl, Germany. Left, the author by the name stone and right, the Wilson Barracks sign post.

I was overcome with emotion as I stared at Alfred's name on the rock. Marie very graciously suggested that she leave me, and we agreed to meet later on in the afternoon. Alone, I stood with Alfred's memorial.

I wrote:

"I have come across two continents and an ocean to stand before this monument in stone. It is a stone, or rather two stones. A quarry that is nearby provided this giant rock base that protrudes out of the ground by about five feet.

"Embedded in the center is a smaller rectangular rock procured by the mayor of Bezange La Petite, France for the Army. By some chance of fate, the stone cutter omitted the first name, Bezange, so the little hamlet is remembered here only by La Petite. A gray marble stone rests at the foot of the huge one. It reads:

WILSON BARRACKS
NAMED IN MEMORY OF
T/5 ALFRED L. WILSON
MEDICAL SPECIALIST 328TH INFANTRY
26TH INFANTRY DIVISION
KILLED IN ACTION 8 NOVEMBER 1944
NEAR BEZANGE LA PETITE, FRANCE

AWARDED THE MEDAL OF HONOR
ON 18 JUNE 1945

"The many buildings that serve as Wilson Barracks range out along this road in the country. My mind tries to grasp the fact that on this quiet pastoral hillside, these buildings were once used as Hitler's school for boys. Young men marched along these lanes, as Hitler's ideology molded them into an army that was almost to have destroyed a world. Now a late morning fog languished peacefully over the rooftops almost obscuring some of them.

One of the buildings of present day Wilson Barracks formerly used as one of Hitler's school for boys.

"The air is stirred ever so slightly and rain drops slowly to the ground. A few cold drops fell on my head. It was a kind of reality check.

"Nestled close to a wooded area, birds flit happily among the trees making a sweet melody. Leaves float gently from the almost bare canopy of limbs overhanging this memorial spot.

"Alfred was a man of simplicity. I think he would have approved of this place the army has chosen. Because it is implanted in the ground, they tell me that "this stone should stay put until hell freezes over." There is a sense of permanence about this rock. Perhaps it shall stand in its present position as long as earth lasts or until man takes upon himself the herculean task of moving it.

"Air caressed my face. It was cold, but I did not feel it. I could not resist touching the stones. My fingers move over the rock reverently, then trail down to the writing on the granite face. I tenderly trace Alfred's name. The stone was cold and the life of this man would seem to be the same as the stone on which his name is carved. But I couldn't believe that. For within my breast stirs the thought that, even in death, this man's life will never lack warmth.

"Somewhere there beats life. Perhaps not in the physical sense, but by far in another realm, within our hearts and souls.

"I believe that no human being exists merely for the

sake of existence. Once we have been created, lived, loved, and touched those around us with our presence and allowed ourselves to be touched by others, we become fused with earth and time. We become part of everything around us.

"I look at the structures around me and contemplated the disparity between what used to be and what now is. Taught here was the art of warfare and hatred. Compassion was for the weak.

"Forty-six years later, it provides comfort, shelter, and security to men and women working in a hospital. It bears the name of a man for whom benevolence was a way of life.

"To help the helpless, to hold high the hope and dreams of home and future were second nature to Alfred. This niece thinks it is more than fitting that the spirit and memory of such a man as Alfred Wilson should live on in this place.

"I know it is time to go and meet Marie, but I find it extremely hard to take my leave of this hilltop. It is as if while being here I have again become a part of Alfred's life, reaching out and touching him in some small way.

"A stone doesn't seem all that much....a few words inscribed down by the carver's hand. But it is everything to me. His presence can never really be forgotten. His physical life lived only for twenty-five years, but his impact is felt in a very real sense, by his own generation, by family and friends, and after all these years, by myself. Even more, there is this feeling, that somewhere out there in the future of time and space, someone will come to know Alfred and be the better for it. His life will live on as if it were yesterday."

In Alfred's hometown of Fairchance, the local VFW is named in his honor, and the Alfred L. Wilson Elementary School is a mile from where his brother Melvin resides.

Other places honoring Medal of Honor winners:

The Medal of Honor Grove
Freedoms Foundation at Valley Forge
Valley Forge, PA. -
    Winners are acknowledged by a obelisk
from each state on which their names appear.

Chattanooga, Tn. -
    Museum for Medal of Honor Winners
Patriots Point, Naval and Maritime Museum,
Patriots Point Road, Mt. Pleasant, N.C.

Organizations Honoring Medal of Honor Winners:
Medal of Honor Historical Society
Congressional Medal of Honor Society United
States of America chartered by the Congress

Books:
Medal of Honor Recipients 1863 - 1973
Published by the United States Printing Office

"In the Name of the Congress of the United States," the committee of Veterans' Affairs of the United States Senate, publishes a book listing all Medal of Honor recipients. As wars add to history, an updated version is printed about every five years.

Immortality? If such a thing can be attained, it has come for Alfred in more ways than he would have ever imagined. But it came with a price tag.

Chapter XVII

Why? Was the Price too High?

On the proceeding pages, the soul and life of Alfred Wilson has been laid bare. The actions of November 8, 1944, and the resulting circumstances, neatly laid out for us like the squares on a checkerboard.

Watching the evening sky one summer night after I had been working on Alfred's story, I observed a shooting star streaking across a moonlit sky. Almost before my mind grasped what my eyes were seeing, it had burned itself out in its short burst of shining glory. Standing in the mantel of darkness, I drew an analogy between the star and Alfred. Both were brilliant for too short a time, both burned themselves out in a final display of dazzling proportions. The two finales leave the onlookers transfixed and wrapped in emotion.

The all too brief passing of the star left me standing there asking myself, "It's all over? It's gone already!" Seconds later an intuitive thought framed itself in my mind. For family and friends, the passing of a man who had everything going for him, must have left a similar pathos in its wake. It is a feeling that eludes the mind and heart for its lack of definition, and tumbles one's emotions into a state of disarray. Death is a risk and expected consequence of war. But when the promise and hope of the young die, our human nature reels in unbelief and cries out at the unfairness of such an abrupt ending.

There is another frustrating twist to this story. While talking with other medics, men who were there, and a letter that Battalion Surgeon, Captain Dedick wrote, we can conclude that Alfred's life could have been spared if proper medical attention had been administered. If taken to an aid station within a few hours or so, the effects of shock and blood loss could have been held to a minimum. Why then did this man die?

What drove Alfred to react to the course of events that were present the afternoon of the 8th of November, 1944? Could I speculate on his thoughts and feelings and ask if he chose to let himself die? Was he simply a victim of the carnality of war? Did he or did he not realize the extent of his own injuries and over or underestimate them?

He had already voiced the statement that he did not want to come home if he lost a limb. Perhaps looking at his left leg convinced him that it couldn't be saved. Could he have perceived himself invincible because of his huge size and strength? Given what I had learned of his character, is it possible that with no intent to literally kill himself, he chose to give of himself to the point that he was willing to surrender his life for his men?

It is absolutely impossible to ascertain Alfred's exact state of mind and his reasoning for his actions that fateful November day.

What we can do, by using rational thinking, God-conscious-ness and human nature, is examine the picture as a whole. Based on fact, we will speculate with different theories and ideas, as to the "why" of his decisions.

When the other fellows heard Alfred was going into the army, he was berated by his friends for going. They asked him why didn't he join the navy? His answer was typical of him, "When I fall, I want to fall on solid ground." Alfred already stood on a rock.

My grandparents had given their children a firm basis for life, a faith in God rooted by a Brethren heritage. Alfred especially had a propensity toward God that seemed to take off in every direction. He became janitor of the church and was involved in the life of the congregation. Almost every letter he wrote home asked how everything was going at church. The church was like a second home to this big gangly kid, and a lifeline to the big strapping man.

Alfred's reputation conjures up the image of a modern day Sir Galahad. A knight in shining armor riding about doing good. Only by this time, the white horse had been replaced by a Model T Ford, and the armor has given way to a miner's hard hat, coal dirt under the fingernails and by 1943, the helmet of a soldier and a medic's red cross. Whether it was a family member needing help, someone in the church or a neighbor, a soldier who couldn't save his money, or a march that was a little too long for some, Alfred was always willing to lend a hand. No wonder Alfred's father pleaded with him to take care of himself that day he left for the army, as if a few words cautioning restraint, would ever deter Alfred from doing what he thought was best. Obviously they didn't.

In considering Alfred's actions it is imperative that we look at his military training. He was a highly skilled medic. He had over a year and a half to hone the skills that the army had drilled into him, and this training was not done in peacetime. We were already at war.

Day after day, week after week, and month after month, these men were taught to kill or be killed. They were taught how to dig a foxhole, and how to survive if captured. Alfred learned how to save lives. He knew to look for a rifle stuck upside down in the ground, for that meant a wounded soldier. As a medic, he knew how to see to blisters, trench foot, and heat exhaustion. He knew how to stop bleeding, give morphine shots, and put on tourniquets. His one purpose was to save lives. He learned responsibility, mostly for the men in C Company, and for himself.

For almost two years, the army had pushed, prodded and pulled the men of C Company into functioning together as a unit. They had lived with each other's snoring and read each other's mail. They had played, prayed, and persevered together in about every situation imaginable and probably some unimaginable ones. By this time, they cared for one another like brothers. The love and camaraderie that bonded them together would last a lifetime for those who survived. For Alfred, it lasted until his last conscious thought.

Alfred had obviously kept himself in good mental and physical shape. He didn't abuse his body with alcohol or tobacco. He rarely even drank coffee. One doesn't get a reputation for extreme strength and stamina by being out of shape. But it is important to note that he possessed more physical strength than was considered the usual, especially for a medic. When one man can accomplish a physical feat that five or six have difficulty with, we can assume that he knew his physical and mental capabilities. There is always the possibility that he over-estimated them or failed to be cognizant of the limitations inherent in all of us. It is the mind set of the young to believe our bodies are invincible, and therefore, can easily be taken for granted.

From an eye-witness account of his injuries, one leg was in pretty bad shape, but he had not lost it. One of Alfred's buddies stated he had expressed the desire not to survive a crippling disability. He felt this would be too much of an obligation to others and put him in the position of being helpless to those around him. Understandably, in theory, it is a noble and practical position to take when one talks about it, but few have the courage to carry it through when the situation presents itself. The reality is that one can live a productive and satisfying life without one or even several limbs.

Alfred's ability traits were strongly defined. He excelled in physical prowess and did well in his job as a medic, thus allowing him to excel and find acceptance as a man among his peers.

Alfred had several strong personality traits. He had a wonderful sense of humor and he enjoyed having fun. Blessed with an easy-going nature, he never took offense at anything the guys did, but laughed and joked right along with them. No wonder Alfred had an abundance of friends, both male and female.

It would appear that his self-image was healthy. He was self-assured enough to do his own thing regardless of whether it was popular or not. It enabled him to stand in front of a barracks of men and tell them he was going to chapel and they could do as they pleased. Call it courage to be a non-drinker in the midst of a drama where most of the players are playing the same scene on the stage of alcohol. Only men like Alfred could have carried it off with aplomb. I'm sure the guys who were depending on him to get them back to base after a pass into town, were grateful he could stick to his principles. We have no evidence that he ever violated his own clear perception of who he was or why he was in a war away from home and family.

Alfred reacted that day to the stimuli around him. These inner urges impel an individual to behave in some manner until reason to do so is reduced or eliminated. Alfred's stimulus ended when the last man left the hill.

Some stimuli are external like an artillery shell. Other are internal: love of nature, acceptance and belonging, and a consciousness of God. How we respond to these innermost promptings depends largely on our experience in reacting to everything we see, hear and touch.

We are an accumulation of what we are taught or conditioned to, through life's experiences. A certain situation does not necessarily dictate our response, but how our minds sort out the set of circumstances we are presented with. Each one of us as an individual is unique and has experienced a different set of experiences and motivations. This explains why, given the same job to perform, a hundred people will find a hundred different ways to do it.

To comprehend Alfred's innate character, I cannot totally use human rationality, but must combine it with a comprehension of his deep faith in God. It can only be noted that man must act according to conscience or else he cannot live with himself.

Alfred had told my mother that he had a special experience with God the summer before his unit was shipped overseas. Not only had he found forgiveness, but now he had a greater sense of communion with God. Now the relationship became deeper and more meaningful. He told Mom that he had always prayed to God, but over there he talked to God. The mystical, non-personal prayer life had been changed into a relational communing between two friends. The superficiality, stripped away, allowed them to walk closely together, almost as one. Perhaps we could say that he had received a sort of ticket, one he would choose to use on a cold November day outside of Bezange La Petite.

The combination of a strong human self, and the power and presence of a being outside the realm of the physical, could have contributed to his choice to stay on the field of battle knowing full well that he was putting his own life in jeopardy. In this way he could have possessed the ability to supersede the thralls of pain, fear, and self preservation with the welfare and needs of others.

Alfred's behavior was consistent with his self-image. A true reflection of who and what he was. A man committed not to the preservation of self but rather, committed to a higher calling from God. Not a calling of subjugation of any one person's rights over another, but a gentle giant who was willing to lay down his life for the lives of his friends. Perhaps for him to have acted other than he did, would have been to oppose the basic premise of his life.

Alfred believed in God and himself, and this clarity of faith never abandoned him.

My curiosity and desire to know my uncle has led me through a most fantastic journey of discovery. Since that long ago day in the attic as I sat reading Alfred's letters, the adventure I embarked upon has not been regretted for a moment. As an inquisitor of the past, I sought to discover who Alfred Wilson was and I have amply satisfied my thirst for that knowledge. I entered the scene in darkness and ignorance of many facts. Now, to the best of my knowledge, I am in possession of as much insight into my Uncle Alfred's life that can be humanly gleaned forty-some years after his death.

No longer does a struggle ensue between the conflicting idea that he could have chosen to let himself be brought in and live, and his decision to stay, help his men, and die.

A comprehension of the transpired events has eased the pain of never having the opportunity to know my uncle in person. It has allowed me to vent my grief and frustration and come to terms with the course of history that I cannot change nor totally reason. Peace now exists within my heart.

His family and close friends have always been proud of him, loved him, kept the memories, and endured the pain of loss.

Alfred Wilson was a man who did his duty, fought the good fight, and finished his course. He asked nothing in return, but silently and stoically accepted his fate. For a man so close to God, death was only a change of residence. Could we choose for a moment to "throw logic to the wind." To see what few people would ever notice. A man with a magnanimous spirit. A man who gave unselfishly of what most of us jealously guard and keep to ourselves. A man who loved God, living, and life, but who gave it all away in one final act of unselfishness.

More than one man has paid the price for the sake of his friends. Can we really say it is ever too high? Can we put a price on an act of heroism like a commodity sold on the marketplace? What would the ten men who Alfred helped make it off the hill say their lives were worth?

Every man I have ever had the privilege to meet in the 26th Division is a hero. They are the survivors of war, and with courage, skill and some call it luck, they made it back home. With wives and sweethearts, they took up their lives once again and made the

United States of America the greatest nation to be written up in the annals of history. My Uncle Alfred is but one more story among many.

Society has always been full of heroes. Heroism at times can be a fragile thing, and at others, it can be outright martyrdom. Any way you cut it, their impact on humanity is immeasurable. They stand before us as an incentive to dream and hope. That going the extra mile no matter what the consequences will never be passe'.

They abound not only on the field of battle, but in every stratosphere of society....from the garbage collector who returns the accidently discarded wallet, to the bank president who coaches little league and buys team uniforms himself, and to the disabled Vietnam Vet who still tries to work despite his handicap.

It is for the living to now share in the tragedies and triumphs that life sometimes brings our way....to allow a tear to flow and, from the ashes of desolation, grief and what-ifs, rise up in faith and courage, undauntable in the face of challenge, changing times, morals, and events which we have no control over.

This story is a salute to all heroes. A recognition for their sacrifice and dedication. The quiet unsung ones and the ones whose tribute of praise have reverberated in their ears through one form or another. May we all be proud to share in the heritage left by my uncle and every other hero who has ever been, who is, and who will be in the future.

There are the Medal of Honor winners who gaze at their medal from time to time and remember. But for those families who stand with empty arms and broken hearts, whose lives have been tragically torn asunder by their act of heroism, my grandfather put it most eloquently when he was presented Alfred's medal in Pittsburgh. "I accept the honor, but the price was too high."

It is the price paid for love and peace. In the bottom of the frayed old candy box, my mother's letters to her brother lie faded with age in similar fashion as those penned by Alfred. But one glaring difference makes these letters stand out from all the rest. They are stamped across the front with a return to sender message. Handwritten in the corner is the word "deceased" with the signature of Captain Kuligowski or Captain J. A. Macaine. I finger these letters as reverently as the rest, and can only imagine the depth of pain felt by my mother when she retrieved them from the mail with the address obliterated by that word.

I leave them in the bottom of the box, unopened as my mother did. They have earned the right to lie in peace. It is finally over.

Postscript

As the golden leaves of fall once again carpeted their way to the floor of our good earth, I traveled east to Lancaster, PA. to another reunion of the 328th Infantry in October of 1993. An ambiguous feeling persisted as I sped along Pennsylvania's turnpike toward my destination. These get-togethers of war veterans always fill me with a mixture of pride, sadness and that of being privileged to be with these men.

I had been forewarned that I was to have a small part in the program that weekend and I was carrying flyers with me about one of their own.

Throughout the weekend I met more men who had known Alfred in some way: Clifford Glazier, whom I did not have enough time with, and I got to meet Malvin Shar, a very articulate gentlemen who impressed me.

After dinner on Saturday evening, and during the program, Patrick Caruso, who had commissioned an oil portrait of my Uncle Alfred, presented it to me on behalf of the 328th Infantry Regiment, and I accepted it on behalf of my family. Alex Pagnotti asked me to say a few words:

"My heart is overwhelmed with thankfulness at the honor you have given my uncle, both while he was alive and now, so many years after his death. Alfred returned that love and honor himself on November 8, 1944.

I thank Pat Caruso and all who had a part in this presentation. It will be cherished.

I want to add that there are no words to describe what being here with you guys means to me. It's not about words, but feelings. It's about sharing a laugh, a hug, a friendship, whether new or old, with a group of men who shared the same experiences that my uncle did. You have allowed me to touch my uncle, to know him through you, to be a part of something he was a part of, and I'm sure would have been a part of again.

The truth is, I've looked into your faces and eyes and whispered to my uncle, this is for you. I don't wonder anymore why he gave his life away for his friends. You are the most exemplary men of character that I have ever had the privilege to meet. I do not ever expect to meet men such as you again.

I would like to publicly thank Robert Clapp, your secretary, and every other man here who helped contribute a memory to the biography of my uncle. This book in part is dedicated to the men of the 26th Division. May the writing of this book and others like it ensure that you heroic men of the 328th will be remembered forever."

HEADQUARTERS 26TH INFANTRY DIVISION

APO #26, c/o Postmaster
New York, New York
28 January 1946

My dear Mr Wilson:-

I know only too well that words cannot bring comfort to your heart in these hours of loss. However, as your son's division commander, I want to tell you that all of us who remain in this division grieve with you in the loss of our comrade.

Your son, Technician Fifth Grade Alfred L Wilson, 33429521, was killed in action 9 November 1944 during our advance near Bazange La Petite, France. He was buried in the Province of Lorrain, France, after an appropriate service at which a Protestant Chaplain officiated. You may secure more detailed information concerning the location of the grave and the disposal of your son's remains and effects by communicating directly with The Quartermaster General, Army Service Forces, Washington, D.C.

He did his duty splendidly and was loved and admired by all who knew him. We will not forget.

He gave his life in battle in the service of his country—these simple words cannot lighten our sorrow, but they bring great pride and inspiration to us all.

Sincerely,

W. S. PAUL
Major General, U.S. Army
Commanding

240

"Was the price too high?"

Alfred's father, Jesse Wilson, contemplates the Medal which so greatly honors his son. "I'll accept the honor, but the price was too high."

Index

Fort George G. Meade, MD. 50
Fort Jackson 108, 129, 172
Fort Jackson, S.C. 51, 120, 125
Fort Meade, MD 49
Fort Riley 220
Fort Sam Houston 56, 222
Freedoms Foundation at Valley
 Forge 229
Frick Coal Company 41

G

Geneva Convention 57
German Luftwaffe 128
Glazier, Clifford 127, 238
Goisse, James E. 50
Goldsboro, J. W. 47, 212
Grandma Tillie 1
Grandpap Jesse 1
Greensburg, PA 48

H

Hawley, Sergeant Bruce 220
Heidelburg 224
Hollen, Robert R. 50
Holocaust 214
Hoone, Harold O. 50
Hopkensville 97
Hughes, Eleanor 78
Hummell, Leonard 49
Hyde Park 109

I

Indian Wars 201
Irwin, Col. Bernard J.D. 201

J

Jenkins, Robert 192
Jepson, Captain 224
Jones, Rev. J.E. 214
Jones, Reverend 53
Jr., John Dobos 173

K

Kaifes, Charles M. 49
Kaiserslautern, Germany 181
Karwatske, John C. 49
Kissinger, Owen J. 50
Kixmiller, Captain 191
Kneff, Rev. Robert 214
Kuligowski, Captain Ed 11, 197,
 205

L

Labin, Richard, Jr. 49
Lancaster, PA 238
Landstuhl Army Regional Medical
 Center 225
Landstuhl, Germany 9, 224
Laurel Caverns 16
Laurel Hill State Park 34
Leadville, Colorado 14
Lebenion 108
Legion D'Honneur 201
Lehman, John W., Jr. 50
Leonard, Ray S. 49
Letters Begin 51
Lewellen, Leona 104
Lewis, Alvin 98
Lezey 191
Lezey, France 181
Lincoln, President 202

M

Maple Grove Cemetery 214
Marker, George E. 50
Marshall, Bob 181
Marshall, Lt. Robert 12, 122, 192
Mayfield, James C. 11
McCormick, Edwin C. 50
Medal of Honor 3, 200
Medal of Honor Citation 208
Medal of Honor Grove 229
Medal of Honor Hall 217
Medal of Honor Historical Soci-
 ety 229